IN
DEFENSE
OF
ACADEMIC
FREEDOM

Sidney Hook

A. M. Rosenthal

Herbert A. Deane

Charles Frankel

Ernest van den Haag

Bruno Bettelheim

Abba P. Lerner

Edward Chalfant

Henry Steele Commager

Jacques Barzun

Frederick A. Olafson

Kenneth B. Clark

Don K. Price

John R. Searle

Arnold Beichman

John H. Bunzel

Paul Kurtz

IN
DEFENSE
OF
ACADEMIC
FREEDOM

EDITED BY
SIDNEY HOOK

PEGASUS · NEW YORK

A DIVISION OF THE BOBBS-MERRILL COMPANY, INC., PUBLISHERS

PREFACE

WHAT unites all the contributors to this volume is a passionate commitment to the value of academic freedom and a belief that it is currently in great jeopardy. This jeopardy has several sources, but chief among them is the belief that the university must become an agency of specific social and political programs and that the techniques of violence and confrontation are legitimate methods of inducing educational change.

The devastating effect of this belief and these techniques upon the educational morale of American universities, their quality of instruction, and bonds of civility have not until now been properly documented. But the costs have been great and tragic. They are continuing.

The editor hopes that members of the academy, as well as intelligent laymen, will find in the essays and addresses assembled here both pertinent argument and evidential materials bearing on the central issues. These may prove useful in helping to turn back the onslaughts against academic freedom and against the idea of the university as an institution whose primary purpose is the search for meanings; clarification and truth rather than the exercise of political power.

The contributors speak only in their individual capacities, not as a group. Their opinions differ. Their differences on a wide variety of political and secondary educational matters illustrate the wide diversity that can thrive on the basis of their primary commitment.

Sidney Hook

CONTENTS

IN
DEFENSE
OF
ACADEMIC
FREEDOM

I
PAST
AND
FUTURE

1. THE LONG VIEW

Sidney Hook

Sidney Hook is Professor of Philosophy at New York University.

I BEGAN my college career in the fall of 1919, almost a half century ago. My academic lifetime spans half a dozen revolutions in American education. But have no fear, I am not going to reminisce. I want to stay young, at least in spirit, and I learned from my teacher, John Dewey, whom I observed closely for the last twenty-five years of his life, what the secret of staying young is and that is *not* to reminisce about the past. Actually, I never heard John Dewey reminisce until he was in his nineties, and that was as a reluctant response to my deliberate prodding in order to extract biographical data from him.

However, there is a way of talking about the past that is not merely reminiscence or idle reverie. It occurs when we make comparisons of the past and present for the sake of a present pur-

Remarks made by Dr. Hook at a dinner celebrating his sixty-fifth birthday and marking his retirement as head of the All-University Department of Philosophy at New York University, May 1968; reprinted with permission, from the *New York University Alumni News*, May 1968; with slight additions by the author.

pose or for the sake of finding a new way out of present difficulties.

Fifty years ago when I began my college studies, it would be no exaggeration to say that the belief in academic freedom was regarded as faintly subversive even in many academic circles. The AAUP (American Association of University Professors), organized by two philosophers. Arthur Lovejoy and John Dewey, was in its infancy without influence or authority. Today, except in some of the cultural and political backwaters of the United States, academic freedom, although not free from threats, is firmly established. In some regions it has the support of law.

Fifty years ago, the power of the chief university administrator was almost as unlimited as that of an absolute monarch. Today the administrator is a much harried man with much less power and authority among faculty, and especially among students, than his forebears. Today there may be temperamentally happy administrators but their present life is an unhappy one. There seems to be an open season on them, and to such a degree that for the first time in history there is an actute shortage of candidates for the almost 300 vacant administrative posts in institutions of higher learning. When I did my graduate work at Columbia, Nicholas Murray Butler was both the reigning and ruling monarch. I don't believe that in his wildest dreams he could have conceived of the Columbia scene today. The strongest argument I know against the resurrection of the body is that if it were within the realm of possibility, Nicholas Murray Butler would have risen from his grave and would now be storming Morningside Heights.

Having been an administrator in a small way myself, I have learned what an ungrateful job it is, and at the same time how necessary. Without administrative leadership, every institution (especially universities, whose faculties are notoriously reluctant to introduce curricular changes) runs downhill. The greatness of a university consists predominantly in the greatness of its faculty. But faculties, because of reasons too complex to enter into here, do not themselves build great faculties. To build great faculties, administrative leadership is essential. In the affairs of the mind and in the realm of scholarship, the principles of simple majority rule or of "one man, one vote" do not apply. The most "democratically" run institutions of learning are usually the most mediocre. It takes a big man to live comfortably with a still bigger man under him, no less to invite him to cast his shadow over the less gifted.

The paradox today is that as administrative power decreases and becomes more limited, the greater the dissatisfaction with it seems to grow. The memory of favors or requests denied remains much stronger than the memories of requests granted. Faculties are fickle in their allegiance. Overnight the most beloved of administrators can become the target of abuse, a figure of obloquy in the eyes of the very faculty, or a large section of it, which he himself has helped to build. In the very year that Clark Kerr received the Meikeljohn medal for academic freedom, the faculty at the University of California campus at Berkeley panicked in consequence of the events resulting from the *fourth* student sit-in.

In effect it repudiated him by adopting a set of resolutions that made him the scapegoat for the student lawlessness that it conspicuously refused to condemn. The faculty even voted down a motion that would have given the students complete freedom of speech except to urge the commission of *immediate acts* of force and violence. Another example: Vice President Truman of Columbia University received a standing ovation from faculty and students at a Columbia commencement for, among other things, opening new avenues of communication with them. Before another Commencement had rolled around he was scornfully booed by a section of the Columbia faculty.

Why any scholar (and administrators are largely recruited from the ranks of scholars) should want to become a *full-time* administrator has always puzzled me. The duties, sacrifices and risks seem altogether disproportionate to the rewards. In speaking of administrators, one is tempted to characterize them with the words Lecky used in his great history of European morals about the fallen women of Europe . . . "The eternal priestesses of humanity blasted for the sins of their people." Well, university administrators are no longer priests, but whenever a crisis arises they are sure to be damned if they do and damned if they don't.

One thing seems clear. In the crisis situations shaping up throughout the country, administrators are not going to enjoy a peaceful life. Their prospect of weathering the storms that will be synthetically contrived for them depends upon their ability and willingness to win the faculty for whatever plans and proposals are advanced in the name of the university. For if they permit students or any other group to drive a wedge between them and the faculty, they will discover the sad fact of academic life that in such rifts the faculty will either play a neutral role or even assume a hostile one.

Not only on good educational grounds, therefore, but on pru-
dential ones as well, the administration must draw the faculty
into the formulation of institutional educational policy. I say this
with reluctance because it means the proliferation of committee
meetings, the dilution of scholarly interests, and even less time for
students. But this is a small price to pay for academic freedom
and peace.

In talking about academic freedom, nothing signifies the distance we have come in the space of my lifetime so much as the
fact that we now are concerned with the academic freedom of
students. For historical reasons I cannot now explore, academic
freedom in the United States meant *Lehrfreiheit,* freedom to
teach. *Lernfreiheit,* freedom to learn, has only recently been
stressed. It does not mean the same as it meant under the German university system that presupposed the all-prescribed curriculum of studies of the *Gymnasium.* If academic freedom for students means freedom to learn, then two things should be obvious.
There is no academic freedom to learn without *Lehrfreiheit* or
academic freedom to teach. Where teachers have no freedom to
teach, students have obviously no freedom to learn, although the
converse is not true.

Second, students' freedom to learn was never so widely recognized, was never so pervasive in the United States as it is
today—whether it be construed as the freedom to attend college
or not, or the freedom to select the *kind* of college the student
wishes to attend or his freedom of curricular choice *within* the
kind of college he selects. Above all, if academic freedom for students means the freedom to doubt, challenge, contest and debate
within the context of inquiry, American students are the freest in
the world, and far freer than they were when I attended college.

I recall an incident when I was a student in a government class
at CCNY. The teacher conducted the class by letting the students
give reports on the themes of the course. All he contributed was
to say "next" as each student concluded. But when in reporting
on the Calhoun-Webster debates, I declared that it seemed to me
that Calhoun had the better of the argument, that his logic was
better than Webster's although his *cause* was worse, the instructor
exploded and stopped me. After emotionally recounting his father's services in the Civil War, he turned wrathfully on me and
shouted "Young man! When you're not preaching sedition, you
are preaching secession!" Whereupon he drove me from the class.
(The "sedition" was reference to an earlier report on Beard's

economic interpretation of the Constitution that he had heard
with grim disapproval.) And this was at CCNY in 1920! The in
cident wasn't typical, but that it could happen at all marks the
profundity of the changes in attitudes toward students since
then. John Dewey's influence has made itself felt even in the college today.

Of course, there is still a large group of potential college students who are deprived of freedom to learn because of poverty or
prejudice or the absence of adequate educational facilities. And as
citizens of a democratic society whose moral premise is that each
individual has a right to that education that will permit him to
achieve his maximum growth as a person, our duty is to work for,
or support, whatever measures of reconstruction we deem necessary to remove the social obstacles to freedom of learning. It is
perfectly legitimate to expect the university to study these problems and propose solutions to them. All universities worthy of the
name already do. This is one thing. But to therefore conclude
that these problems must become items not only on the agenda of
study but for an agenda of action is quite another.

For it therewith transforms the university into a political action
organization and diverts it from its essential task of discovery,
teaching, dialogue and criticism. Since there are profound
differences about the social means necessary to achieve a society
in which there will be a maximum freedom to learn, the university would become as partisan and biased as other political action
groups urging their programs on the community. Its primary educational purpose or mission would be lost. It would be compelled
to silence or misrepresent the position of those of its faculty who
disagreed with its proposals and campaigns of action. Class and
group conflicts would rend the fabric of the community of scholars in an unceasing struggle for power completely unrelated to
the quest for truth.

If the university is conceived as an agency of action to transform society in behalf of a cause, no matter how exalted, it loses
its *relative* autonomy, imperils both its independence and objectivity, and subjects itself to retaliatory curbs and controls on the
part of society on whose support and largesse it ultimately depends.

This is precisely the conception of a university that is basic to
the whole strategy and tactics of the so-called Students for a
Democratic Society. I say "so-called" because their actions show
that they are no more believers in democracy than the leaders of

the so-called Student Non-Violent Co-ordinating Committee are believers in non-violence. And indeed the leaders of the SDS make no bones about that fact. In manifesto after manifesto they have declared that they want to use the university as an instrument of revolution. To do so, they must destroy the university as it exists today.

I wish I had time to list some of the clever strategems they have devised to focus their opposition. On every campus there are always some grievances. Instead of seeking peacefully to resolve them through existing channels of consultation and deliberation, the SDS seeks to inflame them. Where grievances don't exist, they can be created. In one piece of advice to chapter members, they were urged to sign up for certain courses in large numbers, and then denounce the university for its large classes!

Freedom of dissent, speech, protest is never the real issue. They are, of course, always legitimate. But the tactic of the SDS is to give dissent the immediate form of violent action. The measures necessarily adopted to counteract this lawless action then become the main issue, as if the original provocation hadn't occurred. Mario Savio admitted after the Berkeley affair that the issue of "free speech" was a "pretext"—the word was his—to arouse the students against the existing role of the university in society. Speaking at Harvard on October 1, 1968, six months after he had led the "revolution" at Columbia, Mark Rudd said: "Let me tell you. We manufactured the issues. The Institute for Defense Analysis is nothing at Columbia. Just three professors. And the gym issue is bull. It doesn't mean anything to anybody. I had never been to the gym site before the demonstrations began. I didn't even know how to get there."

One of the leaders of the SDS at Columbia is reported to have said: "As much as we would like to, we are not strong enough as yet to destroy the United States. But we are strong enough to destroy Columbia!" He is wrong about this—the only action that would destroy Columbia would be faculty support of the students!—but his intent is clear.

Actually the only thing these groups, loosely associated with the New Left, are clear about is what they want to destroy, not what they would put in its stead. In a debate with Gore Vidal, Tom Hayden, one of the New Left leaders, was pointedly asked what his revolutionary program was. He replied: "We haven't any. First we will make the revolution, and *then* we will find out what for." This is truly the politics of absurdity.

The usual response present-day academic rebels make to this criticism is that the university today is nothing but an instrument to preserve the status quo, and therefore faithless to the ideals of a community of scholars. Even if this charge were true, even if the universities today were bulwarks of the status quo, this would warrent criticism and protest, not violent and lawless action in behalf of a contrary role, just as foreign to their true function. But it is decidedly *not* true!

There is no institution in the country in which dissent and criticism of official views, of tradition, of the conventional wisdom in all fields, is freer and more prevalent than in the university. The very freedom of dissent that students today enjoy in our universities is in large measure a consequence of the spirit of experiment, openness to new ideas, absence of conformity and readiness to undertake new initiatives found among them.

The first casualty of the strategy of the campus rebels is academic freedom. It is manifest in their bold and arrogant claim that the university drop its research in whatever fields these students deem unfit for academic inquiry and investigation. This note was already sounded in Berkeley. It is focal at Columbia. It is a shameless attempt to usurp powers of decision on academic matters that the faculty alone should have. After all, it is preposterous for callow and immature adolescents who presumably have come to the university to get an education to set themselves up as authorities on what research by their teachers is educationally permissible.

Unless checked, it will not be long before these students will be presuming to dictate the conclusions their teachers should reach, especially on controversial subjects. This is standard procedure in totalitarian countries in which official student organizations are the political arm of the ruling party. Already there are disquieting signs of this. At Cornell—*before* the martyrdom of Dr. King—a group of Black Nationalist students invaded the offices of the chairman of the economics department and held him captive in order to get an apology from a teacher whose views on African affairs they disagreed with. Only yesterday, another group at Northwestern demanded that courses in "black literature" and "black art" be taught only by teachers approved by the Negro students.

And there are spineless administrators and cowardly members of the faculty who are prepared to yield to this blackmail. Under the slogans of "student rights" and "participatory democracy" the most militant groups of students are moving to weaken and ulti-

mately destroy the academic freedom of those who disagree with
them.

Let us not delude ourselves. Even when these militant students
fail to achieve their ultimate purpose, they succeed in demoraliz-
ing the university by deliberately forcing a confrontation upon the
academic community that it is not prepared to face and the costs
of which it is fearful of accepting. In forcing the hand of the academic community to meet force with force, the citadel of reason
becomes a battlefield. The students glory in it, but the faint of
heart among their teachers turn on their own principled colleagues and administrative leaders. These militants succeed in
sowing distrust among students who do not see through their
strategy. They also succeed in dividing the faculties.

There is always a small group—a strange mixture of purists and
opportunists desirous of ingratiating themselves with students—
who will *never* condemn the violence of students but only the violence ultimately required to stop it. These students succeed, even
when they fail, in embittering relations between the administration and some sections of the faculty. They succeed, even when
they fail, in antagonizing the larger community of which the university is a part, and in arousing a vigilante spirit that demands
wholesale measures of repression and punishment that educators
cannot properly accept.

How is it possible, one asks, for events of this character to
happen? There have always been extremist and paranoidal tendencies in academic life, but they have been peripheral—
individuals and small groups moving in eccentric intellectual or-
bits. But not until the last four or five years has the norm of social protest taken the form of direct action, have positions been
expressed in such ultimatistic and intransigent terms, have extremist elements been strong enough to shut down great universities even for a limited time.

There are many and complex causes for this. But as I see it, the
situation in the university is part of a larger phenomenon, viz.,
the climate of intellectual life in the country. I do not recall any
other period in the last fifty years when intellectuals themselves
have been so intolerant of each other, when differences over
complex issues have been the occasion for denunciation rather than
debate and analysis, when the use of violence—in the right cause,
of course!—is taken for granted, when dissent is not distinguished
from civil disobedience, and civil disobedience makes common
cause with resistance, and readiness for insurrection. A few short

years ago, anti-intellectualism was an epithet of derogation. Today it is an expression of revolutionary virility.

In the fifties I wrote an essay on "The Ethics of Controversy,"
trying to suggest guidelines for controversy among principled
democrats no matter how widely they differed on substantive
issues. Today I would be talking into the wind for all the attention it would get. Fanaticism seems to be in the saddle. That it is
a fanaticism of conscience, of self-proclaimed virtue, doesn't make
it less dangerous. This past year has presented the spectacle of
militant minorities in our colleges from one end of the country to
another preventing or trying to prevent representatives of positions they disapprove of from speaking to their fellow-students
wishing to listen to them.

The spectacle shows that we have failed to make our students
understand the very rudiments of democracy, that to tolerate active intolerance is to compound it. If we judge commitment by
action, the simple truth is that the great body of our students is
not firmly committed to democracy or to the liberal spirit without
which democracy may become the rule of the mob.

I do not know any sure way or even a new way of combating
the dominant mood of irrationalism, especially among students
and even among younger members of the faculty whose political
naiveté is often cynically exploited by their younger, yet politically more sophisticated, allies. What is of the first importance is
to preserve, of course, the absolute intellectual integrity of our
classrooms and laboratories, of our teaching and research against
any attempt to curb it. We must defend it not only against the
traditional enemies, who still exist even when they are dormant
but also against those who think they have the infallible remedies
for the world's complex problems and that all they need is sincerity as patent of authority. Fanatics don't lack sincerity. It is
their long suit. They drip with sincerity—and when they have
power, with blood—other people's blood.

We need more, however, than a defensive strategy, safeguard-
ing the intellectual integrity of our vocation against those who
threaten it. We need—and I know this sounds paradoxical—to
counterpose to the revolt of the emotionally committed the revolt
of the rationally committed. I do not want to identify this with
the revolt of the moderates. There are some things one should not
be moderate about. In the long run, the preservation of democracy depends upon a passion for freedom, for the logic and ethics
of free discussion and inquiry, upon refusal to countenance the

measures of violence that cut short the processes of intelligence upon which the possibility of shared values depends.

These are old truths but they bear repeating whenever they are denied. Even tautologies become important when counterposed to absurdities.

We as teachers must make our students more keenly aware of the centrality of the democratic process to a free society and of the centrality of intelligence to the democratic process. Democracy has our allegiance because of its cumulative fruits, but at any particular time the process is more important than any specific program or product. He who destroys the process because it does not guarantee some particular outcome is as foolish as someone who discards scientific method in medicine or engineering or any other discipline because of its failure to solve altogether or immediately a stubborn problem.

There is one thing we cannot deny to the intransigent and fanatical enemies of democracy. That is courage. Intelligence is necessary to overcome foolishness. But it is not sufficient to tame fanaticism. Only courage can do that. A handful of men who are prepared to fight, to bleed, to suffer and, if need be, to die, will always triumph in a community where those whose freedom they threaten are afraid to use their *intelligence* to resist and to fight, and ultimately to take the same risks in action as those determined to destroy them.

Yes, there is always the danger that courage *alone* may lead us to actions that will make us similar to those who threaten us. But that is what we have intelligence for—to prevent that from happening! It is this union of courage and intelligence upon which depends hope not only of democratic survival but of the free university.

2. LEVEL OF DISCOURSE
IS A KEY TO THE TONE
OF SOCIETY'S FUTURE

A. M. Rosenthal

A. M. Rosenthal is Managing Editor of The New York Times.

EXCEPT for just one little matter, there really is no terrible mystery as to what the future will be. The future will be the present, as the present is the past.

Science never changes; only the degree of attainment, ^f unlocking, change. The medieval barber who cut into his screaming patient was part of the process of heart transplant, and the Wright Brothers, at Kitty Hawk, were flying toward the moon, in exactly the same sense as Apollo 8 was flying not just moonwards, but to Mars and beyond.

This is the true beauty, poetry and hope inherent in science—the knowledge that it is all there, immutable, and waiting for the proper nerve connections to be made in the brain of man. A scientist at IBM once dismissed with a wave of his hand the intricacies of the computer—they were merely mechanical—and said that far more complicated and wonderful was the mind of an infant discovering his own existence.

Those who were infants not very long ago will, in the next quarter-century, make a few more nerve connections, turn a few more locks, and man will live longer, fly higher, travel faster, see more. The future is entirely discernible; only the details of achievement are to be filled in.

Entirely discernible, except for one little matter—the tone and texture of society. That is quite an open question because it is one thing that does change, and it involves a number of other interesting matters: What will be man's values, standards and goals?

Reprinted, with permission, from the *New York Times,* January 6, 1969.

What will he consider worthwhile and what will he consider dispensable? What will be his style of thought?

These are interesting because they involve qualitative, rather than quantitative, differences. There is a quantitative difference between Kitty Hawk and Apollo 8, but there is a qualitative difference between slavery and emancipation, between illiteracy and reading, between creativity and obedience, between free process and authoritarianism and—decidedly and mostly—between a culture based on standing up and a culture based on standing up against the wall, anybody's wall.

These are interesting, and not really predictable, because while the history of science is pretty clearly a line moving up and forward, the history of man—what he decides to do with his life—is just as clearly a line that rises and dips and curves, moves forward an inch, retreats a yard, moves again.

Put it this way: Assuming for the sake of argument that the world doesn't just blow itself up in a nuclear smash and get the whole thing over with, science won't go back to Kitty Hawk. But there is nobody who can predict that twenty-five years from now any number of free societies or societies moving toward freedom will not reverse and dart backward into despotism.

There are souls who truly still believe that there is a direct relationship between scientific or industrial achievement and political progress. Increased production leads to increased education and increased education leads to increased freedom. Said fast, like a chant, it sounds reasonable. And it is reasonable.

The only trouble is that it doesn't work. Stalin's production record was a lot better than that of the Czars, and Hitler greatly outproduced the Weimar Republic. Political progress is not a matter only of reason, but of attitude, emotion and belief.

And of all attitudes none are more central than those that have to do with individualism and self-expression—freedom of thought and word—because these most determine the texture of society.

The future of society cannot be graphed, but there are some discernible clues and they are not all exhilarating.

Freedom of thought and some form of democratic parliamentary process—the only form yet devised of translating freedom of thought into political action—are quite delicate fruits and require considerable devotion to be kept from falling from the tree.

Opposition to free thought is unfortunately contagious and it is easy to see why. Conformity, of the left or right, removes the uncomfortable irritants that go with free thought—the necessity to argue logically, which can be terribly annoying, and the possibility that one's own emotions and philosophies may be tested and discarded, which is even more annoying.

It requires far more dedication and passion to maintain these delicate fruits than to destroy them. Trying to peer ahead, it seems quite likely that the dedication and passion may come primarily from other parts of the world. In the United States, if it comes at all it will be from those who have not yet fully entered political activity rather than those young people who now consider themselves today's militant leaders.

In any area, the philosophic tone of society is determined by a small group of people, those who have the instinct and talent for political leadership and political action. This has never been more important than in the present and it will continue to be so in the future. Access to television and to thousands of newspapers simultaneously through wire services has given to those who want it a worldwide podium.

The problem, as far as the tone of society is concerned, does not lie in the causes—far more novel and revolutionary ideas have been accepted and built into democratic communities than student participation, black power or even the right of every young man not to get a haircut twice a month.

The problem centers on the simple fact that in the United States the techniques of militancy adopted are those antithetical to discourse among men of conflicting opinion, obviously the one essential to democratic process.

Not much of a discourse takes place when one participant smashes another in the face. And the techniques of present-day militancy often simply are verbal blows in the face.

Obscene epithets are blows in the face, and in political struggle they have a deliberate, thought-out function. To look at a man and speak to him vilely is to throw filth in his face.

Fascists of the right and of the left know that when a man is so addressed he is humiliated and brought down and they know that when filth is thrown the recipient, however decent, suddenly stands amidst the reek.

Obscenity is simply one more weapon in political street warfare, and so is racism, but much more powerful, much more distructive of discourse. Conceivably there is a difference between calling a man a Jew pig and calling him a nigger, but it is rather difficult to see.

Taken separately, obscenity, racism and such allied techniques as breaking up meetings and harassing speakers are weapons in political struggle. Taken together, of course, they amount to a body of thought or anti-thought summed up in the Marcusian philosophy that absolutely everybody has a right to speak—that is, absolutely everybody who is approved by the determining elite who know what is best for the people.

What does all this have to do with the future? The techniques of militancy, left or right, create a climate of violence not simply against those who use them, but within those who use them. The means not only affect the ends, but they affect the user. They warp him and they stunt him permanently.

To the degree, therefore, that the thought-destructive techniques of verbal violence are accepted in any generation, to that degree they prevent the generation from utilizing all its mental and emotional powers in the preservation of thought and discourse when its own future arrives.

A person who has spat upon, kicked or assaulted an opponent—verbally or physically—may recover to some extent from the illness he imposed upon himself, but he can never recover entirely, never be quite as trusted or quite as useful to a free society. He will always be a little crippled.

Unhappily, there is no guarantee that in the next quarter-century today's violents will agree with all this and come limping contritely along and be nice democratic boys and girls.

Quite likely they will be so impertinent as to remain convinced that they are right and people like the writer wrong, and keep pointing out to us our assigned places against the waiting wall.

Quite likely, the next twenty-five years or so in this country will, politically, be a period that could not have been foreseen twenty-five years ago, around the end of World War II.

It will be the period, perhaps more than any other in American history, that will determine the political and social values of American society. The issue will not be attainment of full economic opportunity for Negroes, or ending the closed-circuit concept of the university, or redistribution of wealth and taxes to "help the poor."

All of these goals, and a lot more have been accepted theoretically by American society.

Theory is not enought? Only attainment counts?

Even accepting the answers as taken—which is, not quite so, as anybody who has ever tasted the difference between living under the theory of freedom and the theory of despotism knows—these goals will not be the central issue.

They are not the central issue because not one of the goals is attainable except within a society built upon discourse. In the absence of discourse, society resorts to force and in the entire history of mankind there has never been a society built on force that did a thing about racial minorities, universities or the poor except to manipulate them in the maintenance of power.

But if it does come to a struggle based on force, the betting man of 1969 would have to put his money on the right. Not on the comfortably known and talk-minded right of Goldwater and Buckley, not at all, but on the shadowy and knuckle-minded right that dislikes Jew pigs but doesn't care much either for niggers or unwashed long-hairs and has its own wall in mind for the whole bunch of them.

In a struggle based on hatred, they will discard the Goldwaters and Buckleys as the far left is discarding the McCarthys and the Kennedys; they'll win because when it comes to hate they really are better at it.

The issue in this country will be then that one little matter: the texture of society, the tone of discourse. The question will be: Is freedom of expression really all that important?.

Considerably before 1994 we should have the answers, which will determine not whether Americans will go beyond the moon but whether they will be in much of a hurry to come back.

II

STUDENT UNREST

3. ON THE NEW STUDENT NIHILISM

Herbert A. Deane

*Herbert A. Deane is Professor of Government and Public Law
at Columbia University.*

I HAVE BEEN increasingly concerned in the last year or so about
an attitude (or, perhaps, collection of attitudes), among some students in the present generation, of rejection and hostility towards
many, if not all, established institutions, organizations, and standards. Let me say first that after eighteen years of college and
university teaching I am keenly aware that generalizations about
student attitudes and behavior are exceedingly perilous; today, as
in the past, college students demonstrate at least as wide a variety
of opinions and actions as their elders do.

Therefore, I recognize that the hostility to institutions and standards which alarms me is demonstrated by only a small minority
of students, and it may be that it has not yet appeared at all campuses. Nevertheless, I fear that this attitude of rejection of organizations and traditional patterns of behavior will probably spread
beyond the confines of the small group of students who now hold
it. It has, for youth, all the attraction of an extreme position; it
presents itself under the guise of a highly moral and principled
refusal to compromise in any way with the world, the flesh, and

Reprinted, with permission, from the *Graduate Faculties Newsletter*, Columbia
University, June 1967. The article is based on an address delivered at Muhlenberg
College in November 1967.

the devil; and some aspects of our contemporary society may easily tempt more young people to an outright rejection of the institutions and practices in the world around them. There is hypocrisy, vulgar materialism, expensive ugliness, addiction to high-sounding ideals which are rarely permitted to interfere with shrewd, cold pursuit of narrow self-interest, widespread indifference to those who are not successful in the competitive race—the poor, the elderly, the handicapped, the disinherited minorities at home, and the "stupid" and impoverished masses of Asia, Africa, and Latin America abroad. All these obvious aspects of contemporary American life provide, I believe, a fertile soil for further growth of this attitude of total rejection among a larger number of students, many of whom will be the more intelligent, concerned, and sensitive members of their generation.

Yet, to this negative aspect there may be a hopeful complement. To an extent perhaps unequalled in history, conscientious self-examination is denying us the comfort of pretenses; there is great idealism, which is by no means confined to the young, and new striving to break through the accumulated parochialisms of ages; and in many minds there is concern approaching militant dedication to overcome inequities that have attended civilization from its beginnings. Nevertheless, the young lack sophistication born of experience, and tend, a priori, to resent wrongs and to discount the resistant causes of evil. Therefore the imperfections in the world about us provide ready pretexts for youthful hostility. The cause of that hostility is not so apparent as the syndrome. It is not clear whether the phenomenon is part of a rather fundamental change in basic values among students in general, or a consequence of the rapid pace of social change and the instability of values attendant on a high rate of geographical and social mobility.

Let me try to specify what I mean by an attitude of rejection of standards and institutions, and then to distinguish very sharply between that attitude and a radical critique of existing standards and organizations, no matter how extreme that critique may be. The new student attitude—and for want of a better term let me call it the "anarchistic" or "nihilistic" attitude—seems to reject all existing institutions and patterns of behavior. It seems to reject the state, the legal system, political parties, churches, colleges, and universitites, and seems to deny objective standards of excellence in literature, the arts, and morals. I want, however, to distinguish between the attitude and the students. Although I cau-

tiously use the term "nihilism," I do not wish to describe any of
the students as outright nihilists. A few of them seem to speak
and behave as if they thought destruction were the only suitable
solution for existing ills; but others are less dogmatic, and still
others have more limited targets for their hostility. The attitude
is expressed differently by different students, and is not confined
to those who are adherents of any one ideological position such
as, for example, that of the so-called "new left."

There is much talk about how individuals in the present-day
world of large and complex organizations, find themselves in a
state of "alienation" (a word which has become so amorphous
and vague as its use has become popular that we would all do
well to avoid it). Organizations, institutions, norms are condemned, root and branch, because they stifle the expression of the
free, creative impulses of the individuals caught up in their toils
and turn them into gray, faceless, conforming automata. In particular, our nonrational impulses—our capacities for pleasure,
anger, sexual enjoyment, domination—are said to be in danger of
being stamped out by the rationalism and conformity that are
supposed to be characteristic of organizational and institutional
life today.

Civilization—for that is the shorthand term for the whole complex of institutions, norms, and standards—is the enemy. In the
new "anarchist" gospel, preached, for example, by Norman O.
Brown in his book, *Life Against Death*, which has been popular
reading among undergraduates during the past decade, civilization
and all its appurtenances must be smashed, or at least radically
simplified, in order to liberate the primal human urges and capacities that are now being stifled or blunted by it. A corollary is
that no activity should be organized, planned, or directed—that
action (indeed even art) should follow the dictates of momentary
impulse and "feeling," and that spontaneity, "genuineness," and
the satisfaction of impulse should be the only guides to conduct.
To follow any other path is, at best, to be "square" and stodgy,
and at worst, to surrender one's individuality and integrity to
soulless, dehumanized institutions or to cold, impersonal standards
of behavior.

So, for example, we are now asked to go to the theatre, the
concert hall, or the art gallery to see and hear spontaneous "happenings," whose authors and performers proudly proclaim that
they do not know in advance what is going to happen and, after
the event, are unable to tell us what has happened and what it

all meant. One suspects that some of these "happenings" are not as spontaneous as they are pretended to be. But the terms in which they are rationalized are highly significant. This mood in the world of the arts is not confined to a small fringe group; it has made its way even into the commercial theatre of Broadway; and we in New York have had "happenings" of this sort for the edification of the public in Central Park under the patronage of an energetic high priest of "culture," ex-Parks Commissioner Thomas Hoving (Ph.D., Princeton).

Students who have become converted to this new libertarian or anarchist doctrine now tell us that colleges and universities in the present form are not fulfilling their true function of liberating and developing the potentialities of human beings. Indeed, organized courses and seminars, even regular, organized extracurricular activities, to say nothing of elaborately organized administrative apparatuses—committees, department chairmen, cold-faced deans, provosts, and presidents—constitute an elaborate contrivance to repress all real curiosity, imagination, and individuality that may still lurk within the student, and to turn him into another homogeneous, stereotyped product who will fit neatly into the adult world of "organization men" neatly arranged in corporate hierarchies, and who will never (or hardly ever) suspect that he has sold his soul for a mess of pottage.

In this anarchistic vision the only meaningful education would be found in a deeply personal, sustained, unorganized, and spontaneous relation between a single student and his teacher, who would presumably be available at any hour, day or night, when the student felt the urge to "communicate." There would be no courses, no structured curriculum, certainly no requirements and no grades to mar this ideal relationship.

While this dream is obviously a fantasy, it—or something close to it—is sometimes seriously advanced as an ideal by students who like to consider themselves non-conformist, radical, anti-organization men. Not too long ago one of my College students complained bitterly about the lack of "personal contact" of students with faculty and administration at Columbia—a perennial complaint on most campuses and one that is sometimes justified. I reminded him of the conversations that he and I had had after class, of the office hours during which members of the faculty made themselves available to students, and of the series of informal "fireside chats" which the Dean of the College and members of the faculty had been holding with reasonably small groups of undergraduates in the dormitories. He dismissed all these "contacts" as meaningless or "phony" because they were not spontaneous and "free" but were in some degree organized and planned. When I pushed him a bit on this issue, he finally admitted that the only "communication" with the Dean or a teacher that he would regard as satisfactory would be a meeting that occurred without plan and that led to an hour or so of conversation about life, love, death, war and peace, and basic values. When I pointed out that if this were to be the practice, we would have to reduce the size of the College to the forty or fifty students whom the Dean might be able to see and talk to during a week, he remained completely unshaken in his devotion to his ideal and in his opposition to the present "system."

A weaker but more popular version of this same ideal is the Paul Goodman-supported vision of "participatory democracy" in the university. In this version, there is still a University and there are still courses and seminars, but students share with the faculty the decisions about what shall be taught, how it shall be taught, how the university shall be administered, and how faculty should be chosen and promoted to tenure posts. A few such "universities" have been started in makeshift ways, and provide us with examples of what the "students" and "faculty" have in mind. It might be added that many who attend these have not seen fit to cut themselves off completely from traditional education.

Lest I seem to be an unreconstructed Bourbon reactionary, let me say that I have no objection at all to student concern with college and university administrative decisions. Administrators who consult with student representatives on a variety of issues are likely to make wiser decisions and rules than those who never make any effort to discover what students want or what is troubling them. But I am concerned when some students spend far more of their time in discussions of the problems of university administration than they do on their academic pursuits. I am just as worried when a college student devotes too much time and energy to athletic or non-athletic extracurricular activites and virtually ignores his primary task as a student—his education.

The main responsibility of students, after all, is still studying, just as the primary task of teachers is teaching and of administrators is administering. If students do not want their teachers to decide what courses shall be taught and what should be included in them, if a course is only a discussion on some subject among students and teacher, who are all regarded as equals, if a course is just a sustained conversation or "bull-session," why should the student and his parents waste their time and money on a college education? Why should I (or anyone else) be paid for teaching if all I do is to go into a classroom and ask, "Well, fellows, what do you think about all this?" and if what follows is an unstructured conversation to which I contribute no more than any of the students?

Another facet of this problem is the refusal of some students to admit that there are any valid, objective criteria for determining the worth of an idea or an interpretation of an event or a piece of writing. Personal reaction, sincerity, what one feels deeply—these are said to be the only real criteria. As one of my students said to me last year, "This is what I felt when I was reading Freud. Since I am reporting honestly and sincerely my emotional reactions to the work, you should accept my report as a valid account of what Freud really meant. This," he said, "is 'my Freud.' You are entitled," he acknowledged with great magnanimity, "to 'your Freud,' but don't force me to accept 'your Freud.' " When I asked whether despite all the problems of interpreting and understanding any text, we could not agree that there was a "real" Freud "out there," to whose writings we could both go to see whether his interpretation could be justified, he insisted that there was no such independent entity and that only his (or my) personal, emotional reactions to the words were real. Down this road, of course, lie absolute chaos and nihilism; the "communication" that these students value so highly becomes a total impossibility when nothing except the individual's subjective, emotional reactions are recognized as real and legitimate. Each of us ends up as a totally isolated self, locked in a soundproof room, and unable to communicate with any other human being.

One of the greatest ironies involved in this whole nihilistic critique of civilization and all its works is that the opponents of institutions and standards often rely, as Norman Brown does, on Freud as the basis for their condemnation of artifice, organization, and civilization and for their glorification of individual impulse and instinctual urges. Now it is clear that in *Civilization and Its Discontents* and in other works Freud argued that the whole fabric of increasingly complex institutions has been built up in large part on the basis of instinctual renunciation, especially on the repression or redirection of erotic and aggressive impulses, and that he urged that, precisely in order to preserve the fragile fabric of civilization and rationality, excessive and unnecessary restraints on impulses be lightened or removed so as to minimize the danger of an explosion of repressed instincts which might destroy civilization. But this is a far cry from arguing that the restraints imposed on instincts by civilization, by institutions, and by accepted standards of behavior should be smashed in order to liberate the full force of instinctual energy.

Freud, like Augustine, was far too much the sad-eyed realist to agree with the nineteenth-century anarchist view that human beings were by nature predominantly altruistic, cooperative, and reasonable, and that this essentially good human nature would exhibit itself in conduct once the distorting and warping influences of the political, economic, and legal orders were removed. He would, I am certain, be equally appalled by the views of the contemporary "anarchists" who see in institutions and standards of behavior nothing but forces repressing basically good and cooperative human impulses. For it was Freud who regarded the limited, hard-won gains of human reason in individual and social life as the most valuable achievement of men.

Nothing I have said in criticism of this anarchist or nihilist view should be taken as opposition to radical criticism of existing political, educational, religious, and other institutions, especially on the part of the young. There is always need for vigorous and fundamental criticism of existing norms and institutions, and, given the fact that most of us normally tend to become more conservative and more fearful of change as we grow older, such criticism must come primarily from the young. Without such critical assaults, institutions and standards tend to become ossified and decadent; the spirit that originally motivated them—the concern, ultimately, for the well-being of the individuals who make up the organization or the group—is gradually forgotten or relegated to a position of inferiority to the demands of the organizational machinery itself, and we are left with the dry husks of external forms from which the life has departed. So society needs its radical critics, along with its less radical reformers, and its intelligent conservatives, in order to prosper, even if the young radicals sometimes appear to their elders to be naive, utopian, and simplistic. The attitude of the radical, however, differs sharply from the nihilist attitude that I have been discussing; no matter how vigorous and fundamental his criticisms may be, his posture is essentially a constructive one, since he always believes that he can propose a new set of institutions or standards that will serve human needs and aspirations far better than do existing arrangements.

He may be wrong in this judgment, and he is often mistaken in his too-easy assumption that it is possible to move directly and smoothly from where we now are to where he would have us be (as Marx forcefully pointed out in his criticisms of the Utopian Socialists of his day). But he does recognize the need for some structure or order to give meaning and direction to human life, and his own positive proposals are presented for examination and criticism by those who are more satisfied with existing institutions or who would change them only gradually and slowly. Even if his proposals turn out to be utopian or visionary, statement and discussion of them sometimes help to clarify the present situation and to suggest reforms that were not part of the radical author's intention. The young radical does not propose to smash the existing order of institutions and standards without giving any thought to what shall be put in its place or what the disastrous consequences may be if the fabric of civilization is ripped apart and nothing is or can be substituted for it.

To the members of my generation who have seen the incredible barbarity and destructiveness of which men are capable if the restraining forces of the artifice we call civilization are destroyed, the nihilistic program—smash the constraints of civilization so that blind, spontaneous impulse and instinct may be unhindered and men may be "free"—is an open invitation to anarchy and destruction, and, finally, to tyranny, for men will not long endure the misery of anarchy, and they will prefer even the tyrant's order to no order at all.

At every point in human history of which we have any knowledge, men have lived in organized societies and indeed have not been able to survive outside such societies. A society is a network of institutions—settled ways of behaving and judging—and of generally accepted norms and standards. The society in which we now live is probably the most complex network of institutions, organizations, and rules and norms that the world has ever seen, and, despite the nostalgia that some people exhibit for an older, simpler society, this complexity and multiplicity of institutions and standards will probably increase rather than diminish. Our age, therefore, is the one in which the impulse to break down the institutional framework is most impractical and most dangerous. We have to live with institutions, organizations, and norms. We cannot hope (or wish) to go back to a state of nature or a Garden of Eden. Our task is to improve our present institutional arrangements and to invent new arrangements so that they more adequately satisfy the wants and needs of the individuals who live under them.

In any ultimate perspective, institutions and organizations, like men, are mortal. But in comparison with the lives of individual men, their lives and the influence they exert continue incomparably longer. No one of us can accomplish very much during his brief span of years if he works and strives as an isolated atom. Almost all the accomplishments of our ancestors have been made through the medium of the institutions and the norms to which they have contributed. Our accomplishments, like theirs, can only be made through a framework of institutions and standards.

4. EDUCATION IN FEVER

Charles Frankel

Charles Frankel is Old Dominion Professor of Philosophy
at Columbia University.

IT USED TO BE said of politics on the university campus that it was
the worst of all kinds of politics because the stakes were so small.
We should be able to take at least minor comfort, then, from the
present situation in the educational world: the stakes today are
not at all small. They involve the politics of the country as a
whole and things that go deeper than politics—the country's intellectual and moral standards, its commitment to justice, the tone of
our everyday relationships to one another. We can no longer doubt
that the teachers, students, and educational administrators of this
country are engaged in an enterprise, a struggle, a drama, which
constitutes a major chapter in the history of education and of
moral conscience. And it is a chapter not only in the history of
this country but in the history of the Western world and, in all
probability, of the whole world.

It is not surprising that this should be so. The type of society
known as *modern society*, of which the United States is probably
the most extreme example, is an extraordinary amalgam of daz-
zling achievement and sickening failure, of demanding ideals and
shoddy standards. It is historically unique in its combination of
humanitarianism and violence, social equality and social prejudice, individual autonomy and bureaucratic control, rational planning and irrational waste, convenience and inconvenience, sanita-
tion and pollution.

Where but in schools and universities should the crisis of conscience of such a society show itself?

This, I think, is the large, circumambient fact out of which the
current disorders in higher education have grown. There is much
that is difficult to understand about them and much that is impossible to accept. I do not doubt that many of these disorders are the
work, at the beginning, of a tiny minority of students employing
techniques of provocation and manipulation. But unless we bear

Reprinted, with the permission of the American Association of School Administrators, from *Your AASA*, official report for the 1969 Convention of the Association.

in mind the general condition of our society and its impact on
sensitive minds, we cannot understand what is happening. People
may be throwing matches, but the dry field is there ready to go
up in smoke and flames.

For our society puts an immense psychological and moral pressure on any individual who takes its official rationale seriously. Its
resources are enormous; its conception of human possiblity, of the
condition of life achievable by the great masses of mankind, out-
runs all previous conceptions; the faith it reposes in technology,
social engineering, government, and education as instruments to
realize this conception has the intensity of a religion. And thus
the old question, "If you're so smart, why aren't you rich?" takes
a disturbing twist in our society. If we're so rich, why aren't we
smart? If we're as ambitious and idealistic as our rhetoric suggests,
why are we suffering from a deep malaise? Or is this society simply a study in organized hypocrisy?

It is inevitable that many among us, and particularly young
people, will ask this question. It broods over our national stage
like the ghost of Hamlet's father. And so long as it is impossible
to dismiss it as pure fantasy, we can understand the reactions of
hundreds of thousands of students and teachers who begin as bystanders in campus disorders and who end as partisans and participants. They may not agree with all the specific demands of
those who first provoke the disorders, but they hear that question
behind the demands. And so they find themselves sympathizing
or, at any rate, unable to take a sharp stance in opposition.

And yet, moral indignation and moral fervor are not by themselves a basis for an educational philosophy or a political program. It is tempting to treat them as though they were, and that
is what has been happening. But moral clarity is needed as well
as moral concern. A sense of educational principles is relevant,
and not only the continued use of the adjective *relevance*.

The first step, I think, in coming to grips with the profound
educational crisis we face is to try to restore some precision to the
words we use, to the premises that should guide our thinking, and
to the rules that should guide our conduct. It is with this in mind
that I have composed these remarks to you.

Let me begin by indicating to you my own speculations about
the more immediate causes of present student unrest. I must make
it plain that I claim no superior insight into these matters. We
are in the presence of what is still, in many respects, a mystery—a
sudden outburst of insurgency among the most favored youth in

the world for which little in our theories or our history had prepared us. My confidence in my views is only the confidence of a man who suspects that those who are surer than he is about the answers must know even less.

To be sure, I think the larger background of student unrest is fairly plain. As I have already suggested, it is the condition of our society. But there are also certain special features of this unrest which require a more specific explanation. Why, in the first place, have the young become the most extreme in the expression of indignation at the way things are? Why are the places at which they are concentrated in large numbers becoming the leading centers of protest? Why, indeed, have people who might be regarded as among the most fortunate in our society become the major spokesmen of philosophies of alienation?

Vietnam and the draft, in this country, strike at the young particularly, and undoubtedly they are part of the explanation. But they can only be part of the explanation because, as we know, student unrest is now a phenomenon in most countries, and particularly in the richer ones.

Television and the speed and impact of modern mass communications undoubtedly help to account for this international phenomenon. But again, these too are not enough. The impact of a message or an event is not simply a consequence of the power of the medium by which it is transmitted. It depends on the receptivity of the audience, on its antecedent interests, attitudes, discontents, desires. Rich modern societies, I would diffidently suggest to you, may have a new kind of problem on their hands—a problem that is caused, if I may so put it, by a clash between biology and sociology.

To the general restlessness produced in these societies, both by the character of their vaulting ambitions and by the contrast between their ambitions and their achievements, there is also added a specific cause of restlessness among youth. *Youth*, as such, is—in a way—an invention of modern society. People have been young before, but only in the last century or so have very large numbers of people been held in a position of prolonged social dependency after reaching biological maturity. Youth is that peculiarly marked-off period in life when people, pressed by powerful sexual and psychic drives, and desiring to break loose and live their own lives, are told that, for society's purpose and in their own best interests, they must postpone regarding themselves as fully grown up.

Now, I don't point to this state of affairs to denounce it. I do not agree with those who treat it as though it were a conspiracy of the old against the young. Indeed, if we are to talk about hypocrisy in this society, it seems to me that one of the major forms of hypocrisy is exhibited by people in their forties and fifties who are so anxious to show that they aren't suffering from hardening of the arteries that they talk and act as though age, experience, and study offered no advantages and might perhaps be positive disqualifications in dealing with human problems. Happily, few of the young themselves believe this.

Nevertheless, whether the condition in life known as *youth* is an imposed and arbitrary condition or not, it is a condition that affects a steadily growing proportion of the populations of modern societies. During the last twenty years it has grown dramatically in its duration, in its extent, and in the tensions that go with it. It begins earlier. Changes in mores, the influence of television and mass communications, the urbanization of society, and quite possibly better diets have all conspired to make people grow up faster. Youth goes on longer because people spend, on the average, more years in school. In affects larger and larger numbers of people because high school, and then college, and now graduate and professional school have increasingly become part of the normal expectations of life. And the tensions that go with this status are aggravated by rising demands on one side and by rising frustrations on the other.

Young people today are more accustomed to freedom, more catered to by the fashions, more used to having their opinions listened to and their wants gratified. And yet, in the colleges and universities they live under conditions immensely more crowded and uncomfortable than those that have prevailed in the past. They receive less attention from teachers and very probably less stimulation from their work. And their futures are shadowed by the prospect of service in a war most of them cannot accept as necessary or just. If we were trying intentionally to put the squeeze on a generation, we could hardly do better.

Moreover, the squeeze is being felt by a college and university generation which is different in its composition from its predecessors. Thirty years ago, certainly fifty years ago, the people who went to college fell into two main categories: some were the children of the aristocrats and the rich, and the others were pushing to improve their condition in life. And each of these groups had a reason to submit to the discipline of college life and to think that their apprentice status made sense.

The aristocrats and the rich knew where they were going. They understood that they were being prepared to exercise power, to enjoy deference, to be members of the club. Besides, the discipline of college life was not all that much discipline. They had ways of evading it, or of breaking loose, which were accepted, safe, and even honored. In the end, they knew that a gentleman's "C" would always do.

As for those trying to climb up from below, college obviously was immensely useful. It was a privilege, an opportunity; even those who thought the society evil and wished to revolutionize it would not have thought of attacking its institutions of learning. Certainly the idea that youth is a time of restraint and sacrifice would have seemed to most of them normal and reasonable.

But the present generation in colleges and universities is some what different. A much larger number of them come from families that belong neither to a recognizable elite nor to the ranks of the disadvantaged. They are the children of well-to-do people, but they do not expect to run the country. And neither do they expect to improve very much on the performance or social position of their fathers.

Moreover, a good deal that they have absorbed from their society, whether it be from their parents or their schools, from Salinger or Marcuse or from what they have seen for themselves, has left them profoundly unpersuaded that they want to live as their fathers have or get caught in the same rat-race.

Why, then, are they in college? Why can't they go off on their own? Why can't they show their contempt for ambitions and social disciplines that have nothing behind them but the pressure of an empty social code or the desire for material possessions of which they have already had a surfeit?

"Just one word about your future," says the father's friend to the young man in the film, *The Graduate:* "Plastics. Give plastics a thought." It is a mistake to take a movie as an accurate and balanced account of the way in which the great middle class that has arrived in this era is spending its life. But it is not a mistake to think that this movie may have caught a piece of the truth. And it is certainly not a mistake to think that it expresses—and reinforces—an image of life in this time and place which is widely shared, particularly by the present college generation.

This helps to explain, I think, certain of the more puzzling features of the present student rebellion. It is frequently asked, for example, why dissident students are so extreme in their denunciation of what exists and yet so silent about the reforms they would institute once the revolution takes place. Unlike their predecessors in the thirties, they have no blueprint for a better society. But this is of the essence of their situation: while they may not know what they want, they certainly do not want what they know. And not knowing what they want, not feeling there is anything quite worth wanting, is precisely the basis of their complaint against the society they inhabit.

Similarly, present disturbances on campuses are marked by a disparity between the specific wrongs protested and the emotional tone of the protest. A college that permits the armed forces to recruit but that also permits the recruiters to be picketed can hardly be said to be a committed partisan of the war in Vietnam. One wouldn't know it from what the protestors seem prepared to say about it. A college that refuses to use tax-exempt or public funds to establish racially segregated courses of instruction can hardly be said to be an opponent of civil rights; yet that is what is said. Much of this becomes more intelligible, however, on the assumptions that the grievances that are articulated are articulated not for their own sake but as symbols.

The politics of student protest is, in large part, a politics of symbols, of attitudes, of drama. The point of a demonstration is just that: the demonstration itself, the taking a stand not on small issues but on great ones, the expression of one's emotions not about the college or university where the demonstration takes place but about the system as a whole—the *establishment*, the *biggies*.

I do not mean to say that there are never any real issues on campuses; quite the contrary. But I think it is a mistake to deal with current student protests as though the specific issues that lead to the difficulties are the whole content of these difficulties. They are only a small part of them, and the problem will not be solved simply by dealing with them. What is required is an attempt to grapple with a least some of the issues that lie beneath the surface.

We come, then, to the question of remedies. I would like to be able to tell you I have all the remedies right in my pocket. Long ago, however, as a boy on summer vacation in Atlantic City, a pitchman sold me some soap he claimed would really wash me clean. I tried the soap and ever since I have been careful about what I ask people to buy in Atlantic City. So I shall refrain from passing on my remedies unless you chase me up the Boardwalk to get them. However, I should like to suggest certain major themes which in my own mind seem central to the reform of higher education.

Despite all that I have said about the special position of youth in modern society, and despite what I have said about the special characteristics of the present college generation, the major cause of student unrest remains, quite simply, the objective condition of our society. Vietnam, poverty, and racial injustice are major illustrations of this condition and have been the major targets of protest. But they are only illustrations, and I suspect that even if major progress is made in dealing with them, discontent and trouble will still remain. They will be significantly reduced but the most active and articulate students, along with a great many other people, and particularly those concentrated in academic communities, will continue to believe that our industrial society has a perverse sense of the proper order of human values and is unaccountably wasteful and callous in its use of its resources.

The first order of business for the higher educational community, it seems to me, is to recover, in its educational offerings, a sense of relationship to this discontent and trouble. It must provide an orderly commentary on it, an explanation of it, a discipline for it.

I do not say that this is all that higher education must do, but it is the minimum. And I do not say, of course, that a single orthodox commentary or explanation must be offered. But if people are to take their education seriously, if they are to regard it as more than just a kind of vocational training, it must speak to their social and moral concerns. Too little of this has been done, and often what has been done has been preachy and ignorant.

The academic community has been increasingly divided into narrow specialists who pride themselves on knowing little but knowing it well and intellectual activists who have never studied economics or politics or philosophy or literature but who, nevertheless, hold forth fearlessly on socialism, democracy, moral virtue, or the characters of their fellowmen. Something has to be done to recover colleges and universities from the know-nothings and the know-it-alls.

It is partly with that in mind that I agreed last fall to serve as planning director for a new institute for graduate education which Vassar College hopes to establish. The purpose of the institute will be to produce scholars capable of using in a professional manner the intellectual materials necessary to deal with the problems that concern them. The institute, I hope, will turn out people who know something definite—whether it be the romantic poets, the history of slavery, or the relations of science and government. But they will know this definite thing from more than a single perspective—from a sociological as well as a literary point of view, from an economic as well as an anthropological angle, from a philosophical as well as a political standpoint. The idea of the institute is that the argument or the problem should guide a man's thinking progress and not the bureaucratic, and often artificial, lines between departments.

This will be an institute, if our plans are successful, that will be built around the idea of teaching. For too long our graduate schools have trained young men and women as though their teaching was going to be an afterthought to their scholarship. It is time that this ruinous conception of scholarly achievement be forced to meet some competition.

But this is not the place to go into detail about the Vassar Institute. I mention it here only to illustrate the kind of action which, in my view, badly needs to be taken.

No single experiment will turn out, of course, to have a monopoly of the truth. But major efforts need urgently to be made to turn colleges and universities once again into teaching institutions where scholarship as a humane way of life is exhibited.

The colleges and universities of the country cannot solve by themselves the great social problems that are the principal causes of the disorders within them. But they can try to meet one of these problems directly, because it is peculiarly theirs. This is the problem of recovering the theory and practice of liberal education.

A second major theme with which we shall have to be concerned, I suggest, is the redressing of the institutional frameworks within which young people in colleges and universities spend their days. The massiveness and impersonality of our institutions of higher education are a standing incitement to the young to protest and to seek community and a sense of meaning through protest. And a system of education which excludes them from a chance to be regularly consulted about the conditions of their life and work is bound to aggravate all the special tensions that go with the status of youth.

From this point of view, I see a basic element of strong good sense in current demands for *student power*. Student power cannot extend to the selection of faculty. This is incompatible with a professional relationship between teachers and students and introduces a form of control over teaching incompatible with academic freedom. Nor can student power go so far as to put into the hands of students control over the educational curriculum. The concept of education turns into a self-contradiction if the idea is accepted that people who are less well educated know as much as people who are better educated. But the student's educational experience will almost certainly be richer if he has the opportunity, in a regular and formal way, to sit down with his teachers to appraise his experience and to help design it. Besides, students often do have splendid ideas, ideas that never occur to teachers, administrators, or trustees. We have a need to remake our institutions of higher learning, to turn them from cafeterias into households, from places where education is served up on a conveyor belt to communities where people are in touch about their common business.

In this connection, I would say a word about the present demands for black studies. The history of the black man in the United States is indeed an inexcusably neglected subject. It is a subject which all Americans who have an interest in it should have a chance to study. Indeed, it is not simply a special course of study: America's conception of its past, and of its present, needs to be corrected and enlarged by an awareness, in dozens of different fields of inquiry, of the special experience of black Americans. Black studies, therefore, make sense, urgent sense, in American institutions of higher learning.

But they make sense, I think, as instruments for the education of all Americans, not only blacks. And they make sense only if the standards of scholarly probity and intellectual independence that govern them are as demanding and unequivocal as in any other field. Otherwise black studies will be second-rate studies, and will be known to be so. And this will be to perpetuate, not to cure, the inequities and injustices of racism. The problem of eliminating racism, implicit or explicit, from American education can be solved only if the standards of good education are maintained equally for all.

Finally, we come to the problem which is most immediate and disturbing, and which affects anything else that we may wish to do. This is the problem of establishing, or reestablishing, the codes that should govern the conduct of the academic community.

I said at the beginning of these remarks that we need not only moral fervor but moral clarity. I might have said that we do not need moral fever. A fever may be the body's way of reacting to a bad condition, but it can lead to delirium as well as to a cure. And I think it unquestionable that on our campuses, and off them, something very like delirium has overtaken us.

One of the symptoms is the loss of perspective that marks the present crisis. Small things loom large and fearful, and shadows on the walls are seen as substantial realities. Perhaps universities should not ally themselves, even tenuously, to an Institute of Defense Analysis; the question should certainly be raised. But this does not turn universities, which have been the major centers of criticism and attack on the Vietnam war, into slavish tools of the military-industrial complex. Perhaps it is true that students should have more chance to participate in the development of curricula; I myself think that this is so. But the fact that they do not is hardly a denial of the rights of man.

Indeed, as in a delirium, we have begun to babble. Our political and educational vocabulary is losing its meaning. Scholars who are usually careful, reporters who are normally judicious, have fallen into a use of language that systematically distorts the facts and makes it impossible to deal with them. People speak of *the* students when they mean *some* students, and usually a minority. They use the word *demonstration* to describe disruption and rioting. They describe the polarization of opinion on a campus as a *confrontation* between students and administrators when, in fact, large numbers of other students are also being confronted and affronted. They speak of *repression* of student protest when they mean the enforcement of rules necessary for free and unintimidated study and debate. They speak of *relevance* in education when what is being demanded is the politicalization of education and the dismissal of the ideal of impartiality. And they speak of an *attack* on racism when what is being demanded is the creation of separate and segregated educational institutions organized on racial lines.

Those of us who are forty or older have been here before. We have lived through this kind of double talk from Stalin and his minions, from Hitler, from Joseph McCarthy. Apparently, it is necessary to go through this experience again. But must we be taken in by it? Must we be so generous and forbearing as not to laugh it out of court? Admittedly, the disease of which this fever is the symptom is a real and serious disease. Admittedly, the intentions of many of those who use words in this way are generous, and the contamination of language and thought to which they are contributing is unwitting. But we shall either talk straight or go crazy.

And if the teachers and administrators of the country do not talk straight, what can we expect from our students? To be fuzzy and equivocal about basic principles because the people who are challenging them are young and, as the saying goes, need our understanding is the worst kind of condescension to the young. And to allow the etiquette of civilized discourse to be destroyed in the name of *freedom, humanity,* and *justice* is a sour and ugly parody of moral idealism.

The practical tactics that are used to deal with campus disorders may well differ in different places because circumstances vary. But tactics should not be allowed to leave principles in confusion.

The first and most elementary of these is, I think, a simple one. Administrators and teachers are officers of institutions of learning, and they have one supreme obligation: to be intolerant of intolerance, to protect the conditions for free, unintimidated individual speech and inquiry. They have the obligation to protect this right for all members of the educational communities they serve.

There is much talk in colleges and universities these days about the *legitimacy* of student grievances and student protests. Well, an essential test of legitimacy is available: it is whether the protests are compatible with the maintenance of free universities.

Obviously, I touch here on matters that can be debated at length. I have myself done so on other occasions. But it is enough to point out that, if these are matters to be debated, then the conditions for debate much be maintained. Anyone who is so sure of himself that he feels justified in denying the rights or policies and the consciences of others does not understand what a free university is all about.

These issues go to the heart of what we mean by civility and civilization. They bear not merely on rules and procedures; they have to do with the respect we show, every day and in practice, to our fellows.

If rational discourse disappears from colleges and universities, how shall we maintain or recover it in the larger society? And if we lose the struggle there, what will the youth of the future say of us? Perhaps they will not know enough, or be free enough, to say anything. But I know they will not thank us for equivocating about the value of civilized conduct. I think that most of the young today know this. It is for us, the teachers and administrators, to make it plain that we know it too.

5. THE STUDENT SEIZURES

Ernest van den Haag

Ernest van den Haag is Adjunct Professor of Social Philosophy
at New York University, and Lecturer in Social Philosophy and
Social Psychology at the New School for Social Research.

IT WOULD BE absurd to ascribe the seizures at universities to any single cause, or to hold all participating students and faculty members to be equally ignorant or irresponsible. More is involved than academic versions of millenarianism. "Direct action" is a symptom of a great variety of problems, some chronic, some recent, some basic, some precipitating, some used as justifications, some unavowed.

By definition, adolescence is the process throughout which children exchange their familiar roles for unfamiliar adult, social roles. Even in a peasant community, where roles and transitions were structured by stable functions, and by tradition, where, further, the new roles were pre-established and well defined, transition was not easy. In fast-changing industrial, urbanized societies, where neither roles nor transitions are patterned by tradition, and where there is no stable community to continue any tradition, the task has become quite arduous.

Many adolescents do not manage to go beyond repudiating the parental roles, the established authorities and values. The de-cathexis (detachment) of familiar objects is easier and may not be followed by the more difficult re-cathexis of viable new ones. In some instances, neither is accomplished; and in the worst, the original cathexis was so unsatisfactory that no re-cathexis is possible. A commitment to revolution is ideal in many cases: it produces a comprehensive sense of meaningful action, yet justifies the avoidance of everyday obligations and of discipline.

For students, the adolescent transition is particularly difficult. They must suddenly adapt to a whole new environment which challenges their confidence in received ideas, ideals, moralities, patterns of behavior, and self-conceptions. They are estranged

Reprinted, by permission of the author, from *The New School Bulletin*, October, 1969 from their homes, which are replaced by a temporary, and unduly dependent, relationship to *alma mater*, who seems demanding rather than giving, to the point of grading her children according to performance, and of rejecting those who fail. Students understandably grasp anything that permits autonomous self-identification and solidarity with newly significant others.

Fraternities and sororities used to offer communal support for the necessary transition from the family to individual, independent identification. They have been destroyed, often with the help of faculties who objected to the criteria of group formation (and, therewith, exclusion) and, perhaps, to the influence of the group on its members. The psychological need remains, and group formation continues, even though less formalized. Are the criteria of inclusion presently used, the aims and activities pursued, the influences exercised by socially radical, activist (instead of snobbish) ideologies and groups actually preferable to those replaced?

Poor (and black) students are likely to be least prepared for, and therefore most disoriented by, the college environment. Their initial self-confidence may also be lower; and they receive the least social support in the college. Finally they may feel guilty about their families and friends; for these students can look forward to careers and to comforts not open to their former associates, who are, in every sense, left behind.

Yet poor, and black, students are more interested than affluent ones in careers, future incomes, and advancement for their own group. They have tried therefore to open college to more of their own, while perhaps seeking shelter from academic standards, and obtaining privileges to enhance their status and self-conception.[1] A few of these students dimly realize that even when sheltered, they are unprepared to benefit from colleges with present standards. They are resentful enough to wish to destroy them. They are helped by not a few students able to benefit from college, who

---

[1] The black students do not seem to grasp the self-defeating character of the shelter from academic standards they try to build. Afro-American Institutes are not likely to yield them useful, let alone marketable skills or even prestigious degrees—least when they are student controlled and racially staffed. Some militants, and the staff, might benefit. Other blacks will in time realize that they do not; they will also realize that the universities which endorsed these institutes were derelict in their duty. They did not foster the education of their students but allowed themselves to be pressured by student fanatics and politicans. Children are not grateful, in the end, to meekly permissive parents; they have no reason to be, for the parents did not help them grow up.

feel guilty about it, or bored, or incapable of imposing the necessary discipline on themselves, or of accepting what they need.

Resentment is likely to become more frequent because more
than 42% of college age youths now attend college—while only
25% of the age group have the IQ (over 110) required to benefit
from college education. Many of these students, it is true, are still
protected in community and junior colleges. But this is temporary. They will go on. Since "education" has taken the place formerly occupied by religion in the sentiments of many Americans,
more and more money and people are pumped into it, without
much thought given to the abilities of the participants and to the
qualities and above all, the actual effects of the education given.
Education is felt to be good for everybody—by definition.[2]

Until college education is reduced to high school levels—and
the process has only begun—more and more students will find college irrelevant to them. This is unavoidable unless faculties realize that these students are irrelevant to the college. If they don't,
college will become a custodial institution devoted to bull sessions
and high school level instruction. The process is self-defeating,
just as making national park lands overly accessible defeats their
raison d'être. Americans have yet to learn that some good things
do not remain good when shared too widely or with "irrevelant"
persons, i.e., persons to whom they are irrelevant.

The college inflation was prompted by administrators who
wanted to administer more, and raise their prestige, by faculties
who wanted to be promoted faster, as they will be, when there
are more students (customers), as well as by our paneducational
ideology. Yet it is obvious, to anyone familiar with the situation,
that at present far more people teach and do research than are
competent to do either. Faculties and student bodies expand with
available money, and faster by far than available talent. The
effect on knowledge may actually be negative: pseudo-subjects are
created, and pseudo-scholarship creates obstacles to actual advances. The effect on students is no better.

---

[2] This definition refers to the results hoped for, but confuses them with the
process—schooling—which might but need not produce results such as knowledge,
refinement, wisdom; schooling may leave ignorance unimpaired and produce restlessness, unhappiness, boredom, unrealistic ambitions, or worse. The achievement
of the intended results appears to be exceptional; it requires gifted pupils, gifted
teachers, an appropriate atmosphere—none of which are frequent.

College for everybody necessarily cancels the prestige and relative income advantages which rest on selectivity. Paradoxically, the
disadvantages of not attending increase, as the advantages of attending decrease. The high school diploma today means little, but
the lack of it means a lot. We find a parallel development with
money; as people have more it means less. But not having it at
all, being poor, is more painful than ever. So with the college
degree. Wherefore we find some students attend college because
they realize that a degree is required for anything they might
want to do later. While attending they find out that the education
certified by the degree is not; they learn nothing relevant to their
interests or future occupation. For years they are kept dependent,
and out of the activities they crave, to earn a degree required for,
but not actually relevant to, their employment, or to them. They
are involuntary students, bored, and restless.

Thus, the present population includes, in unknown proportions:

    a) students who actually want (and benefit from) an education in the liberal arts;

    b) students who attend for relevant vocational reasons;

    c) students who attended for irrelevant vocational reasons—
to get a degree required by employers (including the government) although what they learn (or, better, are taught) does
not interest them and is of no actual use in their future
activities.

These involuntary students are demoralized; they also demoralize others and are costly to education and to society. The probably
could learn more outside college.

They would not be compelled to attend if, to the present prohibition of employment discrimination on the basis of race, a prohibition of discrimination on the basis of education were added:
whenever education (or a degree) cannot be shown to be specifically relevant to the job, it cannot be used to discriminate among
among applicants. (The burden of proof would be on the employer.)[3]

---

[3] In most non-professional jobs far more education is required than is used, or
can possibly be useful. And in many jobs—e.g., nursing, social work, teaching–the
educational requirements are of doubtful relevance to the job. Is it beyond our ingenuity to change this? The misuse of the educational system as an endurance
test, or a way to force postponement of entry into the labor market, or of guaranteeing guild privileges is contrary to the public interest.

The students most dangerous to the university, at least in the short run, the students who resent it enough to actually attempt to destroy it through their direct action, are not those to whom it is rationally irrelevant, but those to whom it is emotionally irrelevant—except as something to be defied. The psychological expectations of these students, inchoate and unconscious as they may be, are not met by the university and could not be met by any feasible institution of learning.

They except the university to save them—save them from tedium, from routine, from humdrum work and from discipline. They want the university to fulfill them, to direct them, to love them, to give meaning to their lives—but without imposing discipline. They expect the university to do for them what their parents did not—to listen to them. In short, they expect the university to function as an ideal, progressive kindergarten—and, bitterly disappointed as they must be, they are ready for revolution. With the exception of the blacks, the ideological and activist leaders of direct action are intelligent, affluent, and profoundly dissatisfied students emotionally disappointed by *alma mater*.

In the nineteenth century, Arthur Schopenhauer pointed to two major sources of human unhappiness: deprivation, which frustrates the poor, and surfeit, which causes the boredom of the rich. The poor are stimulated, or at least kept busy, but unsatisfied. The rich are materially satisfied but unstimulated. The poor wish for money and leisure to free them from deprivation; the rich for challenge and meaningful activity to free them from boredom.

In the past the rich were few, and many were still engaged in the activities which tradition and education, if not material need, had made meaningful to them. Now the poor are a minority-wherefore they are more resentful then ever. The many newly affluent people keep busy, but find no satisfying way to engage time, which hangs heavy on their hands. Unprepared for leisure they can no longer kill time altogether by making money—the challenge, and the moral significance, that gave meaning to this activity have diminished too much. Money has lost its authority (though not yet its power). Time stays alive to bore them. It bores their children even more. They never had to work out of necessity and, in many cases, they have found no effort worth their while. The parents and schools who should have led them to meaningful efforts, to the discipline of work, to respect for achievement, have failed them. These children are desperate for the challenge of meaningful activity or, in its absence, at least for distraction from boredom which makes time such a heavy burden to bear.

Sex and drugs serve to distract as does the conspicuous consumption of the self, engaged in by so many. But these do not yield the transcendent challenge and the sense of dedication ultimately required to ward off tedium, as Ortega y Gasset foresaw: "an 'unengaged' existence is a worse negation of life than death itself . . . before long there will be heard throughout the planet a formidable cry, like the howling of innumerable dogs to the stars asking . . . to impose an occupation, a duty." We are surfeited with leisure, liberty, affluence and therewith boredom. The direct pursuit of pleasure turns out to be an onerous task for most of the young, and, in the end, unrewarding.

, Yet many students are unable to pursue anything else. Others fervently insist that everybody follow their ideals, which usually are generous and gentle, and so vaguely formulated as to be unobjectionable: peace, equality, freedom, creativity, love, sincerity, everybody doing his own thing (even nothing if he can't find anything to engage him). There is no understanding of the obstacles to the realization of such ideals, of their mutual inconsistency, of their clash with the requirements of any social order, of their unspecificity and ambiguity which causes them to be beside the point, quite insufficient to solve the problems, to devise the compromises, to settle the conflicts of any feasible society. The only obstacles these students can see are the demons Marx secularized: oppressive capitalists, uptight racists and (via Herbert Marcuse) overly repressed middle classes. More love and more revolution will remedy all that.

Often students do not even wish to understand that to do nothing is to live at someone else's expense, off his labor; and that to demand as much as a right is to demand the right to exploit others. They meet objections with fantasies produced by journalism and science fiction: "scarcity" and, therewith, work could be abolished any day; or with the assertion of a "right" to be paid for a contribution not valued by others, a "right" to be employed to produce something not demanded, or to work at a job not available. It is not realized that this would exploit others by compelling them to give what they value—their work or its fruits—for something without value to them.

Similarly, students asserting the desirability of peace, love, etc., fail to see that no one denies it—that there is disagreement only on how to achieve and preserve peace, love, etc. It is simpler to picture opponents (the establishment) as hateful warmongers. Attempts to confront the actual intellectual issues are as rare as attempts to confront the dean are frequent. High ideals are used by flower-bearing, free, and thoughtless, children to confront the parental generation involved in the sordid realities which made it possible for the children to concentrate on love and flowers.

At first blush one might conclude that instruction about the human experience with alternative organizations of society, has been deficient. Ignorance, undispelled by education, certainly is part of the difficulty and educators cannot escape blame. However, the source of the problem is deeper.

Many students come from highly permissive homes which did not accustom them to value, tradition, effort, discipline and authority. They learned to value intelligence, spontaneity, sincerity, freedom. But they were never taught to ask:

> How but in custom and in ceremony
> Are innocence and beauty born?[4]

Indeed, they think of these as natural qualities. Like the pre-World War I generation of privileged English students they have repudiated "all versions of the doctrine of original sin, of there being insane and irrational springs of wickedness in most men. We were not aware that civilization was a thin and precarious crust erected by the personality and the will of a very few, and only maintained by rules and conventions skillfully put across and guilefully preserved. We had no respect for traditional wisdom or the restraints of custom. We lacked reverence. . . .[5]

Lord Keynes became aware of the precariousness of civilization. Karl Marx did not, perhaps because he lived in times less influenced by his own doctrines (Hitler, and Marx' follower, Stalin, have shown Keynes right). Wickedness to Marx was not in man but in evil social, particularly economic, institutions and systems. Change them, and beauty, honesty, liberty, love, peace and equality will flourish, plenty will be produced, oppression, ignorance, greed and crime will vanish. The students follow Marx rather than Keynes, though with scant information and without his historical consciousness and intellectual rigor.

As often they veer toward anarchists such as Bakunin or Kropotkin. They all believe prelapsarian (precapitalist) human na-

---

[4] W. B. Yeats "To My Daughter."
[5] J. M. Keynes "My Early Beliefs."

ture was good and postlapsarian (after the revolution) human
nature will be. Many of these truly utopian students are naively
religious in sentimental mood and moralistic style, while certainly
chiliastic and antinomian in action. (Marx, by contrast, was
pseudo-scientific in style, certainly a chiliast, but not an antinomian).

The Rousseauean belief in paradise regained by freeing "human nature" has not faded, it has been recolored by e.g. Norman O. Brown, and Paul Goodman, and various Pop-Singer-poets
(not to speak of Herbert Marcuse). All of them appeal mainly to
the students. Stalin's and Hitler's versions of hell, and the purga-
tory of industrial mass society, have merely shifted the search of
the true believers from economic to psychological grounds—while
making them more impatient, irrational and humorless.

The rejection of authority and of discipline, which inspires so
much utopian thinking was generated by many sources, not least
the permissiveness and the affluence in which so many of the militant students were brought up. The suburban middle class, most
emphatically perhaps its Jewish component of *homines novi*, believed in science, and science was thought to newly support permissiveness and indulgence, to oppose frustration and restraint of
children, as well as discipline, punishment, and authority. The
newly affluent parents also wanted to spare their children the
hardships and restrictions they had suffered, the obstacles they
had overcome, so that the children might remain "idealistic."
They did; and now they have to create their own challenges.

Our rate of technological and social change is so high anyway
(and continuously accelerating) that the authority of tradition—and authority itself is never less than tradition—and of
those bearing and transmitting it, was bound to be greatly im-
paired. And, therewith, the authority of all established social
institutions and values, particularly of universities: the institutions charged with transmission of knowledge, tradition, experience
and learning, and with preparing the young for established
social roles. Our life has become too discontinuous—as has our
culture—to grant authority to anything but present power.

When change is slow, the experience of the past seems applica-
ble and its bearers and transmitters are honored, its traditions
revered. But a rapid pace of change makes the experience of the
past seem obsolete. There is a loss of respect for those informed
by it, and a refusal to absorb what is regarded as "irrelevant" to
"now." The old become old-fashioned, obsolete. So does the wis-

dom of the past. Why then learn history, or philosophy, or
economics? Why learn anything from the old generation, why
learn anything old—isn't it altogether "irrelevant" to the "now"
generation?

Actually truth does not change though our knowledge of
it—what we believe—does. Some past beliefs are superseded; but
others are dropped as well, though no more than before known to
be wrong. The attitude toward all ideas of the past—particularly
the recent past—becomes negative. History is ignored. Thus we
are condemned to repeat it by the young who push forward old
discredited schemes that seem new to them. Typically the ideas of
a few generations back are touted as new. Grandfather's European
get-up (as it appears to the young), his glasses, garments and
beard are adopted. One identifies with his idealism and—where
they do not seem restrictive—with his ideas. Thus, parental affluence, and business realism, parental experience and style, are
repudiated in favor of the idealistic utopianism characteristic of
the newly immigrated, who had no hope for improvement, except
by changing "the system." There is, of course, an oedipal air
about this.

Meanwhile the social order is weakened by the increasingly
radical questioning of the legitimacy of any standards of conduct,
achievement and organization. The impairment of the authority
of the past, of the traditions of civilization itself, is a basic cause
of student unrest, and ultimately of "direct action" the world
over,[6] as well as an effect. Some students have become unable
—never having been so taught—to accept any authority. Many
more feel that those now in positions of authority are not credible
in their roles—that they do not actually possess the authority they
claim. Students test them, and often find their suspicions justified.

Authority is a relationship between those bearing it and those
subjected to it, which disposes those subjected to authority to vol-
untarily comply with its orders, and to support enforcement
against those who do not. Such enforcement is regarded as morally legitimate when the authority is, and yet it is seldom required, since people are disposed to obey the decisions of an accepted authority.

Students now see university officials as shorn of authority, pos-

---

[6] In America, the Vietnam war may have made a precipitating contribution.
But it scarcely explains what happened in France, Germany, or Japan.

sessed only of power, which can be challenged and resisted: power bereft of authority invites challenge. When force has to be used against groups, the authority which wields it has lost, at least temporarily, its legitimacy in the eyes of the defiant groups. Timely and resolute use of force may restore authority, if followed by swift punishment of those who defied it, and by measures to reestablish its moral legitimacy. Whereas an early and credible announcement that resistance to authority will be broken by force can reestablish it, concessions erode it. Negotiation under duress, any recognition of a right to "direct action"—even if implied merely by impunity—necessarily weakens authority further. Authority not enforced when resisted, or irresolutely enforced, becomes ineffective. It can be replaced only by naked power—which requires constant reassertion.

Originally just a few students tentatively defied university officials. However these reacted irresolutely enough to discredit their authority in the eyes of all students, so that, when force was finally used, it too was defied. Concessions and amnesties followed and authority de-moralized itself altogether, even in the eyes of those who had not previously questioned it.

The original acceptance of parental authority occurs when the child still depends on his parents emotionally and materially. It is part of the learning process, of the socialization which takes place within the family. With adolescence parental authority decreases and is to some extent shifted outside the family. But authority cannot be shifted later unless it was established earlier.

When pushed too far, permissiveness, which encourages questioning more than the acceptance of authority, may cause the child, and later the adolescent, or adult, to be unable to accept authority altogether, however much he unconsciously craves it. Such persons become anxious, bored, rebellious and nihilistic. They directly or indirectly repudiate the parents who spoiled them, and defy all other authority not just of persons, but of offices, traditions, procedures and customs. Finally, they force society to use the rod the parents spared.

In this sense, many of the students who rebelled against authority, unconsciously rebelled no less against its absence. Theirs was not so much a classical oedipal defiance, shifted to those who stand in *loco parentis,* as it was a defiance of the belated and incomplete imposition of social authority and discipline—when these notions and practices had not been part of their upbringing by their actual parents. Their rebellion was an attempt to organ-

ize their life to find the missing limits, the discipline they were
not helped to impose on themselves, the direction they were not
given. Yet, unprepared, they cannot accept what they need. Adolescents who never were taught to restrain their impulses, to take
directions, may need and crave direction. But they resent the restrictions and directions that universities and societies must impose. They dream of a society without discipline or necessity—of
pure self indulgence ("love"), dedicated to sex, pleasure, and fantasy.

Actions occur only when the desire prompting them exceeds
the desire to avoid the expected cost. That cost may be inherent
(the effort to be made), economic (imposed by others to compensate for their effort), legal (penalties imposed by society to deter
law violations), or moral (pangs of one's own conscience produced
by violation of internalized rules). There are two ways of preventing actions then: by reducing the desire for them; or by raising
the expected cost of fulfilling the desire. The universities took
neither.

The ability of universities to reduce the desire of the students
for direct action is limited. They cannot control suburban education or social boredom; and many direct actions were prompted
by matters beyond the control of universities, such as government
policies. The students protested against university "cooperation"
in such policies. Yet this "cooperation" usually was nothing more
than academic freedom. Students and faculty members were left
the choice of working for or against government policies, or of
doing neither. The students opposed this choice: they denied the
right of some professors to make the choices they made.

Universities as corporate bodies cannot struggle to change the
social order or to oppose or endorse social policies—any more
than the Post Office can. The campus cannot be (nor allow itself
to be used as) an action agency, without ceasing to be a neutral
research and educational institution, which permits each faculty
member to select research subjects, and pursue research (and
publish results, or confide them to some, but not to others, or to
nobody); such research can be financed by the Civil Liberties
Union, the Defense Department, or a labor union—as long as
such financing is acceptable to the researcher. Similarly, the university must allow any career recruitment—or none. It cannot make
choices for its students, or allow individual choices to be restricted
by the wishes of majority or minority groups.

Not even a student directive to avoid investments in South Africa can be accepted. It is not among the university's tasks to exercise pressure on South Africa. The students are free to do so individually, but not to impose their wish on the corporate body. If the student's moral criteria were to determine university investments, there might be few corporations the shares of which could be held; even government bonds might have to be avoided since some students oppose government policies. The money invested does not come from the students who wish to dispose of it. Nor does their enrollment entitle them to such disposal. Analogous arguments apply to construction of buildings, or other non-instructional university policies.

Students enroll to be instructed. Their only legitimate concern as students is the instruction they receive and whatever the university does to affect their life *qua* students. They are entitled to select accordingly among universities though not to decide university policies—just as diners are entitled to choose among restaurants but not otherwise to determine their policies. Research is certainly within the domain of the faculty; and matters concerning the institution over a longer span must be the shared concern of faculty, administration and trustees—and only to a very small extent of any particular generation of students.

Concerning instruction in American universities, I have never heard a respectable argument for letting students influence what is to be taught, or by whom, or who is to be admitted. If the patient (suffering from ignorance) had the competence of the physicians to whom he entrusted himself, he would not need them. If he does not, he should not tell them what medicines are "relevant" to his disease. In European universities, students have a better case (though not necessarily a good one) because usually policies and curricula do not vary from university to university. Students have little choice. But in the United States no student need subject himself to educational policies, or curricula, of which—for good or bad reasons—he disapproves. An immense variety of alternatives is available, and nearly every taste can be served. Student unrest here had more to do with the need of the students to rebel against their own life and their society than with any curriculum.

Perhaps students should have been taught more about the functions of universities. But they do not necessarily learn what they are taught. Moreover, the understanding of many faculty members and administrations of their own academic freedom, and of

58   ERNEST VAN DEN HAAG

the obligations that go with it, is less than perfect. *Quis custodiat custodes?*

Since they could do so little to affect the desire of students to rebel why did the universities not increase the cost of "direct action?" They could have suspended or expelled unruly students. Those who violated laws could have been prosecuted. On the whole, universities preferred to allow their students to learn that their own authority, and that of the law, can be defied with impunity. Why?

The causes which led to the ineffective behavior of faculties and administrations overlap. The general decline of authority already has been mentioned; it is supported by egalitarian ideologies which confuse authority with "authoritarianism": illegitimate authority, or its illegitimate use, or the assertion of authority beyond its jurisdiction or in circumstances in which it is not needed, or finally, the idea that authority must be "total." The confusion between authority and authoritarianism was fostered and, most important, authority was discredited, by the emergence and the careers of Stalin, Hitler and Mussolini.[7]

Many officials further have a vague feeling not only that authority must rest on consent but that each specific act of authority must be ratified by a consensus. Rationally this would be absurd: the authority of laws and courts, or universities, rests on consent, but a particular action, procedure, law, rule or enforcement need not. To think otherwise is to replace law and authority by consensus.

However irrational, the feeling that they could not act against what appeared as consensus, was powerful enough among University officials to make them hestitate. It was also reinforced by the craving for popularity which dominates so many of our officials.[8]

Such attitudes make the assertion of authority against non-consenting groups psychologically hard, unless these groups first have been defined as being beyond the pale. Students clearly are not. On the contrary, administrators, and some professors, treat them as though a political constituency, which must be ca-

---

[7] It is seldom understood that the last two were reactions to the weakening of authority.

[8] These tendencies have become characteristic of American society and were noted alike by de Tocqueville and David Riesman.

tered to, to obtain reelection, or a group of consumers, that must be induced to buy. The youth worship, bordering on pedophilia, which has long been a part of our social life, intensifies this tendency. It is hard for any American to believe that in a conflict between generations the younger generation can be wrong; harder still to punish the young when more than a few deviant individuals seem involved.[9]

All these feelings were quite ably played on by the activist students. Because students seemed disaffected, faculties and administrations felt that they must have been guilty of some crime. The students hastened to define the crime as possession of authority and succeeded in de-moralizing it. Professors and administrators searched their souls instead of asserting the authority of learning. Where did we go wrong, they asked; and each came up with a different answer. Most were eager to blame themselves; but for the wrong reasons.

In the "good" universities where the activists are strongest, professors had been far more critical of the authority of tradition—and of the tradition of authority—than their students. It was hard for them to oppose students who—somewhat indiscriminately—acted on their teaching. Some professors themselves are incapable of resisting actions to which leftist symbols are attached; others hate the administration and "the system" (and themselves) so much that they automatically identify with activist students.[10]

Academicians, moreover, are reluctant to use violence. The students, knowing as much, used little violence (at least initially) but invited it, by taking positions from which only violence could dislodge them. Many universities lacked the means—or felt they did—to deal with physically resisting students. Yet many professors also regarded the university as a sanctuary into which police should not be called. They were willing to trust the students, regardless of their actions: my students, right or wrong. They insisted that rational discourse, not violence was needed—although

---

[9] I am well aware that only about 2% of the total student body were activists, according to John T. Roche (*The New Leader*, June 23, 1969). But they were leaders. And administrations and faculties did not have the wit to isolate them—even though the rest of the student body, if supported by the administration, might well have reduced the activists to impotence.

[10] This professional attitude is well exemplified in Eric Bentley's dialogue with Robert Brustein (*The New Republic*, April 26, 1969, May 17, and ff.) as well as the reaction of professorial letterwriters (*ibid.*).

the students made rational discourse impossible. Obviously, direct action on campus was owed as much to the weakness of faculties and administrations, as to the strength of the students defying them.

It is because of their virtues not because of their vices that the universities have become the first target of direct action. Some of these virtues are connected with vulnerabilities (as are some vices): free speech, teaching and research, independence from outside authority are both the glory and the weakness of universities. Without the virtues they would cease to be the centers of research, reflection and critical intelligence which they are.

But people accustomed to the life of reason find it hard to understand that reason itself is not enough defense against unreasoning force, that freedom can be preserved only by the repression of those who seek to repress it by direct action. The universities hitherto have cultivated reason. Now they are called upon to defend their authority against direct action. Their success or failure will determine the future climate of our society: either we will be governed by persuasion and majority decisions which leave at least interstitial space for reason, or we will be run by the groups that are able and willing to use the strongest physical means of disruption.

6. THE ANATOMY OF ACADEMIC DISCONTENT

Bruno Bettelheim

Bruno Bettleheim is Rowley Professor of Education, Professor in the Departments of Psychology and Psychiatry, and Director of the Orthogenic School at the University of Chicago.

WHILE HISTORY does not repeat itself, and while the present situation in the United States is radically different from that of pre-Hitler Germany, some similarities between the present student rebellion in this country and what happened in the German universities to spearhead Hitler's rise to power are nevertheless striking. Politically, of course, the German student rebels embraced the extreme right, while here the dissenters embrace the extreme left, but what is parallel is the determination to bring down the establishment. In Germany the philosophy which gained the rebels a mass following was racist and directed against a discriminated minority (the Jews), while here the radical students intend to *help* a discriminated minority. This is an important difference, but it does not change the parallel that universities then and now were forced to make decisions with respect to the race of students, rather than on the basis of disregard of racial origin. To use only one example, German universities began to cave in when students coerced faculties to appoint professorships in *Rassenwissenschaft;* that is, professorships devoted to teaching the special aspects, merits and achievements of one race as opposed to others, rather than teaching the contributions to knowledge, whatever the origins of the contributors.

Professor Walter Z. Laqueur (*Young Germany,* Basic Books, 1962) says, "National Socialism came to power as the party of youth." Its cult of youth was as pronounced as that of Italian fascism whose very hymn was called "Youth" (Giovenezza). Hitler insisted all along that his movement was a revolt "of the coming

---

The edited text of Dr. Bettelheim's testimony early in 1969 before a U.S. Congressional Subcommittee probing the causes of student unrest; reprinted with the permission of the author.

61

generation against all that was senile and rotten with decay in German democratic society." Professor Peter Gay *(Weimar Culture: The Outsider as Insider,* Harper and Row, 1968) stresses the prevalence in pre-Hitler days of an ideology that pitted sons against fathers and insisted that the generations cannot understand each other, that they are deadly enemies; in short, an ideology that said exactly the same thing in this respect that our rebellious students, who insist that nobody over thirty is trustworthy, say today. Then, as now, the student rebels were pictured as the new generation, disgusted with the complacency of their parents, fighting courageously for a better world. And what were then the mass media often depicted them as idealists, as young people concerned with the real issues of society. They were, in their time, the wave of the future. And leftist student activists in 1968 burned books they did not like in the same manner and at the same place—Berlin—as did Hitler's youthful followers in 1933.

Then, as now, these youthful followers of the extremists were anti-intellectual, resting their case on convictions based on their emotions. They were fascinated with violence. Their favorite technique was to disrupt meetings, not just because they were not to their liking, but more as a demonstration of their power; and they created disorder which then was claimed to demonstrate that the establishment was unable to function, and hence had to be replaced by one based on their creed.

Having stressed these parallels, one must also recognize the vast differences between the present American student rebelliousness and that of pre-Hitler Germany. It is these differences which should permit us to work toward an entirely different outcome. If I read the signs of the time correctly, I do not think that the rebellious students in and by themselves are a serious danger to this country, although they are a real danger to the universities. The danger, I fear, is rather an opposite one: that the disgusting behavior of a very small group of students—the overwhelming majority of our students are sound and wish nothing more than to take advantage of the opportunities higher education offers them—will arouse a severe counterreaction, so much so that their leftist radicalism may lead to a fascist type of backlash. This is the greatest danger inherent in their efforts to create chaos. To prevent chaos, and in desperation—and the rebels do succeed in creating desperation—repressive measures might be embraced which would be dangerous to our democratic institutions. Because of this danger, student rebellions must be dealt with in the best interest of all society, including that of the rebelling students themselves. But they can be dealt with intelligently and constructively only if the measures adopted are designed to eliminate the causes of the widespread discontent.

To understand this discontent, one has to realize first that many more young people go to college today than ever before, and hence many more are much less prepared for it. Taking advantage of college and being satisfied with the experience, rather than being defeated by it, requires a considerable amount of self-discipline and a high degree of satisfaction with developing one's intellect. Present-day education, both at home and in school, teaches very little self-discipline compared to even very recent times. The expectation now is that education can hand over knowledge and skills, and nearly instantly; and there is a widespread feeling that if students do not do well in school, then this is the failing of the educational system, not the result of a lack of personal application. With each year in school, this feeling becomes stronger in those who do not do well academically. And with it, the system becomes the enemy which deliberately withholds from them what they believe it could so easily give; hence their hatred of the system.

To understand why pressures erupt in adolescence on a growing scale nowadays, and why society's controls seem to grow weaker, we must recognize that adolescent revolt is not a stage of development that follows automatically from our natural makeup. What makes for adolescent revolt is the fact that our society keeps the younger generation too long dependent in terms of mature responsibility and a striving for independence. Years ago, when formal schooling ended for the vast majority at the age of fourteen or fifteen and thereafter one became self-supporting, married and had children, there was no need for adolescent revolt. Because while puberty is a biological given, adolescence as we know it with its identity crises is not. All children grow up and become pubertal; but by no means do they all become adolescents. To be adolescent means that one has reached, and even passed, the age of puberty, is at the height of physical development—healthier, stronger, even handsomer than one has been or will be for the rest of one's life; but to be adolescent also means that one must nevertheless postpone full adulthood long beyond what any other period in history has considered reasonable. And the educational experiences in home and school prepare well only a small minority of young people for such a prolonged waiting, for being able to control their angry impatience while waiting.

It is this waiting for the real life that creates a climate in which a sizeable segment of college students can at least temporarily be seduced into following the lead of small groups of militants. It seems to give them a chance to prove themselves as real men. Thus it is the empty wait for real life which makes for student rebellions. This can be seen from the fact that most of the rebellious students, here and abroad, are either undergraduates, are studying the social sciences and the humanities, or both. There are few militants among students of medicine, engineering, the natural sciences; they are busy doing things that are important to them: they are working in the laboratory and at their studies. It is those students who do not quite know what they are preparing themselves for and why, those students who sit around waiting for examinations rather than doing active work, who form the cadres of the student rebellion.

One example may stand for many. In a class I am presently teaching, a student who was close to the activitists gave me, at first, a very hard time in class. Two months later he was one of my most interested, cooperative students. I asked him what happened. He answered: "A few weeks ago I got a job which interests me, and I also began to be interested in my classes; that did it."

There are today far too many students in college who essentially have no business there. Some are there to evade the draft; many others are there out of a vague idea that it will help them to find better paying jobs, although they do not know what jobs they want. And many go to college simply because they do not know what better to do and because it is expected of them. Their deep dissatisfaction with themselves and their inner confusion is projected first against the university, and second against all institutions of society, which are blamed for their own inner weakness.

To make matters worse, our institutions of higher learning have expanded much too rapidly; under public pressure for more education for everybody, they have increased enrollment beyond reason. The result is classes which are too large, and which are often taught in our large universities by teaching assistants, some of whom, out of their own inner dissatisfaction and insecurity, tend to side with the rebellion. All this leads to the anonymity, the impersonal nature of student-faculty contacts, about which many students rightly complain. And since many of them are essentially not interested in the intellectual adventure, the knowledge which the faculty can convey to them is not what they want. What they do want, essentially, is group therapeutic experiences to help them to mature, to be secure, to find themselves. But since colleges are not mass therapeutic institutions, they disappoint the students where their greatest need lies.

Because of the vast expansion in numbers, moreover, the old methods to lend coherence to the college experience, and to offer students a life geared to the needs of late adolescence, have disintegrated. This the fraternities and sororities used to do by offering group homes to ease the transition from family to society at large. But they no longer can contain the large proportion of students. The demand of some black students for separate black housing should therefore be understood, at least in part, as the consequence of their feeling lost in the anonymous mass of students. Indeed, most white students are similarly lost until they find themselves in their work and study experiences. The old rituals which enhanced student life and bound students both to each other and to their college—the football rallies, the homecomings—have lost most of their meaning and have been replaced by nothing equalling the excitement which the sit-ins and protests provide. The spirit of intimate comradeship—important as at no other time in life—that used to prevail in the fraternity house is now found by all too many students in their demonstrations, where they feel closely bound together, doing things which they deep down know they do also for the emotional satisfaction of simply being together, whatever high sounding issues they think are motivating their actions. Nor should the symbolic meaning of students invading the dean's or president's office, whether violently or non-violently, be overlooked; big in age and size, they inwardly feel like little boys, and hence they need to play big by sitting in papa's big chair. They want to have a say in how things are run, want to sit in the driver's seat, not because they feel competent to do so, but because they cannot bear to feel incompetent.

It is unnatural to keep large numbers of young people in dependency and attending school for some twenty years. This was the way of life for that small elite which always in the past went to universities, but never did they represent more than a small percentage of the youth population, the vast majority of which actively met life early and proved itself as men and women, as real and strong human beings. Now, however, the tremendous push to send everybody to college has brought into the university an incredibly large number of young people who do not find their self-realization through study, or through the intellectual adventure. Yet, still needing to find their early manhood, they try to change the university into something in which they can find it by engaging in an active, sometimes violent, battle against the existing order or all of society. Their victory would change the university into an institution no longer dedicated to the intellectual virtues, to the frontiers of knowledge, but dedicated, rather, to the belligerent reshaping of society; and this is exactly what the militants want—not to engage in study and research, but in political battles. The reason we didn't have student revolts of this kind and this scope before is partly because only those went to college who wanted to be educated, and partly because those students who had to put themselves through school proved their early manhood—at least to some degree—by the very fact that they could do so. I think many of the rebellious students today are essentially guilt-ridden individuals. They feel terribly guilty about all their advantages, including their exemption from the draft, which is a serious guilt. Unable to bear living with their inner guilt, they try to destroy society or certain of its institutions rather than deal with it.

Since all too many students who now go to college have little interest, ability and use for what constitutes a college education, they would be better off with a high-level vocational education closely linked to a work program to give scope to their needs for physical activity and visible, tangible achievement. The complaint of many of these students is that nobody needs them. They view themselves as parasites of society, and therefore come to hate the society which they think makes them feel this way. Here we should learn from the communist countries where studies are combined with work in factories and in the fields. This, I believe, would be a much better arrangement for those students who do not feel a deep commitment to the intellectual enterprise (that is, study and research), and those who are so committed will never constitute more than a relatively small segment of youth.

I would, in fact, urge the creation of a government program of a couple of years' duration—a civilian Peace Corps—in which young people would work on socially significant projects while earning pay for it, and simultaneously receive higher vocational training. After such service and training, only those who really wish to do so would enter the universities, while the rest would feel a much greater stake in a society they helped to rebuild; at the least, they would be well-prepared for permanent jobs. Such a program should be an alternative to the draft. Only those young men who volunteer should serve in the armed forces. And I am convinced that if every able-bodied person were required to serve two years in national service of some kind, there would be no scarcity of volunteers for the armed forces, particularly if military servicemen received advantages in pay or other special advantages at the end of their service. This would also eliminate the draft exemption of college students which, in connection with the war in Vietnam, is behind so much of the student unrest. *If I am exempt from service when others are not, I can live in peace with myself only if convinced this is a vile war.*

In calming the dissent that is so widespread on our campuses now, we should concentrate our efforts on separating the ready followers from the small group of rebellion leaders. Were it not for the widespread discontent, protest leaders would find a scant following, and if they should break the law without such followers, they could be readily dealt with. It is the mass following they can arouse because of the widespread malaise which alone makes them dangerous.

There has always been a small percentage of persons bent on destroying society and on fomenting revolution. In earlier generations there were the Wobblies; later there were the campus communists. But the present brand of campus revolutionaries, who are of anarchist and nihilist persuasion, are much more dangerous because they can point to success after success with their disrupting tactics. And nothing succeeds like success. Two hundred years ago Immanuel Kant warned that we shall never be able to control violence if it is rewarded. "It is far more convenient," he wrote, "to commit an act of violence, and afterwards excuse it, than laboriously to consider convincing arguments and lose time in listening to objections. This very boldness itself indicates a sort of conviction of the legitimacy of the action, and the God of success is afterwards the best advocate."

The greatest danger presently, then, is the readiness with which violence is excused, and the seemingly convincing arguments which are brought forth to justify it before and after the act. Worst and most dangerous of all, there seems to be a tendency in our society to legitimize the results of violence so that, as

Kant put it, the God of success afterwards serves as advocate for the violent action that preceded it, and suggests its future use. On our campuses, those committed to violence (to quote Kant again) "lose no time on considering arguments, or on listening to objections." They refuse to be rational about their grievances and, by violent means, insist on having their way, no matter what. And if they get it, as Kant knew, their success then legitimizes their disruptive actions.

The rebels gain their success by arousing a sizeable number of students through the tactic of confrontation, and by the universities' fear of confrontation. Confrontation has one important aim—to use the reaction of the provoked to generate a new unity among the demonstrators. In its most direct form, militants have stood in front of policemen and denounced them as pigs until the men in uniform hit out. The art of demonstrating then lies in ensuring that the blows are directed against the less-committed demonstrators and, if possible, against completely uninvolved persons. This provides the mass following required for success.

Of the small group of leaders of the radical left, it has been observed that most come from well-educated, very liberal families. Of those whom I know, I would say, too, that they have had their intellectual abilities developed very highly at much too early an age, at the expense of their emotional development. Although often very bright, emotionally some of them remained fixated at the age of the temper tantrum. It is this discrepancy between great intellectual maturity and utter emotional immaturity which is so baffling, often even to the universities, where some members of the faculty fail to see behind the obvious intelligence the inability to act rationally, and most of all, the inability to act responsibly. It is one of the weaknesses of university professors that, as persons committed to value intellectual ability most highly, they are captivated by the intelligence of these students to the degree that they are ready to excuse or brush aside the students' disruptiveness and intellectual arrogance.

As for the discontented students themselves, psychologically I always found them hating themselves as intensely as they hate the establishment, a self-hatred they try to escape by fighting *any* establishment. They need help in overcoming their emotional difficulties, and punishment is hardly the answer. If we bring them to the universities, we should provide facilities for helping them. It is their emotional immaturity that explains both their call for immediate action, and the retreat of the dropout and the hippy into utter non-action; each masks the inability of very intelligent young people to take time to think things out. The militants must want to destroy the universitites because they do not want to be students, for to be a student means to prepare oneself to do something more worthwhile in the future. The militant student's cry is for action now, not preparation for action later. In this sense, he is no longer a student at all, since he clearly rejects knowledge as a precondition of a meaningful activity. Truth, moreover, is no longer sought but "revealed"; the contempt for free speech and free thought is demonstrated as much by his actions as by his words. Were he ever to capture the university, it would cease to be a university.

In their inability to delay action for thought, both right and left extremists, the militants of all colors, are brothers under the skin. This is among the reasons why historically it has happened before that the young followers of the extreme right have become those of the extreme left, or the other way around. The mainspring of the rebels' action is more their wish to prove themselves strong—and less any particular political conviction—superimposed on self-doubt and hatred of a society which they feel has left them out in the cold. In Germany the National Socialists and the Communists voted together and worked together to bring down the democratic Weimar government, and in the same context, it is not so surprising that former Nazis easily involved themselves in the communistic government of East Germany.

But there are also good reasons why it is mainly the children of leftist parents who become hippies or student revolutionaries in our society, just as in other places and other times the children of conservative parents, under similar emotional conditions, spearheaded rightwing radicalism. It was the children of conservative German parents, for example, who first embraced the Emperor's War and enthusiastically went to their death because they felt a need to lay their bodies on the line for ideas their parents had only lukewarmly held; for thus they proved themselves strong, while at the same time proving their parents weak, wishy-washy and unworthy of true respect. They felt, too, that this was a means of rebirth, a way to revitalize an ossified society, to create a new society; with little patience for the voice of reason, they asked for authenticity and confrontation. All these were the main tenets of Hitler's academic youth, as they are now those of our own student left.

Thus, while the emotional constellations which make for very different student revolts are strangely similar, the specific political content of a student revolt depends to a large degree on the beliefs of the students' parents. For in many ways rebellion represents a desperate wish by youth to do better than their parents in exactly those beliefs in which parents seem weakest. In this sense, rebellion also represents a desperate desire for parental approval, but even more it represents a desperate wish that parents had been stronger in their convictions. So many of our radicals embrace Maoism and chant "Ho, Ho, Ho Chi Minh" much as another generation chanted at football rallies. These are strong father-figures with strong convictions who powerfully coerce their "children" to follow their commands. While consciously the students demand freedom and participation, unconsciously their commitment to Mao and other dictatorships suggests their desperate need for controls from the outside, since without them they are unable to bring order into their inner chaos. Such controls, however, must not be imposed punitively, nor for the benefit of others. They must be controls that clearly and definitely benefit the individual, so that he will eventually make them his own.

The inability of militant students to wait and work hard for long-range goals marks them as emotionally disturbed; so does their hatred for their parents who failed to give them direction and set them against the world by exposing their immature minds to criticism of all that could have given meaning to their lives. Indeed, it is their hatred of society that makes it so easy for the militant student leaders to make common cause with another small group that provides temporary leadership for some of the rebellions: outright paranoid individuals. The proportion of paranoids among students is no greater than in any comparable group of the population. But they are more dangerous because of their high intelligence, which permits them to conceal more successfully the degree of their disturbance. And student revolt permits them to act out their paranoia to a degree that no other position in society permits. How understandable, then, that all paranoids who can, do flock into the ranks of the militants. Unfortunately, most non-experts do not know how persuasive paranoids can be, at least until they are recognized. The persuasiveness of a Hitler or a Stalin is now regarded as the consequence of his own paranoia and his unconscious appeal to the vague paranoid tendencies among the immature and disgruntled. I have no doubt that the ranks of today's militants contain some would-be Hitlers and Stalins.

Paranoids make a persuasive appeal to any group in the population which rightly or wrongly feels persecuted, and they seek out such groups because they are most likely to view their own paranoia as true understanding of a persecuted group's particular predicament. Which brings me to the special problems of some of our black students who, fortunately, seem to recognize more and more that sds is using them rather than helping them. (They are not quite as successfully seeing through the motives of some of the paranoid student leaders.)

The overwhelming majority of black students desires exactly the same as does the overwhelming majority of white students: a rightful place in society. Only a very small minority of black and white students wishes to destroy it. Thus if the blacks could be convinced that there is a good place for them in society, their attitude would change and they would part ways with sds, as many of them have already done. But the difficulty is that many black students, because of the nature of the commitment of the university, do not feel that being a student is necessarily the best way for them to find their rightful place in society. It is here that our wish and theirs, that they should become part of the elite, runs afoul of what for many of them is their reality. Many black students in our colleges are often ill-prepared academically and lacking in the skills required for academic success. At the same time, they have been imbued with the notion that it is the fault of the establishment that they are disadvantaged. While this is true to some degree, awareness of such truth offers an easy way out if one does not succeed. All students find the transition from home to college difficult. In past times the student placed the blame for this on himself, and most students therefore tried to do something about themselves and sooner or later succeeded. Today both white and black students tend to blame the faculty for the difficulties they encounter in adjusting to a different way of life and study. The demand for black-study programs originated, not only in the justified feeling that one must be familiar and proud of one's own background, but to a large degree in the feeling that such studies would be easier, and that the faculty would have greater understanding.

The fact is that the preparation of some black students who are induced to go to college is inferior to that of the white majority of the college population. While the faculty is ready to make allowances for this, compensation runs counter to the self-respect of the black student, who rightly does not wish to be treated as a second-class citizen. But if he cannot compete successfully with his fellow students who have had so many educational and social advantages, he is in a terrible conflict. Brought to college to do as well as the other, when he fails his background does not permit him to accept that fact of failure because of his lack of preparation; to do so would make him feel second-class, a position he is seeking to escape by obtaining a college education. Although intellectually able, he has difficulty in adjusting, and he comes to feel that the very place which promised to make him equal fails to do so. Disappointed, he rages against the institution which once more makes him feel inferior, and special programs of assistance only make his feelings of inferiority even deeper. The many black students who are well able to hold their own with the best feel they must not desert their fellow black comrades, and in times of protest, they make their comrades' burden their own.

If we want to bring a large number of black students into our universities, as we should, we must start much earlier than college. From high school on, it will be necessary to educate a larger number of blacks, together with white youngsters from culturally deprived backgrounds, in true prep schools to permit them to enter college as well prepared academically and socially as the more advantaged students.

There is today a fascination in society with sex and violence, with drugs and insanity, which both influences the student militants and provides them with a noteworthiness which they exploit to the full. If students protest in an orderly and rational fashion, they receive little public attention. But if they shed their clothes and walk around naked, this makes news all over the nation, whatever case they may or may not have had; it is part of a dangerous fascination with youth and its extreme positions. What passes for modern literature which these youngsters read in junior high school intoxicates their minds with the appeal of drug-induced madness, with sexual acting out and with violence.

The universities, because of their intellectual prestige, give the student activists a platform for their revolutionary claims which they otherwise would never have. For example, for days not more than some twenty to thirty students recently occupied the administration building of the University of Chicago. They got headlines every day and were prominently featured on radio and television. Had thirty people demonstrated in any other place, they would have received no attention whatever. This SDS knows, and this is why it aims at the universities. The contrast between an institution devoted to the highest achievements of reason, and the obscenity and violence perpetrated there, makes it all the more fascinating, a fascination on which SDS tries to build its revolutionary success.

An idea in itself may amount to next to nothing, but it becomes news by interfering with something else which is considered to be of public importance. In themselves, a couple of hundred demonstrators somewhere in New York or Chicago would amount to very little; but when fifty students march into a lecture hall, seize control of the podium and broadcast their claims and philosophy to people who came to hear something quite different—then they have made news. If someone advocates urinating on graves (as the Fugs did), or if a few girls dress up as witches and put curses on professors (as they did in Chicago), if they did so without reference to politics, people would rightly wonder about their sanity. But when they do so as a condemnation of the Vietman war or in the name of some progressive cause, they win the support of many older liberals and enlightened radicals who invariably consider it all very socially significant. When a teen-ager wrestles with the police for the sake of the moral superiority of a future social order, he cannot fail to obtain the sympathetic attention of radio and television editors, if not psychiatrists. The ritualistic invocation of ideology is thus both an alibi and a defense.

Perhaps it all has made too many headlines, perhaps it has been talked about too much for people to accept the fact, but the truth of the matter is that these rebellions can and do paralyze our universities. Not only are classes interrupted and buildings occupied, but faculty members must devote their energies to calming things down. Even more importantly, the time and energy which should be devoted to more lasting achievements are drained away on plans to forestall new confrontations. A last comparison with pre-Hitler days: In Germany at that time, as Professor George L. Mosse (*The Crisis of German Ideology*, Grosset and Dunlap, 1964) puts it, "professors tended to be either scholars who withdrew into their own specialty, taking scant notice of the world around them, or men who attempted to play the role of prophets. The first kind of academic wanted only to be left in peace. . . . The professor as prophet, with very few exceptions indeed, was to be found on the side of the revolting students." Of the students of that time he says, "They had found a basis for action that opposed existing authority yet remained independent of any political movement directed by their elders." And the faculties, he says, "failed to provide any opposition, failed to use administrative powers and failed to organize effective alternative groups of students. At best they displayed a detached passivity . . . at worst they joined in the harrassment."

In our universities today we have faculty members who are trying to remain aloof from it all, and others who are trying to anticipate even the most radical student demands so as to avoid confrontations. Worse, though, there are few efforts being made to organize effective alternative groups of students. Worst of all, many professors are so intimidated that they cave in even before the students exercise pressure. It is the continuous worry about what the militant students may do next, the anxious efforts to give them no offense, which saps the universities of their strength to the point of paralysis. And this anxious avoidance of taking a firm stand gives not only these militants, but also many non-committed students, the feeling that they have the faculty on the run.

If the colleges and universities would take a determined stand against coercion and intimidation—though always open to, indeed inviting, reasonable and non-coercive discussion about much-needed reform—then student rebellions could be reduced to the point where they would no longer threaten either the universities or society. The university must strengthen its will to resist disruption and coercion. If it succeeds, it will have little need to take recourse to punitive measures, beyond setting into practice the principle that those who do not wish to have any part of our universities should have their will: they should not be permitted to be, live or work in a place they hate, not as a punishment, but because to remain in a place they hate and despise serves no good purpose and is detrimental to their emotional well-being.

7. BLACK STUDIES:
THE UNIVERSITIES IN MORAL CRISIS

Abba P. Lerner

Abba P. Lerner is Professor of Economics at the University of California at Berkeley and formerly economic advisor to the Government of Israel.

I

RECENT DEMANDS for black and "third world" studies and for black and third world control of black or third world departments or colleges in American universities have been supported by arguments ranging from the compelling to the ridiculous, pressed for by means ranging from the ineffective to the intolerable, and inspired by motives ranging from the most noble to the most despicable. The responses by faculties and administrations have covered almost as wide a spectrum, from inexcusable inaction on the most justifiable requests to unprincipled surrender to bullying bigotry.

For rational action in this situation the first requirement is the identification and the separation of the objectives behind the demands. The main objectives as they appear to me are here presented roughly in the order of their justifiability and their urgency. They are:

(1) To remove any still existing discriminations against members of minority groups, thereby increasing the percentage of minority students and faculty in the universities.

(2) To develop more appropriate and more impartial criteria for the admission of minority students and for the appointment of minority teachers and administrators by supplanting or correcting such criteria as may be culturally biased against them.

(3) To provide help and encouragement to disadvantaged and discouraged students and potential students (whose difficulties are in large measure the result of past racial discrimination).

Reprinted, with permission, from *The Humanist* for May–June 1969.

(4) To develop and expand the study of topics of concern to black and other minorities where these have been neglected—possibly because of conscious or unconscious prejudice.

(5) By these and other means to cure black and other minority students of unwarranted feelings of inferiority that are the residues of discrimination against them in the past.

(6) To bring about "reverse discrimination" in favor of members of the minorities in admissions, scholarships, appointments, promotions, etc., as partial compensation for the shameful discrimination against the minorities in the past.

(7) To bring the proportions of minority students, faculty members, and administrators on the campuses into equality with the proportions of the minorities in the general population.

(8) To overcome self-deprecation of black and other minority people—the result of past suppression—and to raise their pride in their color, race, or culture, by playing down, suppressing, or denouncing as "racist" any studies, researches, or criticisms that might tend to weaken such pride.

(9) To limit the teaching of black and third world subjects and the manning of black and third world departments to black or third world people.

(10) To establish departments, colleges, dormitories, etc., that, officially or unofficially, will be basically segregated in their student body and that will instill the habit of seeing all problems in terms of race and foster feelings of racial superiority over other groups.

(11) To combine pride in "blackness" or in "third-worldness" with hatred of all "white" (or nonblacks or nonchicanos, etc.) as intrinsically and incurably racist.

(12) To achieve and escalate confrontations with university authorities by ever increasing "revolutionary demands" (i.e., demands that by their nature cannot be granted) for the purpose of disrupting and destroying the universities as the easiest first step towards destroying the society served by universities.

II

In pressing for some of these and related objectives, militant leaders have tried to shut down universities by so-called "strikes." In this they have universally failed; only small minorities having been peacefully and democratically persuaded to stay away. The militants have thereupon moved from the democratic way of persuasion to the antidemocratic way of intimidation, and have resorted to the disruptive tactics of confrontations and harassment developed by the group that calls itself Students for a Democratic Society. Together with the SDS they have engaged in violence and sabotage "to bring the universities to a grinding halt"—in the now-classic cliché.

In this they have in many cases been able to mobilize all kinds of unrelated discontents and to exploit all kinds of sentimental hangups. They have been able to involve many students and some teachers in staging and in escalating confrontations. They have provided bored students with the excitement of circuses, "rags," and small "social revolutions." They have exploited anger and shame at past discriminations and sympathy with the present sufferers from the past discriminations as well as the concern of all students for more individual attention and their inevitable impatience with the inevitable delays that stem from the ways of even the best intentioned administration (in this context usually called bureaucracy). They have taken advantage of the recent awakening of apathetic students into wholly admirable eagerness for concern for and participation in the conduct of the university. But most of all have they been helped in the escalation of confrontation and violence by an ability to transform an appreciation of campus harmony and mutual understanding that would make police unnecessary, and an abhorrence of interference by totalitarian governments with freedom of speech, into an unthinking hostility to "police on campus" even when their only purpose there is to *protect* freedom of speech, and the general operation of the university, from physical violence.

Surprised by the disruptions and confused by the mixture of worthy and unworthy objectives, the faculties and administrators find themselves caught between unthinking, possibly malicious, conservative politicians on one front and unscrupulous revolutionary demagogues on the other; the two extremes in effect aiding each other. Thus trapped they are sorely tempted to lean over backwards to achieve peace even if it means bending some of their principles or even some of their prejudices.

Some prejudices will have to give, but the bending of principles constitutes just that kind of appeasement of the worst of the objectives that encourages the further escalation of the worst of the terroristic instruments of confrontation. Yet tension tends to cloud our vision, so that what in steadier times was clearly seen as incompatible with the proper functioning of a self-respecting university in a free country tends to be overlooked in the presence of greater threats, and our sensitivity to the fundamentals is warped.

This was brought home to me in looking over a statement of the basic principles as they appeared to me (and to some colleagues) a few months ago, before we were subjected to these pressures (and before the "black" demands had been fused with those of other minorities in "third world" demands). I was shocked to discover that I had not fully escaped the brainwashing by the campus tension or by the howling of the mobs outside as I tried to work in my study. Over twenty years ago I joined Roosevelt College in Chicago (now Roosevelt University) in part because it had revolted against the imposition by its trustees of a quota to limit the percentage of Negro students and had refused to register the color of students. And now I caught myself toying with the thought of buying some peace by deferring to color in selecting a student for admission or a teacher for an appointment.

III

It is in this contrite spirit that I present for consideration and possible guidance in our present crisis this statement of principles, set down in a more peaceful time when they seemed so obvious and so well-established as to be hardly worth spelling out. But in times of stress it is often the most obvious that needs the most emphasis.

(1) We deplore any discrimination in opportunities for study or for teaching or for employment on account of color, race, creed, national origin, language or surname, or any other consideration irrelevant to academic potential or achievement.

(2) We recognize that Negroes and others have been discriminated against, and are still being discriminated against, and that decency and efficiency call for doing all we can to end this discrimination.

(3) Past discrimination is responsible for continuing disadvantages to prospectively successful students, in poverty, in lack of confidence, and in lack of home encouragement and support. It would therefore seem very likely that investment in special encouragement of and financial support to such disadvantaged potential students would be socially profitable as well as morally satisfying.

(4) Such special help should be directed to *all* potential students who are in need of it. Because of the existing conditions

of poverty and discouragement a very large proportion of such help would automatically go to Negroes, even if no attention is paid to the color of the students to be helped.

(5) Paying special attention to color could be perfectly appropriate as a prima facie *indication* of probable need for help. It would not be justified as a *criterion* for help.

(6) Teachers are often tempted to grade handicapped students more leniently, and to use criteria of color, nationality, race, etc., in a "reverse discrimination" favoring members of minority groups. Such temptations should be resisted as strenuously as possible for two reasons. One is that it affects the efficiency of the educational institution by lowering standards and inducing resentments both in those who fail to get the preferred treatment and in those who believe that they have not been favored as much as others or as much as they should have been (as a kind of vicarious compensation for damage done by others to others in previous decades or centuries). The more important reason is that the grades and degrees earned by the "favored" groups become suspect and tend to be discounted and even overdiscounted, so that discrimination against them instead of being diminished is perpetuated.

(7) In the case of the hiring of teachers "reverse discrimination" is even less defensible. In some cases the instructor's special experience or knowledge of the habits, life, and language of certain groups of students may be a genuinely valuable quality, and this may go with his color. But in such cases the special qualification should be judged on its own merits and carefully scrutinized against its being merely an excuse for discrimination because of color, possibly in response to outside pressure—whether this is pressure by governments, regents, alumni, or students.

(8) Such "reverse discrimination" would also have the effect of damaging the status of the "favored" groups. Experience in teaching at an institution would tend to be taken not as evidence of their having been examined by the institutions and found worthy but as evidence of the institution having given in to pressure, and the experience would tend to be discounted or dismissed as of no conclusive significance.

(9) A policy of subjecting purely academic considerations to the objective of increasing (or decreasing) the proportion of the faculty that is of a particular color, creed, nationality, language or surname, or any other nonacademic consideration, would

corrupt the academic community, damage the academic standards of the educational institution it infects, and constitute an attack on academic freedom as severely to be condemned as the imposition of restrictive quotas on the proportion of Negroes or of Jews to be admitted to educational opportunity.

(10) All this is not to deny that great efforts should be made to seek out and encourage available Negro and other minority teachers who have been discouraged or to help such potential teachers to acquire the necessary training and experience.

(11) Minority teachers are more likely than others to be lacking in formal certification even when they are really quite qualified to do the work required. It would therefore be even more useful in their case than in general to have sufficient flexibility to be able to appoint competent people lacking the formal requirements. In many cases this could be achieved by provisional appointments where there seems to be a good enough chance that the appointee could prove himself.

(12) Both of these measures would be severely hampered by "reverse discrimination" such as in pressures to increase the *proportion* of Negro (etc.) teachers so as to correspond to, say, their proportion in the population. Such pressures, if yielded to, would strengthen the fear, often quite justified, that the termination of an experimental appointment, while attracting no attention in the case of a white appointee, would be denounced as racist discrimination in the case of a Negro (etc.). This is likely to make those in authority especially reluctant to make provisional or experimental minority appointments. Feeling that such an experimental appointment of a Negro or other minority instructor would be practically equivalent to granting tenure, they would actually be forced against their own consciences to engage in racial discrimination *against* the minorities.

(13) There have been those who would compromise the principles here stated and undertake to double the proportion of Negroes on the faculty, even at some supposedly minimized sacrifice in the quality of the university, for the sake of relieving the pressure for "proportional quotas." Such compromising would increase rather than decrease the pressure. It would show that the pressure works, and it would strengthen the demands.

(14) Negro (etc.) faculty appointed under especially lowered standards would also find themselves in a difficult and defensive situation. In danger of being charged with having "sold out

to the white establishment" they will experience strong pressures to prove they are no "Uncle Toms" by showing themselves visibly in the forefront of all extremist claims. This is an additional reason why a compromising of standards for the sake of meeting a target would increase rather than decrease the pressures for further compromising.

(15) There is also the danger of chairmen of departments under pressure or imagined pressure from administrators or from black student organizations (direct or through the administration) finding that they can meet quotas only by lowering standards. They would then be tempted to avoid resistance by evading normal faculty procedures in the name of pressure of time or what not.

(16) The issues are clearer still in the matter of pressure for "black" studies. There are courses, and there could be more, that could be considered part of a "black curriculum." The filling of lacunae, if genuine, cannot be objected to, and complete freedom for experimenting in new courses, whether sponsored by students or anyone else, is only for the good. But arguments like that which declares "white" literature to be "irrelevant" to black students of literature, or vice versa, are completely unacceptable. All courses must be open to all students on a nondiscriminatory basis, and should fit into fields where their significance and relevance can plausibly be established.

(17) The university should be especially alert against proposals intended as instruments of black power, and of antiwhite (segregationist, racist) policies within the university. Such proposals seem usually to demand black studies, taught by black faculty, for black students only (or similarly restricted to other minority groups). These proposals strike directly at the heart of the basic principle of free academic inquiry, and must be resisted. The notion, for example, that there should, on these terms, be freshman courses in literature and composition, or in science, taught by black faculty for black students is thoroughly pernicious, to say nothing of extending this principle to more advanced study. We must be scrupulously on guard against any acceptance of black racism as in any way any better than white or yellow racism. It is more easily explained but not one whit more justified.

8. ACADEMIC FREEDOM
FOR THE STUDENT
IN THE CLASSROOM

Edward Chalfant

Edward Chalfant is Associate Professor of English at Hofstra University, Long Island, New York.

I SPEAK AS A TEACHER interested in teaching methods, one who works for the most part with college seniors, juniors, and sophomores, in that order. This article concerns what happens in college classrooms, what doesn't happen in college classrooms, and what perhaps *ought* to happen in college classrooms. Its subject is a change that is taking place in American education. Although I believe that the issues involved in the change are urgent, I do not intend to generalize about issues here. Instead, I shall speak exclusively for myself, confining what I say to the narrow field of my own experience.

My first teaching job was as an instructor in English at Dartmouth College, starting in the autumn of 1947. My teaching load was three courses, with a total enrollment of 59 students. No one coached me in teaching methods. I began to teach by following what seemed to me an accepted set of principles for teaching. I assumed that I should prepare myself for each of my classes by studying the best available books relating to the material of the courses, and by using the brain that God gave me, in the hope that I would arrive in the classroom in possession of some valuable opinions about the subject under discussion. I also assumed that it was the teacher's duty to impart his valuable opinions to his students. So when I was there in the room, and the students were looking at me, and I was looking at them, I told them my opinions freely.

I do not mean that I lectured. On the contrary, from the beginning I resorted to a variety of teaching procedures, mixing intervals of explaining with intervals of questioning; asking the students to volunteer opinions of their own; asking the students to

Reprinted, with permission, from the *Hofstra Review*, Spring 1969.

write in class answers to difficult questions and then to read their answers aloud; making them write papers outside of class; and so on. But the basic thing was that I began with the presupposition that the teacher should tell his opinions to his students.

Before I turn away from those old days, let me mention that the system I used in 1947 did not seem wrong. The students were not in rebellion against it. They were learning—not extremely fast, but fast enough, it seemed, to be pleasing to them. Their attitude appeared to be that teaching was teaching and that I was doing the proper thing.

Much has changed in the United States since 1947. For me, the change has perhaps been less drastic than for the average American. I am no longer teaching at Dartmouth, a school I liked, but at Hofstra, a school I like even better. I no longer teach three courses, but four—plus an extra little seminar thrown in for good measure; and instead of 59 students I have (at the time of this writing) 143. The *big* difference is that I no longer teach the same way. As nearly as I can find out, I am one of several hundred teachers in the United States who, a bit at a time, independently but simultaneously, have discovered during the past two decades that the old methods of higher education are not very good and that better teaching methods are needed.

So I want to tell you, from my own point of view, what a perfect class would be like under a better teaching method than the one I took for granted twenty-odd years ago.

It goes without saying that the perfect class must be a class in a course worth taking. Let's suppose, therefore, that the course requires the students to read the writings of a worthwhile author—for example, Shakespeare. Let's suppose that the enrollment is large, but not too large—perhaps 45 students—and that the students are jammed into a classroom of minimum size, in which the back row is not very far back, and every seat gets used. Let's suppose the teacher is tough and even intimidating about one thing: he wants the students to do their assignments. And let's suppose that the assignment for this class session is to read Act IV of *The Merchant of Venice*.

When the teacher and the students appear in the room and the class begins, the teacher does not lecture. He asks no question. He starts no discussions. Instead, he tells the students to turn to a certain passage he has selected in Act IV of *The Merchant of Venice*, and while the students look at the passage, the teacher reads it aloud.

Then he asks whether anybody has anything to say about the passage, or about Shakespeare, or about anything. If a student does have something to say and says it, the teacher responds by doing something invisible: he accepts the student's statement into his mind. He further responds by doing something audible: he repeats aloud directly to the student what the student has said. Or if what the student has said is long and complicated, he repeats aloud the gist of what the student has said, or perhaps the most striking portion of what the student has said. But if when the teacher asks whether anyone has something to say, the students say nothing and a silence sets up in the room, the teacher bravely faces the silence. He lets it go on.

Should the silence become tremendous, the teacher has several alternatives. He may simply read the selected passage again and ask the students a second time to say something about it. Or he may tell the class he *loves* silence. Or he may mention in dollars and cents how much it costs 45 college students per minute to sit in a classroom. But silence is the exception, not the rule. When college students have done their assignment and then heard part of it read aloud in class, and at the same time looked at the selected part in their books, they will in fact speak up.

Please notice, however, that some strange things are going on. If we compare what is happening in this class to what might be *expected* to happen in a college class, there are some obvious differences:

First, attention has been shifted to a considerable degree away from the teacher to Shakespeare.

Second, a silence that only the students can fill has been created.

Third, before any student fills the silence by saying something, there is absolutely no way for either the teacher or the other students to anticipate what he is going to say.

Fourth, the student who speaks is doing something active, rather than passive—and, moreover, is doing something that might be original, might even be courageous. But the main point is that he is active.

Fifth, because the things that the student says are repeated back to him, they go through a metamorphosis. He hears his own words spoken by somebody else. It is a little bit as if his words were being printed, and he is reading the galley proofs. And while his ideas, in this way, are given a new appearance for him, something similar is happening for the other students taking the course. Most of them are discovering that the ideas they were silently turning over in their minds are different from, unrelated to, opposite to, or strangely connected with the ideas that got expressed by the student who was willing to speak.

I should not need to tell you that in this perfect class, once one thing gets said by one student and repeated by the teacher, more things will get said; that the teacher will accept and repeat aloud every suggestion that gets made; that the teacher will read the selected passage again and urge the class to reconsider and deepen its ideas, if it can; and that the teacher will move the class onward to other passages in Act IV of *The Merchant of Venice*, perhaps very different ones.

The semester cannot be far advanced before it dawns on the students that the teacher is not offended by ideas and suggestions that might be silly or wrong; that the teacher is not in the room to criticize; and that, each time the class meets, the teacher is hopeful that before the hour is over he and the students will exchange the opinions they came into the room with for better opinions on the same subject.

What this means is that the students will discover that there are interesting and serious problems implicit in Shakespeare's writings; that these problems can be recognized and defined by less highly educated people just as well as by more highly educated people; and that extremely rapid progress toward solving these problems can be made through the help of cooperative thinking.

Understand that what is going on in the class I have been describing is not mere discussion. From the day the course begins to the day it ends, the teacher brings into the classroom an attitude that forbids mere talk and chitchat and "exchange of views." In fact, a lot of things are forbidden. The students are not permitted to smoke. Neither is the teacher. The students are not allowed to whisper to one another. They are required to pay attention, strict attention, to Shakespeare. They .cannot escape the sound and sight of the passages that the teacher reads aloud, nor the sound of each other's voices making suggestions. They are also required to write papers setting forth their opinions at length—one paper about each play by Shakespeare that is taken up in the course—and that means a lot of papers, each of which may require a great deal of toil and agony to write. So where, one may ask, is the freedom? I have entitled this article "Academic Freedom for the Student in the Classroom," but it may seem very unclear where the freedom comes in if students are put under such pressures as these.

I believe I can tell you where the freedom comes in—because the class I have been imagining in the preceding paragraphs is not just a hope for me. For many years now, I have been running classes much like this one. Thousands of hours in the classroom—not to mention innumerable conversations with students outside the classroom—have removed all doubt from my mind that *when students are taught with the help of such procedures as these, they are not only free in the classroom but know they are free.* Furthermore, they welcome their freedom like a great breath of fresh air, and they react to it by becoming more active persons, not only while the class is in progress, but outside of class while reading their assignments, writing their papers, and doing whatever else they may do. In short, the method makes possible a liberation, and this liberation carries over into many parts of the students' lives.

Let's study this liberation more closely. The first thing we'll notice is that the liberation begins when the student finds that his role in the classroom is not to be the passive one of being told opinions by a qualified *speaker,* but rather the active one of being urged to offer opinions in the presence of his fellow students, as well as in the presence of a qualified *hearer.* Please note that last phrase; I do not want to give the impression that I have stopped preparing for classes and just wander into room, hoping the students will have something to say. No. In connection with each of the courses I teach—for example, the Shakespeare course—I am taking greater pains to develop opinions that are truly sensible and well informed. The students know that I *could* give lectures; they even try, without success, to worm my opinions out of me; but they are also immensely relieved that I won't tell them what I think, because they are eager to have a chance to get going on what *they* would think if they could just master Shakespeare by means of hard study and cooperative effort.

To be frank, I must admit that the students themselves refer to our classes as "discussions." But I much prefer to avoid the word. As I understand the term, "discussion" can go on forever without getting anywhere, without advancing toward new conclusions, without involving discovery. When the teaching procedures I have described are put into use, it is almost impossible for a class *not* to get anywhere, *not* to reach new conclusions, *not* to make discoveries. The liberation, the freedom, goes hand in hand with rapid—almost painfully rapid—learning.

The liberation of the students certainly makes classes exciting. The teacher, with respect to what will be said next in the room, deliberately throws every class completely out of control; and, partly as a result, the ideas put forth by the students are often upsetting, unexpected, or extremely original. But because everyone present knows by instinct that chaos will ensue if a general effort is not made to preserve order and maintain good manners, the classes tend to be exceedingly civilized. They turn into interesting blends of explosion and control, of energy and restraint, irritation and harmony.

Such classes keep the teacher unusually busy. He must never stop communicating to the students the feeling that learning is possible. He must watch several dozen faces at once and try to read the meaning of the changing expressions. He must vary the torment of the system by saying apt things on the spur of the moment—apt things that will vigorously push the students' inquiries forward—and by devising and asking, instantly and without hesitation, highly relevant and well-worded questions that will not distort the students' efforts or give away his own opinions. He must be prepared to go on with this strenuous process even when he discovers that the opinions he himself has brought into the classroom won't stand up under the battering of cooperative mental work by young and talented minds. Above all, he must curb every impulse to get into the act himself by intruding his own opinions. If he does that, he will wreck the class.

Because the role of the students is active, they grow interested in what they are doing, often with the unlooked-for result that all sorts of troubles that have dogged them for years begin to clear up, as if of their own accord. Bad spellers start to spell very much better. Poor concentrators sit down and read books over and over. Timid writers begin to write in assertive, decided ways. To the gratification of both teacher and students, the fact grows clear that every student in every class is intelligent. There are no dumb ones; there are only different degrees of positive performance. Learning becomes athletic. The teacher feels more and more a coach and less and less like a pedant. The students feel less and less like involuntary bookworms, and more and more like a team.

The students recognize the teacher as a learner like themselves; and the teacher may well have the illusion—only perhaps it is not an illusion—that he is holding on to his youth. In turn, observing the teacher, the students may begin to grasp the inspiring idea that human beings do not need to grow old (at least, not in all respects) and that it would be for the best if they kept mentally active, if they kept learning, all their lives.

A great advantage of the procedure I am describing is that the students taught with its help spontaneously solve, in all but the most exceptional cases, the problem of "relevance" that is now so much talked about in discussions of education. *The individual student finds the relations* that exist for him or for her between the texts we are studying and the student's other concerns, both academic and non-academic. What is more, in practically every instance, the students seek and find this "relevance" at a very fundamental emotional and intellectual level. There is nothing superficial or merely verbal about the meaning that the texts gain for them, just the reverse. The risk involved in the procedure, if anything, is that the student may become so deeply concerned about a particular play of Shakespeare, or a novel, or an essay, or whatever the text in question may be, that it becomes difficult for the teacher to persuade the student to write a paper on *that* text without delay, in order to go on to the next text. Instead of erring on the side of carelessness, the students tend to err on the side of perfectionism—a tendency which has the added, bonus value of teaching them the urgent importance of self-discipline and the ability to keep to strict schedules, with only occasional variations.

I don't want to suggest that these teaching procedures are perfect for everyone. A few years ago, I was assigned to teach a graduate course in the evening at Hofstra. The subject of the course was the writings of Herman Melville and Emily Dickinson. At the beginning of the first class, I explained my methods to the students, one of whom, without saying anything, made up his mind that such methods were wrong. He was good enough to stay quietly in the room until the class was over. Then he went straight to the Dean and told him that one of the university's teachers was insane, since he did not understand that the first duty of a teacher is to tell students what to think. He demanded his money back—and got it, Hofstra being a reasonable institution. (The moral of the story may be that it costs a university money to keep people like me on the payroll.)

Neither do I intend to suggest that my teaching method is fixed and unchanging. It is true that none of my students seem to want me to change it; they keep telling me it ought to be kept just as it is. But because I want to improve it, I do keep changing it all the time.

I would be giving a wrong impression if I said that I use the method in pure, undiluted form. The truth is that I often water it down, chiefly by devoting part of the class hour to asking difficult questions that I prepare before the class begins. But there is a disadvantage to the so-called Socratic method which Socrates probably noticed, and which we can notice, too. The disadvantage is that questions channel attention. They deprive the student of his freedom to decide which aspect of the matter under consideration should be turned to first, and how that aspect should be approached. So I mainly use prepared questions at the beginning of the term, while the students are getting gradually accustomed to academic freedom.

Let me add that I do supply my classes with small but highly useful packages of information in connection with each subject we take up. But the information I supply is invariably selected to aid and encourage—not to block, short-circuit, or undermine—free inquiry. Similarly, I do tell the students my opinions about minor matters not worth cooperative study.

I must also warn you that a method of the kind I have described, which has unfailingly worked well for me, might be worse than unworkable for another teacher. There is an unwritten law in the universities that we teachers will not try to teach each other how to teach, and it may be that the law for the most part is a good one. When teachers are young or inexperienced, for example, they are likely to be deeply afraid of their students. They may put on a false front of courage, and I hope that they do; but it is naturally quite terrifying to have to match wits all alone with twenty, thirty, or even fifty minds at a time. In such emergencies, teachers can perhaps be forgiven if they defend themselves in the classroom by lecturing, by building brick walls made of words behind which they can stand until their terror begins to recede. So I would not necessarily be willing to recommend my methods to another teacher, even if he said he wanted to try it. The methods I have grown to prefer presuppose that I am no longer afraid of students—not even slightly afraid.

Yet I have to confess that I'd be happier if more of my colleagues would resolve to transform their courses in ways that would set their students free in the classroom. It is my belief that the option of freedom is always there, directly in front of the teacher. It does not matter whether the subject is English, or medicine, or accounting, or psychology, or engineering; if the teacher wants to liberate the student, he can do so.

If my gropings toward a better procedure have taught me one thing conclusively, it is that the teacher who wishes to free his students must begin by teaching himself to stop talking. He must *form* valuable opinions, but he must keep some or all of them *quiet*. He must be prepared to have his wonderful ideas go with him, unexpressed, to the grave. He must get his main satisfaction from seeing his students do better work than he himself could have done at the same age—or at any age.

* * . * * * *

The following dialogue is transcribed verbatim from the tape recording of a recent class conducted by Dr. Edward Chalfant. The class is composed of college juniors and seniors engaged in the study of Shakespeare, and the assigned reading is Act IV of *The Merchant of Venice*. Professor Chalfant begins by reading a few lines from one of Shylock's speeches in the courtroom scene:

> And by our holy Sabbath have I sworn
> To have the due and forfeit of my bond.
> If you deny it, let the danger light
> Upon your charter and your city's freedom.

Teacher: Does anyone have anything to say at all? Anything? [There is a long silence.]

Student A: I have a question here.

Teacher: What's the question?

Student A: Why did Shylock swear to have the forfeit instead of the bond?

Teacher: Why did Shylock swear to have the forfeit instead of the 3,000 ducats? Well, can anyone answer that question? It would speed things up tremendously if someone could tell us. Why does he want the pound of flesh instead of the money?

Student B: Because the pound of flesh represents the love of Antonio, and that's why he did it. I mean, he wants his love.

Teacher: He wants Antonio's love, good opinion, regard. And this pound of flesh corresponds to that?

Student B: Right. And it means more than money to him—to be loved.

Teacher: We have a suggestion from the front row which, judging from the frowns on many faces, meets with instantaneous disapproval. [To Student A] What's your trouble?

Student A: When you love someone, you want to cut out their heart?

Teacher: Well, the heart stands for love, doesn't it? If I remember right. [General laughter breaks out.]

Teacher: It might be that we are trying to deal with this question in too few words. [To Student B] Could you explain at length what you're talking about?

Student B: Well, all right. What happened was, Antonio needed the money very much, and he had to go to Shylock. Now, he does not approve of Shylock's way of doing things, of usury—he calls it usury—and exacting, you know, making profit on a loan, because this is not the Christian thing to do.

Teacher: I hear you.

Student B: So . . . he [Shylock] tells him [Antonio] in the first act of the play, "What I really want is your love and your friendship. And to show you that I mean it and that I am not such a horrible person, I will give you the 3,000 ducats and not make a profit on you, but if . . . your love and friendship doesn't mean anything and you don't give me back the 3,000 ducats at a certain time, I want a pound of flesh."

Teacher: You're satisfied that the original impulse was friendly?

Student B: Right. . . .

Student C: I can't see the being friendly or wanting love. First of all, Shylock continually repeats how much he hates Antonio.

Teacher: Maybe Shylock can clear this up for us. Shylock goes on to say, and I suppose he was given these lines for a purpose:

> You'll ask me why I rather choose to have
> A weight of carrion flesh than to receive
> Three thousand ducats. I'll not answer that!
> But say it is my humor—is it answered?
> What if my house be troubled with a rat,
> And I be please'd to give ten thousand ducats
> To have it baned? What, are you answered yet?
> Some men there are love not a gaping pig,
> Some that are mad if they behold a cat,
> And others when the bagpipe sings i' th' nose
> Cannot contain their urine. For affection,
> Master of passion, sways it to the mood
> Of what it likes or loathes. Now for your answer.
> As there is no firm reason to be rend'red
> Why he cannot abide a gaping pig,
> Why he, a harmless necessary cat,

Why be a woolen bagpipe, but of force
Must yield to such inevitable shame,
As to offend (himself being offended),
So can I give no reason, nor I will not,
More than a lodged hate and a certain loathing
I bear Antonio, that I follow thus
A losing suit against him. Are you answered?

You look puzzled. Are you puzzled?

Student D: Yes. I wonder why. Why did Shakespeare write a puzzle?

Teacher: Why did Shakespeare write a puzzle? Is it a puzzle?

Student E: Nothing I've ever read of Shakespeare ever was a puzzle. You know, it's usually straightforward, and usually means what it says. I guess Shylock is a very embittered man at this point, and he always was an embittered man, but now it's reaching extremes. And what he says here . . . I guess it does make sense if you put it in a context of someone who is wholly alienated, embittered, and wants some type of revenge, but really does not know how to get it in a world where no revenge is open to him, because he's put in a position where he is always on the defensive. Now he wants to take the attack, and this might be a way to let out the steam that's been building up in this man for forty years, or fifty years.

Teacher: Sixty years. Isn't he sixty?

Student E: Sixty years.

Teacher: Seventy-five years. Isn't he seventy-five?

Student E: Yes.

Teacher: We need more ideas. Has someone got a different idea?

Student A: I don't quite agree that he, Shylock, has given an answer.

Teacher: Are you saying that the main words in what Shylock said were, "I'll *not* answer that"?

Student A: Yes.

Teacher: The main words, she [Student A] says, are "I'll not answer that."

Student A: He does have an answer, but he's not giving it, and he's hoping that this speech of his will suffice.

Teacher: She says he has an answer which he won't give, and instead is saying something which he thinks might suffice. Let's run through this again.

[The teacher rereads the same passage, beginning, "You'll ask me. . . ." After much further struggle with the problem discovered in the text, the class is interrupted.]

Student A [suddenly]: Ohhhhhhhhh!

[There is a general burst of laughter.]

Student A: I couldn't figure out if Shylock knew what was going to happen at the trial, but now I see! Maybe Shylock *knows* that he is going to do what he [Student E] said—kill Antonio. . . . And maybe he wants it that way.

Teacher: Does he want a sort of holocaust?

Student A: Yes. He wants to bring Antonio down with him.

Teacher: He wants to bring Antonio down with him.

Student A: He, Shylock, is so upset about losing his daughter that he doesn't want his own life anyway.

[The class continues, going on through many other possibilities, toward conclusions that will emerge in the students' papers.]

III

THE
CRISIS
OF THE
UNIVERSITY

9. THE CRISIS OF THE UNIVERSITY

Henry Steele Commager

Henry Steele Commager is Professor of History at Columbia
University and Amherst College.

THE CRISIS of the university today is a tribute to its importance.
Within a quarter-century the university has moved to the very
center of American life; the center of ideas, the center of research,
the center of criticism and of protest. Students who once went to
the university to prepare for a career or, as we amiably say, "to
prepare for life," now find that the university *is* life. Parents who
looked upon the university as a golden interlude before their
children faced the hard realities of life are confronted by the fact
that college years are not an interlude, but the real thing, and
that they are not golden but iron. The public, which thought
students should be protected from disturbing ideas and should
provide vicarious happiness and public entertainment for those

Reprinted, with permission, from *Newsday*, June 7, 1969.

94

outside the university, is discovering that students are far more interested in making people unhappy than in making them happy.

Student population has grown to six million—rather larger than the total number of farmers—and university teachers probably number over half a million: a formidable phalanx. If professors ever thought of the university as an Ivory tower (which may be doubted), they no longer do: they are involved in everything from advising Presidents, who rarely listen to them, to conducting seminars for businessmen, attending conferences in Asia and Africa or mediating between capital and labor and between whites and blacks. The scientists, said Lord Snow, have the future in their bones, but it is no longer the scientists alone, it is the whole army of scholars, in all areas. The future promises no relief from this situation, but rather more of the same: the university population is bound to grow, and as society and economy become increasingly complex, scholars, who stand at the levers of control of a technological society, will play an increasingly vital role.

No one bothers to attack institutions without significance or power. As long as the college was small and pastoral it could be ignored or tolerated, but not taken very seriously. Now that it occupies the vital center of society it is inevitable that the winds of controversy should swirl about it, that the din of national politics and international controversies should shatter its peace; that all of its members, students, faculty and administration, should be shaken out of their complacency and required to justify themselves.

The student protest against the university is, in a sense, a flattering gesture, though there is no doubt that more universities would gladly forego the flattery. What students are saying, in their somewhat incoherent way, is that they no longer have any confidence in government, politics, business, industry, labor, the church, for all of these are hopelessly corrupt. Only the university is left. Clearly it is corrupt, too, but not hopelessly; it can still be saved and if it is saved, it can be made into an instrument to reform the whole of society.

Student dissent and revolt in the United States has two clear dimensions, though the student themselves are aware of only one of them. Vertically it is rooted in some two centuries of American experience with colleges and universities, experiences quite different from those of Old World nations. Horizontally it reflects the pervasive frustration, outrage and despair of the young at the

Vietnam war, the draft, the armaments race, the destruction of the environment, racial injustice—at all that is implied in that epithet "the establishment."

It is the heritage that largely explains why the revolt of youth against the establishment is directed against the university rather than against government, or parties, or the military, or Dow Chemical or Chase Manhattan or the Automobile Workers of America; it explains, too, why students who revolt against the university claim special exemption because they are part of the university and demand that it protect them and care for their every need.

The university, as it emerged out of medieval Italy, France and England, and developed over the centuries, had three clear functions. The first was to train young men for essential professions: the church, the law and medicine, and perhaps teaching. The second was to preserve the heritage of the past, and pass it on to future generations intact. The third—first clarified by Göttingen and her sister universities in Germany in the eighteenth and nineteenth centuries—was to expand the boundaries of knowledge through research. The two ancient universities of England added a fourth which was never quite clear: to train a social elite to the tasks of governance.

Because the American colonials were unable to establish genuine universities, they created instead something quite new: the college—and the college remains, to this day, a unique American institution, occupying a twilight zone between the high school and the university. As American students were very young—boys went to Harvard or Pennsylvania or Yale at the age of twelve or thirteen, though a really bright lad like John Trumbull could pass the entrance examinations to Yale at the age of seven—they had to be treated as children: hence the early practice of *in loco parentis* and its persistence through the years and even the centuries. As they came from simple middle-class households, without (for the most part) learning or sophistication, they had to be taught elementary subjects, and the plan of study had to be laid out for them with utmost circumspection. Hence the long tradition, still very much with us, that the college is a kind of extension of the high school, that students must be taught everything in formal courses, and that students were intellectually, as well as socially and morally, *in statu pupillari.*

These characteristics of the American college persisted into the nineteenth century and when, in the 1860s, Americans created their first universities, they established them not as substitutes for the colleges, but as continuations of the college, and adapted them, very largely, to collegiate rather than to university standards.

Just as the antecedents of the colleges had been Cambridge and Edinburgh, so the antecedents of the university were Göttingen and Berlin and Leipzig. But this could not last, or, where it did, it produced a kind of academic schizophrenia. Actually the university was bound to develop differently in a democratic and equalitarian society than in an aristocratic society. Because the United States did not have the scores of other institutions to carry on much of the work of science and research, or even of ordinary cultural activities (as did most Old World countries), almost everything that society wanted done in these areas was handed over to the university. Thus the schools of agriculture, of engineering, of library science, of nursing, of hotel management, of business administration, of almost anything that society or government wanted. Thus, too, came the multiversity, the university that did not confine itself merely to four faculties, nor to the traditional functions of professional training and research, but took on the most miscellaneous activities, academic and otherwise.

Thus by the twentieth century the special character of higher education in the United States was pretty well fixed. It was an education that was to be open to all, that was dominated by the collegiate idea, that inevitably took on the habits of in loco parentis. It was required to teach everything that society wanted taught, or that special interest groups in society were strong enought to get taught; and it was expected to acquiesce in the democratic notion that all subjects were equal; it was expected to respond to all the demands of government or society, to serve these masters in every way that it could serve—as a sanctuary for the young, as a moral training ground, as a social and matrimonial agency, as a social welfare center, as an agency for entertaining the community, as a center for research in all fields and as a handmaiden of government. Some of the private institutions escaped the most onerous of these demands, but even they fell easily into the habit of accepting them.

This pattern of the college-univeristy worked well enough as long as almost all elements in the community agreed on the basic assumptions that were implicit in it: that the university was to "reflect" American life (the current formula is that its student body is supposed to be a reflection of the whole of American society), that it was to train character as well as the mind, that it was to inculcate all the going "values" of American life, that it was, in short, an integral part of the establishment, and that the establishment itself was sound, just and enlightened.

Now the situation is different, and the mood is different. Students no longer accept the establishment, but repudiate it. They are too old and physically too mature for *in loco parentis*. They are not interested in the historic functions of the university, and are revolted by the dependence of the university on government, or its ready response to economic interests or social demands.

They no longer believe in these traditional functions nor do they accept these traditional objectives, but they cannot free themselves from them, or from the expectations which they have encouraged. They reject the right of the university to interfere with their private lives, insisting that they be treated as adults, but they reject with equal fervor the notion that when they violate the laws, or public mores, they are to be treated precisely as other adults. They say, in effect, that as long as they are students, trespass isn't trespass, arson is not arson. They reject the tyranny of courses, but assume that they cannot possibly learn anything unless some professor (preferably of their own choosing) gives a course in it, and they clamor for more and more courses. They reject the connection of the university with government and with the establishment, but demand that government support the university—and its students, too.

What they are really concerned about is not, in fact, the university, but society, government, the economy, even the moral order. They know perfectly well that the university did not make the Vietnam war, and cannot end it. They know that the university did not institute the draft, and cannot end it. They know that the university is not responsible for the Cold War or the armaments race, not responsible for the destruction of the environment, not responsible for racial injustice, and cannot cure these ills. Even more, they know—most of them, anyway—that in the past two decades it is from the university that has come the most penetrating and effective criticism of all of these things, and that long before they themselves were old enough to protest against the shocking evils and immoralities of our society, university professors were voicing such protests. But they still direct their hostility and their attacks on the university. For the university is *there*, and it is *theirs*.

Nothing is more depressing than the gap between the evils that the young object to and the changes which they propose to the university—nothing except, perhaps, the pervasive triviality of the "demands." If every academic demand that student rebels have made were to be granted tomorrow, nothing would be any different—nothing, that is, that they really care about. The war would still rage, the draft would still work its injustices, the environment would still submit to ruin, the cities would still decay, racial discrimination and racial injustice would still flaunt themselves everywhere. For the students do not, on the whole, have a program, certainly not one that they have been able to make clear to the university or to society. They are passionate in protest but paralyzed when it comes to constructive achievements.

This is not to say that the demands on the university itself are inconsequential. Here the students are, for the most part, either misguided or pernicious. Consider, for example, the *cri de coeur* of the young, that the university be "involved" and that what it teach be "relevant."

Consider this matter of involvement. Students assume that it means being involved in all the things that *they* suppose important—involved, that is in the opposition to the war, in opposition to the antiballistic missile proposals, involved in the plight of the cities and in racial discrimination and in the lawlessness of government. And so it does. But if this were all that meant, why bother with the university? It cannot, after all, in the nature of things, make decisions in these areas; these are the areas of government, and for government.

But university involvement is something quite different. It is the duty of the university to be involved with the past, and to preserve it and its contributions to civilization. It is the business of the university to be involved with the welfare of future generations, as far as imagination can reach. It is the business of the university to be involved in the welfare of the whole of mankind, not just of this local segment of it.

Suppose all the great geneticists and biologists turned away from their laboratories and went into the hospitals: they would doubtless alleviate much suffering, but we should never find the cause of cancer. Suppose all the great jurists left their legal studies and enlisted in the work of the legal aid societies: they would doubtless help many a poor wretch now the victim of racial discrimination. But we would never come to an understanding of the law, to a reassessment of the penal code, to construction of an effective system of international law. Suppose the painters and musicians turned from their easels and their pianos and devoted themselves to work with deprived children, or, for that matter, to playing folk songs designed to inspire youth revolt. All very well, but would we have any Serkins or Rubensteins, any Krieslers or Elmans, any Lili Kraus or Clara Haskel in the next generation? And without these, and their equivalents in every area of art, would we have any civilization?

No, the obligation of the university is not that of the doctor or lawyer or engineer or social welfare worker. It is to train doctors and lawyers and engineers and welfare workers, and this it does. It is to create an intellectual and moral atmosphere which will persuade the young to study medicine and law and to serve mankind, and this it does. But more, it is an obligation to the great commonwealth of learning, an obligation to the past, and to the future.

There is this to be said, too: it is perilous for the university to be *involved* as a university. Involvement is a personal affair. Professors have always been, and doubtless always will be, involved: indeed, just a few years ago it was a familiar charge that professors were neglecting their scholarly duties and involving themselves far too much in public concerns. But just as the university cannot be permitted to speak for its members, certainly not for its professors, so professors cannot be permitted to speak for and thus commit the university, nor can presidents nor trustees. It is the essence of the university that each of its members speaks for himself.

So, too, the demand for relevance misconceives the nature and the function of the university. What do students mean by relevance? What they mean is that the university has failed to make clear the relation of what it teaches to their own deep interests and anxieties, that it has failed to excite their minds or to lift their spirits; that it has not brought them that warm and sympathetic relationship with their society and their fellowmen that they had hoped for.

Insofar as this is true, and insofar as the failure is not in the student himself, this is a just criticism of the university, or of its teachers and its administrators. Students at large universities who are fobbed off with graduate students rather than learned scholars, who are treated impersonally, who are not taught to use the resources of the library, or of the museum, or of the record collections, or of the scores of other enterprises through which the university attempts to widen the horizons and deepen the sensibilities of the young, have a right to be outraged at what they consider a betrayal.

But usually students mean something a good deal more specific than this. They mean that the university is not relevant to their own concerns, that it is not relevant as, say, the New York Times or a television documentary is relevant.

But it is not the business of the university to be relevant in the way that a newspaper or a television station is relevant. It is not the business of the university to allow itself to be captured by the immediate, the momentary, the sensational. The university has other relevancies. It is—or should be—relevant to the whole of the past and the whole of the future. It finds a place for scholars who think classical archeology or the civilization of the Incas is relevant. It finds a place for those who are sure that there can be nothing more relevant than art, music, philosophy. It has, too, another very special function. It must create an atmosphere in which students can discover what is relevant to them, and provide the facilities for them to enlarge that relevance. For relevance is essentially subjective. It is something that happens to an individual, as a result of experience. That experience may be hearing a Mozart trio, or solving a difficult problem in mathematics, or getting to know Voltaire or Goethe; it may be falling in love; or having a child, or writing a poem. Do the young really suppose that only Prof. Herbert Marcuse or Stokely Carmichael are relevant, only sociology and black studies? All experience is against them, including their own.

Now, how does a university go about creating an atmosphere in which students can discover what is relevant to them? This is a very complicated business, and one that cannot be summed up in a formula. It may do it, as Oxford and Cambridge do, by antiquity and beauty. It may do it, as Harvard and California do, by attracting great scholars and building up great libraries. It may do it as so many of our smaller colleges do, by teaching that helps students to find themselves: teaching by a Robert Frost at Amherst that made poetry relevant, teaching by a Lionel Trilling at Columbia that made criticism relevant, teaching by a David Riesman at Harvard that makes sociology part of philosophy. The university is not an institution which is, itself, relevant to any particular time or place or interest; it is an institution where students and scholars can discover what is relevant to them and find encouragment and guidance in exploring and possessing it.

There is, to be sure, one area where students want not more involvement, but an end to involvement: that is the area which the university and government occupy jointly. Disillusioned by what they see of university tie-ins with the Defense Department, the State Department, the Central Intelligence Agency; outraged by university cooperation in research on chemical or bacteriological weapons, they turn to violence to dramatize their indignation. They demand that the university break with the government, that it break with all branches of the government that are themselves tainted by participation in an unjust and immoral war.

But all European universities and most American are in fact supported by government; all have in the past cooperated with government on research in a thousand fields. Nor has this research always been designed only for the purpose of peace. Universities enlisted, as it were, in the struggle against Nazi Germany; their scholars and scientists threw themselves into governmental service, and their administrators hastened to make available their library and laboratory facilities. None demurred at the time, and few now would have had it otherwise. The explanation of the alliance between the university and government in World War II was not innocence. It was rather the all-but-universal assumption that the war was a just war, and one that had to be won if civilization were to survive.

What this experience suggests is the danger of absolutism in judging the relation of government and universities, even in time of war. For there are wars, and wars. Some, like World War II, had to be won. Others, like the war in Vietnam, have to be lost if we are to survive. It was right for scholars to enlist in World War II; it is wrong for scientists and universities to suppose that no moral issues are involved, or that they are to be neutral in moral issues, or that the government can decide these issues for them, and thus to defend participation in the Vietnam war.

Here protesting students—and professors (who were after all, first in the field)—have performed an invaluable function. They have resisted the automatic conscription of the university to the purposes of government in time of war. They have rejected the immoral principle of secrecy in scientific research. They have insisted that the university itself must be in charge of its scientific investigation, and have repudiated the efforts of government to bribe, seduce, tempt or intimidate scholars and administrations to serve on terms the government lays down. They have steadily reminded the government, and the public, that the community which the university serves is not just the immediate local or national community, but the larger community of man and the longer community of succeeding generations.

As for the minor, though vexatious, problem of recruiters on campus—recruiters from the military or the CIA, recruiters from Dow Chemical or others of that ilk—here, too, there is a fairly simple formula that will resolve most of the difficulties. The university is not an employment agency. It is not under any obligation to supply facilities to any organization that comes along and asks for them. It is an educational institution. It should open its gates to all who are engaged in the business of education; it should close them to those who are engaged in making money or in fighting wars or in other irrelevant activities. That there are borderline cases here is, of course, clear; there are always border-line cases in life and law. But sensible administrators and faculty committees can be trusted to deal with these.

What students want of the university is that it be independent, and that is just what professors and administrators have been fighting for for many years. Students reject what they call the establishment, and ask the university to divorce itself from this. No great segment of society can wholly divorce itself from that society, but allowing this, must it not be said that for centuries the university has stood aloof from society? Students, and critics, charge that the university is itself part of the establishment and that it is therefore corrupt. But the university has been for generations the chief critic of the establishment, and still is. It is the university that has been the generator of new ideas, the powerhouse of new programs: that is the reason it is always in trouble with the establishment, always being attacked by the stout defenders of the status quo.

Independence means independence of all improper pressures—improper pressures from students as well as from government or industry of patriotic organizations. And in the past few years, the pressures from students have been more grossly improper than those from any other element in society.

One thing that should be beyond dispute is that the university is a citadel of reason; if it is not that, it is not a university. The use of force—closing buildings, assaulting or intimidating members of the faculty setting fire to chapels or libraries—these are the very antithesis of reason and the deepest repudiation of the university.

There is a sobering analogy between the use of force by students against the university and the use of force in Vietnam by President Johnson and his associates. Johnson, Dean Rusk, Walt Rostow and others were sincerely convinced that the cause they espoused—the cause of containing communism—was good. So, too, students are no doubt sincerely convinced that their own cause—the attack on the establishment—is good. The Johnson administration did not, however, whether out of prudence or out of cowardice, attack communism at its center: China. Instead it attacked communism on its periphery: Vietnam, which was innocent and vulnerable. So rebellious students do not attack Dow Chemical or Chase Manhattan Bank, nor do they boycott labor unions that practice discrimination; they attack the university, which is both innocent and vulunerable. Johnson and his associates were convinced that because their cause was just they were justified in disregarding international law, flouting existing agencies for the adjudication of international disputes and using terror against the enemy. So students, sure that their cause is just and their hearts pure, think it entirely proper for them to ignore the potentialities of discussion and debate—which have never been refused—to repudiate due process and to resort to force.

They hate Johnson, and perhaps President Nixon, too; they hate the war in which they find themselves involved. But as so often in history, they have succumbed to what they hate, and have adopted the methods of those they reject and despise.

What we are witnessing now is the most reckless attack upon academic freedom in our history. In the past, academic freedom has been threatened by the church, the state, and private interest groups. Now for the first time it is threatened not from without but from within, and that is perhaps more a betrayal than a threat.

Student assert now that they are to dictate courses and even appointments and tenure. That is precisely what the Nazis said to the universities back in the 1930s, and the state dismissed Jewish scholars while bands of Nazi youths roamed the universities attacking professors who were supposed to be unsympathetic with Nazi racial creeds. Students tell us now what is to be taught, and their demands are not based primarily on intellectual considerations but on nonacademic considerations. Students demand now that others be admitted not on the basis of intellectual or artistic capability or potential but on the basis of color: that is, in reverse, the equivalent of excluding students on the basis of color. Students ask now that the university dispense with grades and even with standards. Grades themselves are of little importance, but standards are: imagine dispensing with standards in medicine or law. If the academy is to put the stamp of approval on students not on the basis of competence but of race, or of needs, or of compassion, then it can no longer maintain any standards at all.

Once you accept the assumption that powerful minorities, using intimidation and force, can dictate university policies and faculty appointments, prescribe courses of study, select students—that they may even take over the universities physically to enforce their demands—you have established precedents that it will be very difficult to resist at a later day. You have, in effect, endorsed the principles of totalitarianism, the principles which made a mockery of higher education in Nazi Germany, in Fascist Italy, in Communist Russia.

The university is the most honorable and the least corrupt institution in American life. It is, with the church, the one institution that associates us with the past and the future, the one institution that has, through all of our history, served, or tried to serve, the interests of the whole of mankind and the interests of truth. No other institution can perform the functions which the university performs, no other can fill the place which it has for so long filled, and with such intellectual and moral affluence. If we destroy the university we will destroy a unique institution. As the integrity of civilization depends in part on the university, we will be dealing an irreparable blow to a civilization now in moral peril.

10. CONFLICT AND CHANGE
IN THE ACADEMIC COMMUNITY

Sidney Hook

AMONG THE current myths that circulate about the American college and university is the view that they have been very conservative institutions, hostile to educational change and cloistered off from the tumults and troubles of the marketplace. On the basis of my own experience as student, teacher, and administrator, covering a time-span of more than a half-century, I testify to the injustice and inaccuracy of such a characterization. Much of that period I have spent, together with colleagues, in prolonged and agonizing reappraisals of the objectives of higher education, particularly liberal arts education, and the refashioning of the curriculum to achieve these objectives. The diversity of our institutions with respect to methods, content, requirements, and standards of instruction is weighty evidence of the experimental nature of American education, and its sensitivity to a wide variety of educational needs. From the multiversity to the denominational college, all are in need of educational improvement. The present ferment within them may provide the occasion for continued improvement but only if we do not assume that every change *is* ipso facto an improvement. Institutions, like human beings, change for better or worse.

At the same time, during the last half-century, the governance of universities and colleges has on the whole been transformed from administrative absolutisms with respect to educational issues to academic communities in which faculties possess preponderant powers if and when they choose to exercise them. The problem of the structure, legal and otherwise, of our colleges and universities is today in debate and in transition, but the proper resolutions of this and allied problems seems to me to be clearly dependent upon the prior determination of the educational function or goal of the institution.

Prepared especially for this volume

The history of American higher education, then, shows no hostility to change. The all-important question today is how changes are to be effected—by coercion and/or the threat of coercion or by reflective discussion and debate. Unfortunately, there is a widespread tendency to introduce reforms not in the light of a considered analysis of basic issues but in terms of what seemingly might restore order and prevent further physical disruption of the campus—as if this were the primary criterion of what the best higher education for modern man should be; as if the absence of physical turbulence—the freedom from arson, bombings, violent confrontation—could be anything more than a necessary condition for the *locus* of a liberal educational experience.

I have been a lifelong critic of American higher education mainly on the ground of its deficiencies as an instrument of liberal education, whose ideals I regard as perennially valid. (The "perennial" must not be confused with the "eternal".) In my *Education for Modern Man*, I have offered a program of positive reconstruction of the college curriculum along the lines of John Dewey's educational philosophy, whose validity seems to me more apparent today than when it was originally published.

Before addressing myself to current challenges to the ideals of a liberal education, I wish to take sharp issue with those who confidently assert that today's graduates are better educated in the values and traditions of a liberal arts education than their predecessors. If the perduring quality of the liberally-educated mind is the pursuit of freedom through the arts of intelligence, then by and large we must frankly recognize that liberal arts education has failed dismally. When arson, obscenity, violence and the threat of violence, confrontations, classroom disruptions, hooliganism, and cognate activities are present, the legacy of liberal education is absent. (I find it significant that some apologists for radical student activism contend that, despite the means it employs, this movement is designed to *reinstate* the traditional values of liberal arts education betrayed by its faithless faculty servitors! This reminds me of nothing so much as the contention of advocates of almost all totalitarian philosophies that despite their dictatorial means they are "really" committed to democracy in a "higher" or "truer" sense.)

By a liberal arts education I mean an education whose curriculum has been designed to help students develop those powers and resources—intellectual, emotional, cultural—than will enable them to acquire in a greater or lesser measure:

(1) a perspective on the events of their time with which to meet the challenges of present and future experience;

(2) a constellation of values or a set of meanings or a calling or a developing center around which to organize their lives;

(3) the knowledge, ideals, and techniques necessary for them adequately to perform their duties as free citizens of a free society;

(4) a cultivated sensiblity and inner landscape so that they can live a rich and significant personal life, renewed by a continuous process of self-education.

These are generic ideals whos connotations embrace an indeterminate number of special and temporal goals. It should be quite clear that the commitment to a liberal arts education does not entail a single and fixed curriculum for everyone. On the contrary: just as the ideal or pursuit of health is comparable with quite different regimens of hygiene and diet for different individuals, so a liberal arts education will have not only an historically varied content as society becomes more and more complex but will be reached by varied paths reflecting the experience, capacity, needs, and interests of the student.

Today this conception of a liberal arts education, which I regard as a necessary basis for—and sometimes as a proper accompaniment of—all higher professional education, is under attack from many different quarters. I wish to consider some of them.

The first of the many threats to liberal education is the popular view that the curriculum of our colleges should be oriented to meeting the *crises* that periodically arise in society, that threaten to set the world aflame, or to imperil our national survival or the health of our economy. This crisis-oriented approach to education assumes that the course of liberal study can and should be so organized that we can thereby win a war or end it, prevent recessions or inflations, extend civil rights, rebuild our ghettoes, stop the population explosion, prevent environmental pollution— whatever may be the "good cause" which we as citizens rightfully deem to have overwhelming priority at the moment. But in view of the extent to which the colleges and universities of the country have responded to appeals to gear their curricular offerings to special situations and emergencies, the complaint that institutions of higher education have been academic cloisters and ivory towers, uninvolved and unconcerned with the troubled fate of man and society, borders on the grotesque. It is typical of the looseness and irresponsibility of much of the writing about the state of American higher education today. If anything there is a greater need of ivory towers for competent persons who wish to live in them, especially when we recall the great benefits to mankind made possible by those who inhabited ivory towers in the past.

Even practical effects are best achieved by indirection. By any but the most philistine standards of human culture, the larger community has an ever present need for seers, prophets, and lonely men of vision—persons whose findings may seem maddeningly irrelevant to the intellectual and social fashions of the moment. We cannot breed such men, but we should not prevent them from functioning by denigrating them or depriving them of a hospitable environment. They are all too rare under the best of conditions.

It is one thing to aim to develop through curricular means the attitudes and capacities necessary to think and act intelligently in periods of crisis; it is quite another thing to believe that the special knowledge and skills required for the mastery of specific crises can be acquired in advance of their appearance. It is one thing to plan a curriculum of studies with an awareness of the social trends and problems that are shaping the future and that are certain to affect the lives of generations to come; it is simply Utopian in the bad sense of the term, i.e., unrealistic and self-defeating, to imagine that a curriculum must necessarily keep up with all the specific trends and changes that are cried up as important in the great news media—changes that often emerge into and fade out of public consciousness with bewildering suddenness. It is one thing to develop *a readiness of response,* an ability to move promptly and intelligently in grappling with successive problems; it is quite something else to become petrified in a specific posture, however excellent it may have proved with respect to some previous complex of problems.

This particular myth—that colleges and universities can anticipate and help to master, through curricular panaceas, the specific *crises* of the future, not to speak of crises of the present—overlooks the most patent truths about the history of past crises and of the kind of social action necessary to resolve them. It is a myth which has been attributed with some jutification to modernists who have invoked Dewey's name but have either not read or not properly understood him.

The opposite of a myth can be just as mythical. Some traditionalists argue, in contradistinction to the above, that the best preparation for social change is the immersion in a fixed curriculum or program of studies. For example, Robert Hutchins writes: "If one neglects history in favor of current affairs, first he will never know history, and second he will not understand current affairs." (Oscar Wilde put this more felicitously a long time ago when he wrote: "He to whom the present is the only thing that is present, knows nothing of the age in which he lives.") We should applaud this recognition of the value of knowledge of history and the plea for its intelligent study. But then Hutchins goes on to add: "The part of the schools is not to expedite current affairs but to initiate students into timeless affairs." One cannot help asking in reply: How can the study of timeless affairs help us to understand historical affairs which by definition are *not* timeless? Surely there is a distinction between the enduring, which is part of historical existence, and the timeless!

An intelligent modernity does not require that we redraw the maps of learning each year or decade or even generation at *every* level. The past—even interpretations of the past—does not change that much. Intelligent revisions and adaptations of the curriculum are always in order, and if better methods and techniques of learning and teaching are available, let us employ them as soon as possible. But not all knowledge becomes obsolescent at once!

There are additional serious threats to the future of the liberal arts education which are allied to this ill-conceived notion that the university be crisis-oriented. These additional threats are more serious, in that they challenge the supremacy of the authority of reason, or better, the authority of intelligence, which gradually has emerged as the *ideal* of the secular university, however much it has been decried by different pressure groups, who in behalf of some private faiths or vested interests have struggled against its recognition. This ideal is intimately related to the conception of the university—in the words of Karl Jaspers—as "the place where truth is sought unconditionally in all forms." It is an ideal which, like the value of intelligence in reflective moral experience, is the only valid absolute, because it is self-critical, aware of its own limitations. The view that American institutions of higher learning stress intelligence and the rational process too much is simply a bizarre notion of the educational underworld for which no rational evidence is advanced. A much more formidable case can be made for the opposite view.

Today the challenge to intelligence takes the form of the renewed cult of raw experience, of glorification of action, passion, and sensual absorption, as if the latter were immediate avenues not only to excitement but to truth and wisdom. Hoary errors in the history of thought have been revived to undergird this view, when those immersed in this cult deign to defend it. "We learn by experience," it is said. "We learn by doing. We learn by going into the fields, streets and factories—by marching, demonstrating, fighting, etc." One might just as well say we learn by living, and that the longer we live the more educated we are. This is absurd on its face. But even if it were not, it is apparent that one does not need a university to acquire this kind of education—if one calls it education.

Life is not a school except as a dubious metaphor. There are many ways by which reality may be experienced or encountered, all legitimate in their context, but the knowing which gives us understanding and truth is a distinctive mode of experience. It is not true that we learn *by* experience. We learn *through* experience, and only when we have the capacity to learn. And what we learn *through* experience is more likely to be valid when we confront experience with a prepared mind. It is the cultivation and development of the prepared mind, and its attendant functions of trained observation and disciplined imagination, which is or should be the objective of all schooling, and especially schooling on the college and university level.

It is true that ultimately we learn by doing. But it is not true that all doing is a form of learning. Here, too, the role of ideas or hypotheses is central. Their presence is what distinguishes the intelligently learned man from the learned ass, from the dogmatic autodidact, and from those long on experience but short in wisdom.

Lest the reader think that I exaggerate the extent to which the cult and glorification of raw experience is cried up today by those who pander to popular life-styles among students, I quote from a college reader, *"Starting Over,"* hot off the press, edited by Frederick Crews and Orville Schell, two professors at the University of California at Berkeley. "We don't rule out the possibility," they tell us in their Preface, "that Lenny Bruce may have more to teach us than Alfred North Whitehead." With characteristic lack of precision, they fail to tell us what, aside from obscenity, Lenny Bruce *can* teach us, more than Alfred North Whitehead—one of the profoundest thinkers of the twentieth century. As for obscenity, whatever its uses, one hardly needs to attend a university to learn it. And although the editors complete their sentence by say-

ing, "We include both of them just in case," surely the bare
possibility that one may learn something about anything is hardly
an appropriate principle for including subjects for study. For it
excludes nothing!

Effective schooling of the prepared mind requires clinical experience that may take the student out of the classroom to am-
plify the meaning and test the validity of what he or she has
learned within it. But it must be intelligently planned, supervised,
and carefully assessed. Emphasis on clinical experience, where
appropriate, cannot be overstressed. It is analogous to the experimental approach. It is a far cry, however, from current demands
that uncontrolled, diverse, helter-skelter forays into "life and experience" be recognized as integral and valid elements of university education. The demand that "action Ph.D's" be awarded,
that graduate students receive credit for leading rent strikes, organizing the unemployed, or fighting pollution, and that undergraduates be granted academic recognition *merely* for the experience of traveling or living abroad is a *reductio ad absurdum* of this
view. One may as well give them academic awards for sex and
marriage!

Another challenge to liberal arts education is implicit in the
demand that research, teaching, scholarship—in short, all curricular activity in whole and part—be "relevant." What nonsense is
embraced by that term! The cry for relevance extends from the
simple demand that the teacher talk sense to the demand that
what he teaches, regardless of his subject matter, help achieve the
classless society. Strictly speaking, the term "relevant" is rela-
tional. We must always ask: "Relevant to what?" Normally, in
the life of mind, what is taught, if the teaching is good, is relevant to a *problem*. Problems themselves are relevant to domains of
experience. The problem of *who* first propounded the theory of
organic evolution, or the labor theory of value, is irrelevant to the
problem of its validity. On man's problem may be irrelevant to
another man's purpose or interests without affecting its
significance in its own field. In a well-ordered university in which
the scholarly faculty decides, the existence of certain fields of
study is prima facie evidence that the field is deemed to have
educational significance, in the light of the objectives of liberal-
arts study. Any attempt to control the relevance of studies except on educational grounds is an intolerable interference with
academic freedom.

Most claims that higher education be "relevant" are either politically motivated or inspired by narrow utilitarian considerations. I shall discuss the political motivations below. The other motivations are open to the easy retort that narrow utilitarian considerations are irrelevant not only to the ideals and delights of a liberal arts education but also to the multiple, indirect, and enlarged social uses of theories which at first are *not* immediately useful. Einstein's special theory of relativity had no earthly use when it was first propounded. But it was highly relevant to a genuine problem—the negative findings of the Michaelson-Morley experiment. The current demands for relevance would have driven Einstein and many others out of the university. Whitehead used to celebrate the perpetual uselessness of the theory of numbers and symbolic logic. They have now found a use, but they always had a sufficient justification in the eyes of those who enjoy the games and beauty of abstraction.

Related to these challenges to liberal arts education is the critical challenge that stresses the importance of immediacy—the demand that the curriculum offer solutions to complex problems that can lead to early, if not overnight, transformations of our society, economy, law, or culture. Radical-activist students are properly aware of the distance between the goals of the American dream and our current achievement—a distance which they have learned about in large part through the despised curricular offerings of the present. They are not properly aware of—indeed, they aggressively ignore—the fact that American society has again and again raised its sights and periodically redefined the goals of the American dream. They have, therefore, systematically ignored the distance covered in removing the obstacles to political and social equality, and, despite the great problems and injustices still remaining, the magnitude of the social gains. Disregarding the fact that American colleges and universities have been the great centers of outspoken criticism and dissent in American life, they have pictured them instead as exploitative agencies of the Establishment. They have caricatured the whole notion of an Establishment (itself a vulgarized Marxist view of "the ruling class') with the charge that the organized working class is part of it. In consequence, they have demanded not only that their instruction be relevant in relation to their purposes but also that it be oriented to reformist, even revolutionary, objectives vaguely defined but completely and explicitly critical of every aspect of American history and culture.

The truth tends to be the first casualty of every war and crusade. One-sided criticism can distort the truth every whit as much as apologetic accolades. On several campuses, *enragés* students have disrupted the classes of professors who have not—in their eyes—taken a sufficiently critical stance towards one or another aspect of American culture. There is no record of interference (which would have been just as deplorable!) with the instruction of teachers openly sympathetic to the Viet Cong or to the totalitarian despotisms of Castro, Mao-tse-tung, or the Kremlin, with their holocausts of victims. It is not surprising, therefore, that these radical activists and their faculty allies have denounced the ideal of "objectivity" as a bourgeois myth. To challenge as a chimera the ideal of objectivity, difficult as it may be to reach, is to renounce the ideal of the truth which is the *raison d'être* of the liberal university. To deny that the concept of objectivity is intelligible is incoherent and self-contradictory, for it would prevent us from distinguishing between historical fiction and historical fact, and make groundless and arbitrary even the radical activist's litany of alleged American crimes.

An unexpectedly formidable challenge to liberal arts education has been nurtured by some *liberals,* so acutely aware of the failures of the liberal tradition to achieve its promise, that *they* have betrayed its perennially valid ideals, sometimes out of simple confusion and sometimes out of cowardice, moral and physical. I refer to the failure to recognize the human experience or the human condition as the basic source and orientation of the curriculum. It is mainly this failure that has caused the growing fragmentation of the curriculum into isolated blocks of studies, into "Black Studies," "Afro-American Studies," "Third World Studies." The black experience, the African experience, the Third World experience, the Jewish experience, the Irish experience, etc., *are* each part of the human experience and as such worthy of inclusion in those areas and subject matters whose understanding is required to achieve a proper liberal education. The revision of the traditional liberal arts courses in history, literature, art and the social studies to do justice to the various ethnic expressions of human experience has long been overdue and is currently being undertaken. That is one thing. But the organization of special blocks of study, often open in effect only to members of minority groups among the study body—groups organized and controlled by members of those same minorities—breaches important assumptions of liberal education as well as the principles of academic freedom. Here I stress only the educational aspect of the question.

There *are* no class truths, national truths, or racial truths as distinct from truths, objective truths, *about* classes, nations and ethnic groupings. The black experience is neither necessary nor sufficient to understand the truth about slavery, any more than the experience of white Southerners is necessary or sufficient to understand the truth about the Reconstruction Period, or experience in Fascist or Communist countries is necessary or sufficient to learn or teach the truths about their terroristic regimes. I find it highly significant that the powerful criticisms of the proposals for *separate* courses of study for black students made by distinguished Negro educators like Kenneth Clark, Sir Arthur Lewis, Bayard Rustin, and others, have provoked no considered replies, but only derisive epithets. Many administrators who have supported the demand for autonomous Black Studies programs have done so not on supportable educational grounds but out of fear that their campuses might be torn apart. Professor Henry Rosovsky, has done pioneering work as Chairman of the Harvard Committe on African and Afro-American studies, in devising a college major in Afro-American studies with the *same standards of academic excellence* that obtained for other majors. He has flatly charged that the action of the Harvard faculty reversing the report of his committee, and in effect giving black undergraduate students "powers hitherto held only by Harvard *senior faculty* and denied to junior faculty, graduate students and non-black undergraduates," was adopted in the face of threats of violence.

To make exceptions to principles of equity as well as valid educational policy in order to compensate for historical injustices is an inverse form of racism just as objectionable to sensitive and intelligent members of minority groups as traditional forms of racism. To lower standards of judgment and excellence, to dilute content and subject matter as a form of intellectual reparations, is to restore and compound the infamies of the double standard. The student is just as much a second-class academic citizen if an institution discriminates in his favor on the basis of his skin color as he is when it discriminates against him on the same basis.

There are dangerous tendencies in the admission policies of some institutions which mistakenly assume that in education democracy requires that all groups in the population be proportionally represented by students and faculty in every course of study. A case can be made for the view that in American democratic society everyone has a human right to the kind and degree of schooling from which he can profit, and which will facilitate the

growth of his intellectual and cultural powers to their fullest. But
the right to an education no more carries with it the right of everyone to a specific kind of education or to a certain degree of
education than the right to medical treatment carries with it the
right to one kind of medical treatment, no matter what one
is ailing from. Just as no one prescription can adequately meet the
medical needs of all people, no one special curriculum or method
can adequately meet the educational needs of all students. Quack-
ery both in medicine and education results from this denial. Here
as elsewhere individual need, interest, capacity should be the determining considerations. Democracy does not require belief in
the moral equality of those who are the same or alike but, rather,
belief in the moral equality of the *different*—whether they are
physically different, racially different, or intellectually different.

The liberal arts conception of higher education is based upon a
belief in the community of educational interest among
teacher-scholars, learners, and administrators. This conception is
being threatened by something analogous to a "class struggle"
view, according to which the university is a factory in which students are processed and exploited by their teachers and administrators. But knowledge is not a commodity of which one can say
that the more one has of it the less remains for others. It belongs
to the family of values of which it is true to say that they are not
diminished but enchanced by being shared. Education is not in
the first instance a quest for power, whether student power or
faculty power, but instead is a quest for truth and a means of
growth, of spiritual enlargement and maturation. Where a community of educational interest prevails in the university, it does
not preclude difference, sometimes sharp differences, about a mul-
titude of things. And, so long as the "class struggle" conception of
education does not enter to disrupt the rational exchange of views,
all of these differences are negotiable in the same way in which
we seek to resolve scientific differences. That is why the university
can be a conservator of values and attitudes and at the same time
an innovator.

All of the challenges to liberal education I have considered
come to a head in frank espousals for the politicalization of the
university. By the politicalization of the university is meant the
direct involvement of the university as a *corporate* institution in
the controversial political and social problems of the day. The
radical activists of our time speak out of both sides of their
mouths on this question, sometimes condemning the university

for allegedly already being politically involved, and as guilty of betraying the ideal of noninvolvement, and sometimes—the real burden of their song—condemning the university for being involved on the wrong political side. Not content with having won the right of the individual faculty member to espouse any political cause he may wish without prejudicing his position in the university community, they seek to draw the university *as such*, and *officially*, into the endorsement, teaching, and organization of programs for social reform and/or revolution of the society on whose largesse and support the university ultimately depends. Since the radical activists assert that no program of social reform or commitment can dispense with an ideology, they are proposing that universities cease making a fetish of objectivity and neutrality and become ideological institutions.

This is a recommendation which if acted upon can result only in educational disaster. If the universities attempt to politicalize themselves, and instead of studying, proposing, and critically analyzing programs of social action, seek to implement these programs as parts of an agenda of social action, the unconverted larger community will not only withdraw its support but purge or suppress the universities that are thus self-politicalized. The universities will in this way lose their hard-won relative autonomy and become politicalized with a vengeance, but from an ideological quarter hardly congenial to the radical activists, who will be ruthlessly swept away, together with their liberal allies. Although I am convinced that the consequences of politicalizing the university would be suicidal, I do not wish to base my criticism of the proposal mainly on this very practical ground, but rather upon the values of the liberal arts tradition.

The attempt to line up the university *as such* behind some particular program of reform or revolution testifies to a failure to establish a consensus or win agreements to positions on the basis of argument and evidence. There is very little that a university can do as such that a faculty of persuaded individuals cannot do as well. Where a university takes a stand on capitalism or socialism, or war and peace, or methods of urban reconstruction, in the nature of the case the position of the minorities which cannot accept such stands becomes precarious. The outvoted minorities appear as malcontents and troublemakers, sabotaging the larger commitment of the university.

Once the university becomes politicalized, the students, too, become politically polarized—if they have not already reached that state. Students and faculty then join forces in ways already familiar to us, not only in the universities of some foreign countries, but on some of our own campuses. Factionalization among extremists leads to a kind of competition among them to implement corporate policies more vigorously and to push the university into the very forefront of the struggle to radicalize society. The consequent effect of ideological commitment on particular departments—especially on the appointment and promotion of faculty personnel—can easily be imagined. The normal frictions and conflicts that operate even when the university is uncommitted and permits all the winds of doctrine to blow freely on the campus become exacerbated to a point where professional competence, which should be the first and main criterion in matters of this kind, is subordinated, under all sorts of pretexts and rationalizations, to ideological considerations. The canons of professional ethics and integrity are celebrated in the holiday rhetoric of convocations and commencements, only to be abandoned in practice.

That politicalization of the university constitutes a threat to academic freedom is acknowledged. Sometimes in an effort to minimize the danger, advocates of politicalization narrow the scope of the "political" to grave issues during periods of crisis. But the definition of grave issues depends on how intensely human beings feel about them, and the world is always in crisis. More often, and especially among students and junior faculty, academic freedom is regarded as a kind of class privilege of professors that can readily be sacrificed or compromised to further larger ideological goals or purposes.

It may sound harsh, but there is convincing evidence that it is true: Academic freedom in the United States today is threatened not so much by fundamentalist churchmen, reactionary businessmen, and political demagogues, as it is by ideological fanatics among students and faculty. It is ironical that they owe their presence in the university and the guarantee they are given of an opportunity to proclaim their ideological wares to the very principles of academic freedom which they violate and undermine. They ignore the truth that genuine tolerance does not require tolerance of the actively intolerant.

No one can reasonably defend the status quo in American higher education. For one thing, there is no such thing as the status quo. For another, the growth of American universities in the past has not always been guided by a critical and self-conscious philosophy of education. Many activities and enterprises now housed in our universities could more appropriately be housed elsewhere. The university cannot be all things to all men, an instrument of every purpose, without losing its intellectual dignity and authority and ultimately its honesty. Everything depends upon the method of change and the direction of change. I take it for granted for the moment that the method will remain one of rational and autonomous decisions by the faculties, uncoerced by political groups from within or without. If I am mistaken about this and the fate of the university becomes a function of which political groups happen to triumph in American life, academic freedom—both *Lehrfreiheit* and *Lernfreiheit*—will be eclipsed.

The direction of change which holds the greatest promise for deepening, enriching, and developing the great humanistic and scientific legacies of university education is the liberalizing of the curriculum, and of processes of teaching and learning, in the light of the ideals of the liberal arts tradition. These legacies may stem from the contributions of socially privileged and elite groups of the past. But today our technology makes it possible for all men and women who are willing and able, to partake of them, to contribute to them, and to find meaning and enjoyment in them. The liberal arts tradition is strengthened by the principles of academic freedom and in turn draws support from them. Both keep open the pathways to new truths and new visions of excellence in man's unending quest to understand himself, society, and the environing world.

11. TOMORROW'S UNIVERSITY—
REACTIONARY EITHER WAY

Jacques Barzun

*Jacques Barzun, formerly Provost and Dean of Faculties of
Columbia University, currently is University Professor at
that institution.*

Now THAT the open season on college presidents has come around
again, appointed bodies and self-appointed seers are busy defining
the right way to govern academic places. I hope they hit upon
useful ideas. But if its primary aim is *study,* there are not sixteen
ways of running a college or university. Except for interesting but
inessential variations, there are only three, and not all three yield
to the same extent the conditions favorable to study.

Let us look at the earliest—student power. We've had it, quite
literally: it marked the very beginnings of universities. Since it is
returning, full- or half-strength, into the American system, it deserves attention in some detail. The typical precedents are Bologna and Paris. Bologna shows the internal relationships; Paris
the day-to-day workings.

In both universities the idea was participation. Authority lay
with the general assembly. There was no distinct central organization, but a loose collection of units. The *universitas* or corporation was the name of this grouping, which implied nothing academic. At Bologna, the students soon seized control, thereby expressing the burghers' control of the city. The sons dictated to the
professors, and the city fathers backed up the youthful will by
law.

For example, professors and doctors could not leave the university, under penalty of death, or even go out of town without permission. They had to swear absolute obedience to the student-
elected student rector, who at the behest of the general assembly
could pass or change any rule. The students collected the fees,

---

Reprinted, with permission and with the title originally intended by the author,
from the *Saturday Review of Literature,* November 15, 1969.

paid the salaries, and issued the working rules: If the teacher cut a class, he was fined; likewise, if he could not draw five students, if he skipped a chapter or a difficulty, or if he kept on talking after the ringing of the bell. At any time the lecturer could be interrupted by a beadle summoning him to appear before the rector and learn of his misdeeds.

As the great historian of universities, Rashdall, puts it—and notice in passing that boycott is the true name for student strike or sit-in: "By means of the terrible power of boycotting which they could bring into play against an offending professor, the student clubs were masters of the situation." Not until Bonaparte conquered Italy five centuries later was a professor again considered fit to be rector of a university.

Rashdall's reference to student clubs brings us to the situation at Paris. Medieval students were divided into "nations," just as the teachers were divided into subject-matter faculties. But the nation soon ceased to denote birthplace and became an arbitrary aggregate. The French nation at Paris included Spaniards, Italians, Greeks, and Levantines; the English took in Flemings, Scandinavians, Finns, Hungarians, Dutch, and Slavs—no British insularity then! These clubs were further divided into cliques, usually based on parish allegiance. Here was no compact group of bourgeois fathers' sons, but an international and vagrant crowd of large proportions. The results for university governance were to be expected—incessant quarrels, shaky alliances, jealous betrayals.

For each nation had to vote as one unit in the assembly and elect a new rector *each month*. They voted also on proctors, beadles, financial officers, examiners, and deans. They also had to choose one ad hoc committee after another to look into endless charges and abuses. In the great year 1266, the papal legate Simon de Brie tried in vain to get the rector's term extended to six weeks, in hopes of reducing the number of contested elections and student defiance of the rectors and the rules. At one time two rectors claimed authority. Simon finally got them both to resign in exchange for a statute permitting a nation to secede and thus escape disputed rules. This feud of 1266 lasted a good fifteen years.

The suggestive point in this truly flexible system is that it went on all fours with the prevailing theory of government—"what affects all must be by the consent of all." It was democracy to the full. A representative body was not supposed to express the collective will of its constituents but to give every individual will a chance. Three students (out of several thousand) could ask for a change of statutes, and officers were elected who specialized in statute-changing.

The frequent elections fitted in with the reigning philosophy. Aristotle had said that no one should be entrusted with any but the briefest tenure of office and that the whole assembly must not only legislate but administer. And student control obviously meant a deal of administering—collecting fees, paying salaries, renting or buying school buildings, watching the financial officers, approving student lodgings, supervising book publishers (copyists), issuing summonses, levying fines, and seeing to the taking of oaths on an unprecedented scale.

All this plus the fights of town and gown and the internal feuds that, according to one authority, were "akin to later international wars in their ferocity and destructiveness," must have made the student life rich and exciting. Everything was an issue, including the hiring of messengers, of which the several nations had from twelve to 160 each. A touching detail of organization was that the rector might bring to the meetings of the assembly his bosom friend as bodyguard.

This elaborate structure so far was all for administration. Not a word yet about the *studium,* the classwork. The rector, students, and (elected) deans looked after it very much as was done at Bologna, that is, by supervising the professors. This arrangement called for certain abilities in the rector, and since the freshmen, who were eligible, often were under the entrance age of fourteen, the Paris rules came to stipulate that the rector must be at least twenty years old.

With these provisions in mind and knowing the ways of youth, one can get a sense of the student-run university of the middle ages. One sees these eager, free-lance, turn-and-turn-about administrators as belonging to the somewhat older group of students and apprentice teachers, the bold and daring, handsome and articulate—those who, like M. Cohn-Bendit in our day, glory in the feeling of "we do what we like."

One can imagine them angry at the previous administration, impatient with the snarls of bureaucracy that they could so quickly fix by some further rules, exhilarated at the thought of the coming meeting with a good fight in prospect, and ready always for the actual bloodshed on the narrow winding street, if townsmen or a gang from the wrong parish or nation should debouch from the next corner.

And as one describes the scene, one is suddenly hushed at the

thought of François Villon gathering up his genius amid the confusion and surviving as the symbol of an emancipated day. Was
he perhaps one of those excluded as "vagabond scholars" from
taking part in the making of the curriculum, the degree requirements, the class schedules and examinations, and the plan of
festivities? Or was he one of the many non-scholars, those hang-
ers-on mysteriously called "martinets"? No one knows, but some
of his brilliance and energy must have existed elsewhere in the
mass, or there would have been no medieval university, no medieval mind to write about.

University administration by student groups is not to be
sneezed at. It is cheap and never monotonous. By controlling the
faculty it certainly prevents the flight from teaching, and it
affords the young the pleasure of making their elders hop, skip,
and perform. In fighting all of society and themselves, too, the
medieval students preserved minority rights to a degree otherwise
unexampled. That is, such rights were freely enjoyed by the vic-
tors and survivors of the scrimmage. The rest—well, there is a
price to pay for every good thing, and the good achieved was the
very appealing, youthful kind of life: the free-for-all.

Besides, student power need not be as perpetually violent as it
was in the glorious thirteenth century. It can be had at the somewhat lower price of a lack of continuity and a repetition of hopeful errors, for in one student generation experience hardly has a
chance to accumulate and make a difference; and who cares in
youth about the confusion that comes of injecting practical and
political action into the rather different atmosphere of study? So
let's gaze fondly back at the happy days of student power.

The second mode of managing universities is illustrated by
what happened when the confusion became too great—or at least
when it seemed to the neighbors to have got out of hand. A historian of the time who, as legal representative of the university,
cannot have been prejudiced against it says: "Studies were in
chaos . . . the rooms on one side were rented to students and on
the other to whores. Under the same roof was a house of learning
and of whoring." There was no reason in the nature of youth itself why this boisterous exercise of self-government and
self-indulgence should stop. But by 1500 the scheme was swept
away in the collapse of the medieval theory and practice of government. In one short generation—by 1530—a new University of
Paris was in being.

The force at work was the rise of the nation state, the move-

ment that gave "nation" its modern meaning. The One Hundred
Years' War had shown the country's need for an effective central
power to put down disorders and stop the waste. That power was
the king, and it was the king who put an end to student power
within the university. In 1450, he restrained their excessive feast-
ing. He then ordered the papal legate to reform the university
from top to bottom. By 1475 he was imposing a loyalty oath and,
soon after, threatening students with a kind of draft. Finally, in
1499, he prohibited their boycotts and strikes.

From then on, whether under king or revolutionary government, dictator or Parliament, continental universities have been
ruled by the central authority. The degree of control has varied
widely with time and place. Still, out of ancestral respect for
learning, the European university has always enjoyed certain privileges. For example, even under the Russian czars the police
were forbidden to enter the university, a tradition that curiously
persisted through the Russian repression at Prague in the summer
of 1968.

No one needs to be told that in times of trouble since 1500
universities under central control have been threatened, dictated
to, or shut down; professors suspended for sedition, exiled for refusing to take oaths, prosecuted and shot for political crimes, and,
from the beginning of the twentieth century periodically heckled,
insulted, or physically attacked by their own students. These appear to be inevitable by-products of making the university political through its link with the state.

Central control is, of course, the opposite of student power, but
they have one feature in common—the multiplicity of rules.
When codes and tribunals regulate university affairs, the legalistic
outlook and the contentious temper prevail and warp the emotions appropriate to study. And contrary to expectations, even the
management of the university's material concerns is not thereby
improved but worsened. The reason is plain. Both these styles of
administration—the anarchical and the autocratic—bring to the
fore people whose temperaments are the reverse of systematic and
studious.

Imagine the American university going down the road it has
lately chosen and becoming thoroughly reactionary, which is to
say, going back to either of these earlier modes of governance. In
the one case, that of student power, we should see the emergence
of a new type of academic man, wanting and achieving power at
a much younger age than his predecessors—in fact, a graduate

student or beginning teacher. He would be a man of strong feelings, caught by some sort of doctrine, ready to drop his work at any time for the turbulence of mass meetings and the stress of political strategy, and not averse to exchanging blows when denunciation, blackmail, and obscenity fail—a man, in short, prepared to strike in all senses of the word; a man given to the life of impulse and self-will, like the old-fashioned duelist, and also given to the heady pleasure of moral indignation; a man ever suspicious—and with good reason; a partisan, but restless, dissatisfied with all arrangements including his own, because his idealism and his strength alike drive him to find a life totally free of *conditions*.

We need not ask whether men such as this in a reactionary university would wield their power in behalf of an outside political party, as in the Japanese university, and use professors as indentured servants closely supervised. The texture of the straitjacket might be looser owing to the presence of diverse student leaders similarly moved to have their way.

But we cannot doubt that an opposite reaction to central control would bring with it the enforcement of a political orthodoxy. The type of man who would rise in such a system is quickly described: the commissar with a Ph.D. And he too would be a poor provider of the complex physical arrangements prerequisite to study: His mind would be incessantly on things so much higher. Indeed, if one absolutely must have rule from on top, it would be better to put there a retired member of the Mafia seeking to make his peace with God by good works. For he would have no doctrine but order, and after a few faculty-club shootings, seminars would meet on time.

The third mode of university administration is the one we have so rashly abandoned over the space of a few months. The American university was a characteristic creation. Drawing on the old English collegiate model for its best habits, it assumed that the faculty *was* the university, and as such the protector of two great treasures—students and learning. Learning was something to be transmitted to the young and added to when possible. Study was thus the single aim for both faculty and students.

The running of academic affairs by a faculty through a mixture of convention and consensus was, of course, easier when the faculty was small and its members lived close together. But the triumph of the American universities is that between 1890 and 1950 many of them grew to the size of a town yet kept the spirit and action of the original free university, the university governed not by the one or the many, but by principles.

These principles were simple enough: influence and deference; rationality and civility; above all, reciprocity.

Most people, including some academic men, had, of course, no idea how American or any other universities were run and could discern no principles whatever in the day-to-day operations. So when the cry of tyranny and revolt was raised, they rushed to pull down the fabric, on the assumption that where there's a complaint there must be an evil. The questions of what evil and where it lay precisely were never thought of. Indignation in some, passivity in others conspired to establish as a universal truth that the American university was an engine of oppression, rotten to the core, a stinking anachronism. So down it came.

That is must stay down for a good while appears inevitable from the nature of its former freedom. How was it free? Not because its members were angels and its statutes copied from Utopia but because its concentration on study had brought the world at large to respect its autonomy—hence, no interference from the state—while freedom of thought and speech, academic freedom, had generated within the walls the principles listed above. The free university is that in which the scholar and teacher is free to learn and to teach. He is free because society values and keeps its hands off the double product—the educated student on one side, new knowledge on the other.

Principles, of course, need devices for their application and protection. The American university had evolved some fairly good ones for the purpose:

1) The trustees (or regents or legislative committees), whose defined role showed that they did not own the university, nor were employers of employees: they bestowed tenure as a guaranty against themselves.

2) The administration, conceived again not as bosses but as servants; easily removed if unsatisfactory; in practice, a body that worked like slaves to suit faculty wishes and that protected scholars against trustees as well as against parents and alumni.

3) The professional associations—learned, accrediting, or self-serving like the American Association of University Professors—all upholders of academic freedom.

4) Public opinion and notably the press, which until very recent years could be counted on to respect and defend the individual scholar, researcher, discoverer, expert.

At each level, the attitude of the imperfect beings entrusted with administrative responsibilities was that they could only influence the action of others, not command it; that decisions must be rational and discussions civil; that any signs of strong reluctance after discussion must be deferred to, and that rights and duties, like concessions, must be reciprocal.

This is not to say that the institution always worked like a dream. Friction, abuses, injustice beset all human undertakings. But no one can deny that compared with other institutions, universities enjoyed a government in keeping with their high purpose—government by separation of powers, by consent through committees, and by extensive self-restraint. Within the best universities and colleges there was continuous consultation, a wide tolerance of eccentricity and free-wheeling, a maximum of exceptions and special attention—and these had long since been extended to the students.

In recalling this fast-waning institution, one may indeed think of occasions when the principles were violated. But one should also think of the great diversity of opinion and of purpose that was permitted to flourish, even when challenged. For example: boards of trustees, generally Republican and conservative, allowing leaves to professors working in Washington for the New Deal or for John Kennedy; or in the thirties ignoring the Communist affiliation even of junior officers without tenure. Go back fifty years and you will think of the protectors of Veblen and his work, of defiant instruction in Marxism, of research and indoctrination in contraception. You will think of President Lowell saying: "If the Overseers ask for Laski's resignation, they will get mine." Lowell was not exactly a socialist defending a fellow member of his party.

Nor should we forget the common realities of the last half century—the open campus, receptive to all the shocking modern literature and subversive speakers; the college newspapers receiving subsidies from administrations they denounce and insult by name; the frequent public championing of dissent, as when President Brewster of Yale stood between angry alumni and Professor Staughton Lynd.

Fifteen years ago, Walter P. Metzger, the leading authority on academic freedom, summed up the extraordinary character of the American university: "No one can follow the history of academic freedom without wondering at the fact that any society, interested in the immediate goals of solidarity and self-preservation, should possess the vision to subsidize free criticism and inquiry, and without feeling that the academic freedom we still possess is one of the remarkable achievements of man. At the same time, one cannot but be appalled at the slender thread by which it hangs."

When certain students, with encouragement from many sides, cut the thread, they did it (as they thought) in the name of still greater freedom. They wanted a "voice," and, with a trifle of self-contradiction, a "dialogue" on "non-negotiable demands." Sentimentalists believed that the university "bulldozed the student," carried on "a war against the young." The truth is that for years student opinion had been exerting an influence on curriculum and campus rules and habits, not only through free expression in the sacrosanct student paper, but, more importantly, through free access to faculty members and ease of deportment with them. Go to Europe and Asia and see how they "interact" there. Here student reports of bad teachers have affected promotions and choice of men—a force acting from day to day and not only in annually published evaluations.

The common faith in education as an indivdual right had also made the student's free choice among programs and courses the accepted thing, while the combining of programs, the multiplicity of certificates and degrees, the preservation of credits through all changes of mind—all these practices encouraged the development of the untrammeled self.

To be sure, this student freedom was only freedom to be a student. As long as parents believed in certain mores, there were parietal rules and library fines and some fuss made over cheating at examinations or stealing books from the bookstore. But that was not because the university was tyrannical; it was because, rightly or wrongly, students were thought young and inexperienced and in need of guidance.

Before 1900 and the free elective system, the ancient discipline and professorial control had made students rebellious. From Jefferson's University of Virginia to Charles W. Eliot's Harvard, student hostility and violence were a recurrent problem. It seemed to be resolved by letting the student choose his courses and preparing him for them sooner. He became docile, which means teachable, and he was believed to acquiesce in the fact that he knew less than his teachers, did not own the university, and benefited from what it stood for.

Such was the institution that a couple of years' violence have made into a historical memory. True, the American university had begun to lose its soul through misguided public service, and students had grievances they should have analyzed and publicized. But by organizing hatred instead, by assaulting and imprisoning their teachers, dividing faculties into factions, turning weak heads into cowards and demagogues, ignoring the grave and legitimate causes for reform, advocating the bearing of arms on campus, and preferring "confrontation" to getting their own way, hostile students have ushered in the reactionary university of the future, medieval model.

For it is clear that once the traditions of deference and civility are broken they cannot be knit up again at will. No one can be sure of the future, but the past is not dumb. Medieval student power met its quietus when the aggressive traits of its leaders were, so to speak, taken over by the state. The students, losing their privilege, became subjects like any other and were put down. For the American university there is no telling whether the return to the Middle Ages will not be halted at the phase of royal repression. Already more than half the states have passed acts of control, mild yet menacing by simply being there.

Nobody with a heart and a mind can look forward to the fulfillment of either reactionary hope—it took so long to develop the republic of learning in which *study* was the sole aim and test of the institution! Who can bear to think of reliving 1266 and All That? Still, it will be interesting to watch what happens to the university during the next seven hundred years.

IV

LEARNING

AND

SOCIETY

12. STUDENT ACTIVISM AND THE
SOCIAL ROLE OF THE UNIVERSITIES

Frederick A. Olafson

*Frederick A. Olafson is Professor of Philosophy at the
School of Education, Harvard University.*

AMERICAN COLLEGES and universities are currently facing a problem of very considerable gravity. During the past five years a movement of student protest has been developing on many campuses across the country; and while most students remain largely uninfluenced by this movement, it can on occasion command wide sympathy within the student population and has succeeded in bringing major universities like Berkeley and Columbia to a complete, if temporary, standstill. The acts of disobedience that have been committed have included violations of both university regulations and statute law; and in the latter case there have often been connections between the on-campus activity of some student organization and the illegal acts which have been committed be-

Reprinted, with permission, from *Education and Ethics,* ed. Blackstone and Newsome, University of Georgia Press, 1969 (papers presented at a symposium held in May 1968).

yond the campus. Most of the acts in this category have been in
the nature of protests against policies of the national government
which the participating students believe to be both dangerous and
wrong. The question such activities raise for the universities is
whether they should penalize students for involvement in such
illegal actions that take place outside the university. This question
is difficult enough; but the problem raised by acts of disobedience
directed against the universities themselves is even thornier. The
leadership of the radical student organizations which engage in
such actions seeks to compel the universities to alter what is said
to be their relationship of complicity with the policies of the
wider society which are under attack. To their considerable shock,
the universities thus find themselves accused of implicit racism
and militarism by reason of their collaboration with the federal
government and their financial involvement in the business
community; and this challenge comes from within—from a group
of students who regard themselves as an exploited proletariat
which is entitled to use any weapon in order to compel a corrupt
and guilty institution to change its ways. Whatever one may
think of these accusations there can be little doubt that they
express the sincere convictions of at least a minority of students
and the less explicit and intense views of many others; and I
think we must also concede that the very strong feelings and
beliefs thus engaged are often of a moral character. That fact does
not, of course, suffice to justify either these beliefs themselves or
the actions to which they lead; but a recognition of the moral
inspiration of at least a significant portion of this movement of
protest does, I think, create an obligation on the part of
universities and those within them who are concerned for their
future to formulate their reaction to these events with great care
and without undue attention to the side issues and personalities
that tend to distort much public discussion of these matters. In
this paper I will attempt to make a contribution to this task.

One way to deal with this theme would be to consider the
forms of protest currently being used by students as a special case
of the more general problem of civil disobedience, and secondly to
attempt to develop some judgement on the legitimacy of such disobedience both generally and in this special academic case which
has some features that may differentiate it in important ways
from other forms of civil disobedience such as that directed
against the draft. There is, of course, an initial difficulty here
since it is no longer clear that all the disturbances taking place on

our campuses are properly classifiable under the heading of civil disobedience. As that term is commonly understood, it designates a deliberate violation of some law or regulation for the purpose of drawing public attention to its iniquitous character through the arrests that become necessary in order to enforce it. Civil disobedience is, of course, distinguished from crime by the public because of the unconcealed way in which it is carried out and by the fact that the persons who engage in it do not seek to avoid apprehension and punishment. It is also distinguished from rebellion by this same avoidance of resistance to the authorities who enforce the statute that is being violated. Whatever persons engaging in acts of civil disobedience may think of the legitimacy of the government in power, their actions do not take the form of an overt challenge to its authority in the way that a rebellion does. Clearly, however, when an element of violence is associated with civil disobedience, the line between it and rebellion becomes much harder to draw; violence in one form or another *has* become a feature of many campus demonstrations. It might well be rewarding to undertake a detailed examination of these distinctions between civil disobedience and crime and rebellion, as well as certain other forms of social protests such as strikes. Nevertheless, while such an analysis might help us to categorize more accurately the disorders that have been occurring on our campuses, it does not seem likely to supply a judgment on the justifiability of these manifestations of student activism or a formula for handling them. There may be, after all, rebellions which are justified and which we should join instead of preventing or suppressing them; and if that is accepted as a premise, then the only way to reach significant conclusions in this matter is to evaluate the case that is being made in their own defense by the student activists themselves.

What I am suggesting, then, is that a judgment as to the way this movement of student activism should be met by the universities requires an antecedent judgment on the goals that movement has set itself. We must ask whether the broad political and social objectives which are being pursued by illegal means are of such importance and are so unlikely to be achieved by other means that would be consistent with a preservation of legality that they must command our support. I am assuming here that breaches of legality *are* involved and that this fact by itself does not suffice to condemn the movement that is responsible for them, although it does create a presumption against it. That presumption could be overturned if a very strong case could be made on general social and political grounds on behalf of the goals of student activism; and if it could, then it would not be enough to judge campus disorders solely in the light of existing rules. Those rules themselves and indeed the university's whole conception of itself would then have to be judged in a higher court of social utility. From that review the revolutionary party might well emerge as the true and legitimate authority within the university and what previously appeared as its illegal actions would have to be reinterpreted as justifiable forms of resistance to a spurious and socially retrograde authority. On the other hand, if it should appear upon careful inquiry that the objectives of the student activists would be purchased at a very heavy social cost without substantial compensating gains, then the universities would be justified in refusing to comply with the demands that are being made upon them. By that I do not mean that the universities would be justified in turning a deaf ear to specific proposals for internal reform or in refusing to create permanent forums in which student views can be presented and discussed. What I do mean is that the administrations would have a right to treat many manifestations of student activism as what in the first instance they are, i.e., infractions of the universities internal regulations; and would have the further right to punish the offenders accordingly.

There is one further respect in which I wish to limit my treatment of the objectives of student activism. I do not propose to discuss those objectives which are in some sense purely internal to the life of the university—matters such as the abolition of parietal regulations, examinations, or admission requirements. These matters are certainly not unimportant and it may be that they enjoy the highest priority among the great mass of the students who participate in campus demonstrations though not, I would guess, among those who lead and organize them. The efforts of the latter, or at least of the most radical among them, are concentrated upon the function of the university within the wider society it serves, i.e., upon the relationship of the university to other institutions in the society and especially to constituted political authority—a relationship which they believe to be a form of tacit collaboration with policies that are both evil and catastrophic. The universities are called upon to change that relationship in a quite radical way and to assume a political and social posture which in the circumstances would unavoidably be one of opposition and challenge to those policies. This is to say that the universities *as institutions*, through the policies they officially adopt and carry out, are to commit themselves to positions which are political in character. By political I do not mean association with a specific political party but the identification and sponsorship of concretely defined social undertakings which are needed if we are to realize the goals of peace and democracy of which university presidents invariably speak in glowing terms, but which usually remain quite abstract in terms of what a university may and may not do by way of collaboration with political authority. In short, the universities are no longer to confine their social role to that of an agent of public authority as when they train peace corps workers or carry out medical or military research; and they are not to assume without any real independent judgment that the tasks assigned them by these authorities are in fact in the public interest. I think it is clear, moreover, that the critics whose views I am trying to state are not simply calling for a withdrawal of the universities from their present involvements with government and business, but are advocating the development of new social initiatives which will be consistent with the requirements of a new critical self-consciousness on the part of the university. It is equally clear that when these same critics call for "student power," it is because they believe that the universities will radically change their social role only when effective power within them has been reallocated in such a way that students acquire a major role in policy formation.

Now some of this has a quite familiar ring to it. Americans, perhaps to an even greater extent than other peoples, have traditionally thought of education as a highly moral undertaking and of the school and the teacher as having a quite special responsibility for the moral development of the citizen and thus of the society as a whole. A conception of the school as the moral crucible of society has found wide acceptance; and some rather extravagant statements on the subject can be found scattered through the literature of American education. Even in the writings of the normally sober John Dewey there occasionally erupt passages of the most unrestrained moral enthusiasm in which Dewey assigns to the teacher and to the school a role that plainly transcends the sphere of normal instructional activity:

> The teacher is engaged not simply in the training of individuals, but in the formation of the proper social life. . . . He is a social servant set apart for the maintenance of proper

social order and the securing of the right social growth. In this way [he] is always the prophet of the true God and the usherer in of the true kingdom of God.[1]

At the same time, however, it remains obscure just how and through what specific kinds of activity other than inspired classroom teaching this high vocation of the teacher will be realized. There seems to be a kind of gap in Dewey's rhetoric at this point since the more familiar and humbler activities that normally fill a teacher's day scarcely seem to qualify for description in these terms if they are what Dewey has in mind; and if something more is intended, as one is tempted to think it must be, then we are not told what it is. The teacher is consequently left with the grandiloquent assurance that he is a servant of the true God but he still spends most of his time sweeping out the temple. At the same time, it is interesting to note that it is the teacher to whom Dewey assigns the task of moral and social renovation, not the students. For all this emphasis upon the importance of understanding and utilizing the interests of the student at whatever stage of development he has reached, the role of the teacher remains primary. It is the teacher who embodies the type of free and enlightened intelligence which students are to develop within themselves, and it is the teacher who presides in his own flexible and permissive way over that development. The notion that the authority of even such a friendly and uncoercive supervisor might be found onerous is one that Dewey appears never to have contemplated.

This same primacy of the teacher is even more openly asserted in the well-known essay by George Counts, "Dare the School Build a New Social Order?" which dates from 1932.[2] Counts argues vigorously against the view that the school should maintain an attitude of benevolent neutrality in matters of social concern; and he urges teachers not to try to deny nor avoid the element of imposition, as he calls it, which is necessarily implicit in all education. They should, he says, use the authority that is inherent in their position and in their relationship to their students to build a more humane social order. When read from the perspective of today's events, Counts's plea sounds unmistakably like a demand for "teacher power"; and while he is critical of those

---

[1] John Dewey, "My Pedagogical Creed," reprinted in R. Archambault, ed., *John Dewey on Education*, New York, 1964, p. 439.

[2] John Dewey Pamphlet No. 11, New York, 1932.

who believe that "the school is an all-powerful educational agency, he quite unambiguously calls upon teachers to "reach for
power and then make the most of their conquest."[3] He even
holds out the hope that "teachers, if they could increase
sufficiently their stock of courage, intelligence, and wisdom might
become a social force of some magnitude."[4] The schools would
then "become centers for the building and not merely for the con-
templation of our civilization."[5] This sounds a good deal more
radical and more concrete than does Dewey's statement because it
really seems as though Counts were proposing that the school
become the primary agency for planning and executing the necessary reform of our society. But from this suggestion he draws
back. Counts says that his conception of an active social role for
the schools does not "mean that we should endeavor to promote
particular reforms through the educational system." It turns out
that the building of a new social order that is to go on in the
schools is really the preparation of those who will issue forth into
the world to do the actual building. To this end, "we should . . .
give to our children a vision of the possibilities that lie ahead and
endeavour to enlist their loyalties and enthusiasm in the realization of this vision. Also our social institutions and practices, all of
them, should be critically examined in the light of such a vision."[6] The power that teachers are to seize proves to be power
to govern the school and to teach in accordance with their own
vision of the social good; and no *direct* intervention of educational
institutions in the affairs of government or of other institutions is
really being proposed. Again, from the vantage point of our own
current preoccupations, it is interesting to note that Counts speaks
of a vision that is to be "given" to children and of an enlistment
of the latter in a cause that has apparently been defined for them
by their elders.

It is clear, I think, that in spite of a rhetorical radicalism which
they share with the student activists of today, both Dewey and
Counts remain well within traditional conception of the way in
which a school or university can properly attempt to influence the
policies of the political and other insitutions of the society it
serves. This is the view that the teacher and the school affect the

[3] *Ibid.*, p. 23.
[4] *Ibid.*, p. 28.
[5] *Ibid.*, p. 37.
[6] *Ibid.*, p. 37.

society as a whole indirectly. They form the mind and character of the child who then issues from the salubrious moral climate of the school and, in the various civic capacities he assumes, proceeds to modify and, if necessary, to reconstruct the society. No doubt the thinking of the teacher or professor and the critical perspectives on society which it proposes will exert an influence on adults as well through the public discussions in which academic figures participate; but, even so, the mediated and indirect character of their influence remains. In short, the university is not itself to be an operational agency in any field except that of education itself; and if Dewey and Counts propose that teachers are to have more power over the school and more freedom to give a political and economic content to the moral and intellectual attitudes they seek to form in children, it is still the latter *in their eventual capacity as citizens* who are to translate their mentors' social vision into social reality.

Now if I have correctly interpreted the statements that have been made about their objectives by leaders of the current movement on the campuses, it is precisely against this limited and indirect role of the universities that some of their strongest objections are directed. In part, this impatience may be due to the fact that the "teacher power" movement of the thirties failed, with the result that the universities remain to a considerable extent under the control of the very social authorities whose policies are so repugnant to the radicals of then and now. But the latter are not primarily interested in making the universities self-governing; or rather to the extent that that *is* one of their aims, it is because they expect such an autonomous university to be animated by their own political ideals and controlled to a very considerable extent by them. A university in which student power had become paramount in this way could then be used as an institutional base from which pressure could be exerted upon the unreformed segments of society. In the wilder fantasies of the New Left the university appears to figure as a kind of urban Sierra Maestra from which the student-guerillero will make sorties into unredeemed territory. Once again I hasten to add that this goal which I am imputing to the most radical leaders of student activism is one that very few of their followers and even fewer among those who are influenced by them really share. Most of them have been drawn into that movement by dissatisfaction with one or another aspect of university life which could be corrected within the existing organization of the universities. Still others, perhaps, are expressing through their participation a more diffuse malaise that springs from their bafflement at academic life and their inability to use the university and the opportunities it offers for purposes of their own. But students whose primary complaints are directed against housing regulations or the grading system or even the sheer immensity and impersonality of the modern university rarely mount demonstrations of the kind we have witnessed during the past few years unless these relatively specific discontents have been focused in a general indictment of the universities along the lines I have been describing. There is obviously a certain danger that by turning inward, at least temporarily, to concentrate upon the internal organization of the universities and the current grievances of their immense student populations, the activist movement may lose touch with the wider struggles that are going on outside the universities. A number of observers have in fact pointed out that certain forms of student protest bespeak nothing more clearly than they do a persistence in projecting a child-parent conflict pattern upon all institutional arrangements that involve any element of authority or hierarchy. I do not propose to take up this line of criticism, however, and I will assume that even in this parochial theater of action student activism remains a movement that is directed outward toward the society as a whole. The question I do want to raise is one that concerns rather the effectiveness of the university as an institutional base for radical social reform. In other periods, other institutions have been selected for this role as were, for example, the labor unions in the 1930s; and they have served the purpose assigned to them with very different degrees of effectiveness. As far as I know, no previous attempt has been made in this country or in most others to make the university the *principal* instrument of political action; and the decision to treat it as such undoubtedly reflects the increasing unsuitability and unavailability of the institutions which have traditionally served this purpose. But just how sensible is it to assign this new role to the university and how compatible will it prove with older and more familiar functions it discharges?

From the standpoint of their possible function as agencies of social action, our universities as they are presently constituted have one crucially important defect: they are dependent institutions. By dependent I mean that universities derive their resources from the society they serve, and they lack any power, in fact or in law, to command or coerce such support. In the case of publicly maintained universities, this dependency is patent and each year such universities are reminded of it in a rather obvious way when the state legislatures consider their budgets. But even the great private universities with their endowments are heavily dependent for current gifts upon their alumni and upon the government for grants that sustain many research activities. This support, both public and private, is given with the understanding that the universities will operate in a manner that is consistent with legal requirements and that they will not use the resources allocated to them for the purpose of influencing public policy or that of other institutions in any way that has not been explicity authorized by public authority. There have, of course, been many violations of that understanding, some of which have been tolerated and even encouraged by governmental authorities themselves. It is also hard to draw the line that separates partisan intervention by the university in the affairs of the community from the subtler kind of influence that discussion and research within a university exert over a period of time on public affairs; and the enemies of academic freedom have not been slow to equate the two and to insist that unorthodox thought in a university is tantamount to the treasonable subversion of our institutions. But whatever ambiguities have surrounded this distinction between permissible and impermissible forms of influence by the university within the wider community, its acceptance in some form by the community has been one of the chief safeguards of the freedom that universities effectively enjoy in this country. People, it seems, are not entirely averse to the kind of influence that gradually permeates a society even if it emanates from a university; but they are very quick to resent any institution that officially sponsors and seeks acceptance for policies that involve major social innovation. As a result, American universities have on the whole assumed wider social responsibilities only as the agents of public authority; and they have carefully distinguished between the social views and proposals that are put forward by members of their faculties and the official position of the university as a corporate body which has usually been one of neutrality.

In the eyes of many student activists this neutral posture of the university is its chief sin, and the freedom that is bought at the price of such neutrality is felt to be a degrading form of servitude. To cite just one example of the kind of demand that is now often made on universities and that manifestly requires the abandonment of such neutrality, I would mention a recent denunciation of the university at which I teach for its failure to come out officially against the mayoral candidacy in Boston of a woman whose stand on racial questions was rightly condemned by the critic in question. (In my opinion such an action by the university would have insured her election but that I concede is a tactical consideration and tactical considerations are not currently enjoying a good press among student activists.) In any case, it is very clear that a university could abandon its neutrality and embark upon a program of social activism outside the framework of public policy only if it were prepared to do without a very large part of the support that it now receives. Some private universities might be able to do that although at great sacrifice; but it is scarcely imaginable that a publicly maintained university could survive if it were to adopt such a course of action. There have been a few attempt to found new and, as they are called, "free" universities for this purpose; but as far as I know these have remained largely parasitical upon the established universities from which the members of the free universities seceded. Naturally, I am not suggesting that survival is always the highest imperative that a university should obey. At the beginning of the Nazi era the German universities should surely have spoken out and in their corporate capacity, even if the price had been their dissolution which would at least have been more honorable to them than their extraordinary passivity under a barbaric regime. I would point out, however, that such action by a university will be largely symbolic in character though not necessarily ineffective for that reason. A free university could have survived in Nazi Germany only underground. Happily that is not the situation in our country at the present time; and the issue that faces us is whether the university as we know it should be reorganized for another quite different social role which would entail the sacrifice of a large part of its current support, and not whether the university, in order to defend even its present degree of freedom, must defy the government and challenge the validity of its laws. Nevertheless, the issue this poses for the universities is quite grave enough; and if a decision to transform the university were to be taken, much thought would have to be given to the creation of new bases of power and support for this new kind of university.

A university which is maintained from voluntary outside sources of support, however inadequately, and which as a condition of this support is required to remain nonpolitical in the sense which I have been trying to indicate, is also a place, at least in intention, in which persons from quite different groups within the society, with different political attitudes and different social interests, can come together for the purpose of study. This is, I concede, the ideal conception which American universities have of themselves, and a few universities and colleges may in actual fact have become special preserves in which only those who are prepared to hew to a given political line are welcome. But in general this has not been the case; and the student populations of our universities are probably as diverse socially as any in the world. Their students unquestionably segregate themselves in various ways within the universities and often achieve disappointingly little contact with or understanding of one aother. That fact can hardly be an argument for abandoning even the ideal of political noninvolvement on the part of the university, however, unless it can be shown that the impact of life in a university community is in fact negligible from the standpoint of the political and social issues that dominate our national life. I do not believe that this is in fact the case, and it certainly cannot be established by such facile arguments as often appear to underly the conviction that the university's institutional neutrality is simply a form of feckless passivity. No doubt the kind of "rationalistic universalism" which our best students often assimilate as a life style in many of our universities often hides a deeper class partisanship which asserts itself when the student assumes his place in the social world, if not before.[7] But there is much to suggest that the attitudes of the educated class, while overbalanced and particularly absorbed by the partisan requirements of particular social affiliations, maintain themselves to some degree as a force for moderation, intelligence, and cooperation in our social and political life. If so, and if in spite of the disesteem these virtues are currently suffering we persist in believing that this residue of disinterestedness and universalism is a precious resource in our national life, then we must ask whether they would be likely to receive much encouragement in a sectarian university, so heavily engaged in the social contests of the surrounding society as in effect to invite only one kind of constituency. My own feeling is that they would not and that in this respect what appears from a partisan standpoint as the marginal position of our universities—in the consecrated phrase, their "ivory tower" aspect—is a condition of a distinctive social benefit they confer.

---

[7] An interesting discussion of this life-style can be found in Christopher Jencks and David Riesman, *The Academic Revolution* (New York, 1968), p. 12 *et passim.*

It is not at all easy to imagine what a university that deliberately politicised itself would be like; although it is clear that in
matters of support and constituency profound changes would be
involved. Nor are there many precedents that can help us to understand what the situation of such a university in relation to society as a whole would be. Nevertheless, the experience of the
various Christian churches over the centuries may cast some light
on the matter. At the present time, the relationship of most
churches to social action and policy is, like that of the universities, indirect in the sense that the church is expected to shape the
character and attitudes of its communicants who then, individually and without any authoritative control by their church, are
supposed to bring the beneficent influence of their faith to bear
on the daily business of life, both private and public. With a few
notable exceptions, churches are not themselves agencies engaged
in bringing about social and political change; and while churches
tend to be classified to some extent as liberal or conservative in
social matters as do universities, this polarization has not reached
yet the point where most churches can expect support exclusively
from those who share one or another of these orientations. Not
surprisingly, this reluctance on the part of most churches to become directly engaged in political struggles has earned them the
contempt of some of their own communicants who have been
pressing for a more activistic stance on the part of the
churches—a contempt that is justified insofar as the churches' refusal to become involved in social controversy has been a mask for
a deeper partisan commitment. I am not concerned, however, to
form any judgment on the social role of the churches, but to contrast their present role with others in the past when the church
was in some sense an executive social agency. In part by reason of
an historical accident—the long hiatus in effective secular government following the dissolution of the Roman Empire—and partly
because Christian doctrine claimed a comprehensive control over
all aspects of the life of its communicants, the early Christian
church assumed direct responsibility, not, to be sure, for social
reconstruction in any modern sense, but for a detailed supervision
of the lives of its members and in practice of all members of the
society. Sometimes this supervision became a direct assumption of
the powers of secular government; but later, with the revival of
secular government, the church's position was that of a kind of
state within the state—enormously powerful through the financial
support it exacted as a matter of right and exerting a steady pres-

sure upon secular government in defense of its own special position which was justified by the church's claim to final authority in spiritual and intellectual matters. Indeed, until far into the modern period ministers of the crown were often drawn from the ranks of the clergy who thus acted in an essentially similar capacity to that of our present-day "in-and-outers," the academics who move so smoothly from the universities into government and back. Of course, the story of the church's involvement in the secular world had an unhappy ending when the revolutionary upheavals of the late eighteenth and nineteenth centuries stripped it of much of its wealth and social power and in many countries returned it to the status of a voluntary private association; and the church was despoiled in this way precisely because it was, and was regarded by the revolutionary party as being, a great and antagonistic social feudality, actively engaged at the primary level of social action in defense of its own interests and its own conception of how society should be ordered.

Now it may seem that the parallelism I am suggesting between universities and churches is fanciful indeed; and so it is in certain obvious respects. The universities in our day are, after all, many, while the church in the medieval period was one. There has been no lapse of secular power that would permit other institutions to intrude upon its normal sphere of competence as there was at the end of the ancient world. And above all the social influence of the church was for the most part profoundly conservative while that of the universities tends to be markedly innovative and liberalizing. But there are equally impressive respects in which these institutions are alike; and among these the most important is a tendency to claim for themselves a kind of monopoly of intellectual and moral authority. This claim, in turn, exposes both to a temptation to pass beyond the confines of a purely advisory role in relation to the executive institutions of society and to assume direct operational responsibilities. In this paper I have been drawing attention to the demands of the student left that the universities move in this direction; but I might equally well have cited the kind of rapproachement of the universities with government that has proceeded so far under the auspices of academics who belong somewhere in the center of the political spectrum—those fabled figures that *Life* magazine has hailed as the "action intellectuals." I am reminded here of Lionel Trilling's charming fantasy in which the walls of separation between government and university disappear entirely and the chief officers of government are known under such titles as "Dean of Defense" and "Dean of State." It would in fact appear that the main difference between left and center activists in this matter of the social role of the universities is that the former envisage the university as an embattled dissenting church and the latter, as an orthodox established church; but both quite emphatically, though in different ways, represent the church militant. The largest question of social policy that seems to me to have been raised by the current unrest is whether the universities *should* be transformed into a kind of secular equivalent of the church militant, whichever subvariety of the latter appeals to us most.

To that question my answer would be "No"; and my reasons are the very simple and obvious ones that are reflected in the comments I have been making on the activist proposals for the reorganization of the university. As I see it, the universities have two major social duties: the duty to increase human knowledge and understanding and the duty to educate, i.e., to prepare young people to assume positions of special responsibility by helping them to acquire both the specialized competence and the broader critical perspectives which such positions require—ideally, if not as a matter of actual employment criteria. If to these duties we were to add a further requirement that the universities intervene as independent and partisan agencies in the social and political contests of our time, we would change in unforeseeable ways both the material basis of support for the universities and the social constituencies they serve. It seems very likely to me that these changes would be such as to interfere significantly with the discharge of the first two duties I have mentioned; and that the loss to our society thus entailed would not be balanced by any substantial achievement that can realistically be expected from institutions as weak as our universities really are. They are weak because they have no resources of their own and because they have no natural allies in other social groupings whose strength might compensate for the universities' weakness. In these circumstances, a politicization of the universities could be expected to lead only to their destruction or their suppression and while there are those who accept this consequence and declare that they prefer no universities at all to universities that do not stand in overt opposition to the main trends of our society, their views are not likely to be widely shared. Polarization of opposing points of view may have its utility in the political sphere; but the militance and rigidity it brings with it would be the death of the universities. It seems obvious to me that their demise as free institutions of learning would not benefit the social cause which they would have vainly attempted to serve and that a distinctive institution that contributes in its own way—however indirectly and imperfectly—to the sanity and decency of our society would simply have been sacrificed at the behest of an *enragé* mentality which it is becoming harder and harder to distinguish from the other forms of brutality and violence that fill our lives today.

I wish it were possible to claim that in arguing against these demands I am defending the autonomy of the universities. In a sense of course that is just what I am doing, but I would be less than candid if I left the implication that all would be well and that autonomy intact if only these student radicals would stop trying to push the university into a social role that will make it extremely difficult for it to make its own distinctive sort of contribution. In fact, that autonomy has already been very seriously compromised by the faculties and administrations of our great universities; and I suspect that the demand that the university become engaged in the struggle for radical reconstruction of our society would not have been made or would not in any case have proved as persuasive as it has if it were not for the fact that the universities have so readily accepted a *de facto* alliance with government and industry—an alliance which tends to preserve and strengthen the social status quo at points with respect to which the universities might have been expected to maintain a more independent posture. If student activists were calling the universities back to a saner conception of their own true function instead of insisting that they become engaged on the other side of social conflicts in progress, I would have no criticism to make; and even though they are not, I think it is legitimate to excerpt a negative critique of current university practices from the context of their wider proposals for redeployment of academic resources to another front in the same war. The point of that critique is simply that the universities have not made and apparently have not wished to make effective use of that margin of freedom in relation to other institutions of our society—especially government—which I believe they could validly maintain is theirs. They have been avid petitioners for a share of the public largesse; and they have shown scant concern about the effects of the resulting involvements upon the integrity of their instructional programs and on the possibility of any independent judgment on the public policies in which they cooperate. I submit that it would have been wiser for the universities and in the long run for the country as a whole to assign many of the research and operational responsibilities that the universities have assumed either to governmental agencies or to new nongovernmental organizations on the Rand Corporation model which are now being used more and more for this purpose and about which I will have more to say farther on. The object of such a shift would not be to divert them entirely from work in the same areas in which government is and should be active, but rather to insure that the work the universities undertake is dictated by criteria of intellectual interest and long-run social value that are their own rather than those of the clients of such research.

I am aware that the line I am taking makes me vulnerable to the charge that I am separating thought from action; and that is a very serious charge, especially at the present time. It will be said that American universities have long since transcended the limits I seek to impose; and that their vitality and "relevance" are dependent upon their close involvement in enterprises that require an irreversible commitment of thought and resources to the cause of the betterment of human life. This charge has at least a surface plausibility about it since no one can reasonably dissent from the demand that thought and action be effectively related to one another; and it is easy to pass on, as is often done nowadays, to the more questionable claim that intelligence and moral concern can be meaningfully associated with one another only in the context of the kind of undertaking we call a "cause." I would be the last to deny that there have been superb examples of the way intelligence can function within a commitment to such causes; but we all know how often the imperatives of conflict have exerted a distorting influence over thought that is unconditionally subordinate to them. It is, of course, entirely proper that scholars and scientists who concern themselves with matters of public policy should be asked to keep in mind the situation and the priorities of those persons who actually have to make decisions; but this demand can all too easily pass over into a requirement that they keep their inquiries within limits that are dictated by the current strategic convenience of the institution they are to serve. Historically, neither established nor dissenting churches have proved very hospitable to the kind of inquiry that claims the right to ask and to answer questions that may not be convenient from anyone's point of view; and the charge of irresponsibility and lack of social concern has often been used against those who exercise that right. It is being used again today by those who wish to force upon the universities the dicipline and the homogeneity that are characteristic of a militant and partisan social force.

There are, over and above these general reasons for rejecting the charge of social irresponsiblity, more specific and more specifically contemporary grounds on which a defense of a restricted social role for the universities can be based. As many observers have pointed out in recent years, our society and especially many of our leading national institutions are taking on an increasingly "cognitive" cast. The qualifications necessary for various kinds of work tend more and more to be centered on the certified completion of some course of advanced academic work; and educational level has become a very important element in the assignment of social status. Moreover, business and industry—the traditional hold-outs—have been steadily drawn into this evolution; and research departments and independent research firms of all kinds, drawing on very variegated types of rarefied intellectual expertise, have become a prominent feature of the national scene. To an important extent, technological innovation and economic growth are now dependent upon the contribution that such organizations make. Most of these were the offspring of the universities; and the latter—the original "cognitive" institutions—now find themselves in the company of a growing number of foundations, research firms, laboratories, etc., many of which employ very highly trained products of university study in research activities that are contracted for by private business or government. It seems likely that in the near future many of these organizations and others yet to come will move into the field of social inquiry and planning in a much more ambitious way than they have hitherto done; but here too the organization of work around specific issues of policy will presumably distinguish what these institutions do from the more traditional preoccupations of university scholars.

One large question posed by these developments is what the special position and function of the university is to be within this new family of "cognitive" institutions and whether the creation of these new task-oriented research firms does not make possible a more satisfactory delimitation of the special function of the universities to which, in the absence of these other instrumentalities, a great many very heterogeneous responsibilities have been assigned. Many university people view the growth of these nongovernmental firms with considerable reservations, and distrust of the "Rand mentality" is common among academics. Not surprisingly, continued activity by the universities in the same fields in which these firms are working is often regarded as the sole safeguard against the victory of technocratic intellectuals in the service of big business and bigger government. But while people in the universities have an important critical role to play in relation to these new institutions and a yet more important one in training the people who go on to staff them and while manifold informal relationships between those institutions and the universities are highly desirable, it is still clear that universities have a special responsibility which distinguishes them from other "cognitive" institutions and which can be combined with extensive external responsibilities only with great difficulty and strain. This is their responsibility to their internal constituency—their students. I would be inclined to argue that scholars and scientists who are so interested in pure undisturbed inquiry or in the actual formulation and implementation of social policy that they are either ineffective or uninterested in that responsibility should properly find their place in another kind of cognitive institution, whether a research institute or an operational agency. The primary social duty of the universities in relation to these task-oriented agencies and research firms and to government as well is to prepare the people who will staff them; and while this function is now often said to place the university in the humiliating position of a subcontractor to the dominant industrial and governmental institutions, I cannot see any reason to think that what is apparently assumed to be the inevitably corrupt character of the latter will be remedied by an assumption of executive responsibilities by the universities in the same areas. Nor do I see why, in restricting the external responsibilities they assume in order to conserve their resources for their prior social obligations, and in seeking to do what they can to raise the level of performance in all the principal institutions of our society by raising the level of training that is given to those who will staff them, the universities would, in any reasonable view of the matter, be either cutting themselves off from the contemporary world or accepting a wholly passive and uncritical attitude toward the performance of the executive agencies they serve.

Returning then to the topic from which I set out, I would offer in the way of a general conclusion the view that the demands that student activists are making for a politicization of the university are ill-advised and that the universities should not yield to such demands. This is not to say that they will be justified or wise in adopting a harsh and repressive policy on the occasion of pro-tests and demonstrations or in turning a deaf ear to what these students—even the most uncivil among them—have to say. And by itself a refusal to yield is not likely to lead to significant changes in the moral atmosphere of our universities unless the latter find ways of reasserting through important internal reforms their in-terest in their students and their interest in education. Only by doing so and by associating the training they give with humane and critical perspectives upon the world of practice in which the competencies thus formed will find their place, will the universi-ties be truly justified in saying to the student activists that their distinctive social duty is being discharged and that a policy of promiscuous intervention in the political and social affairs of the larger community would, in addition to its other disabling effects, make the discharge of that duty difficult or impossible.

13. EFFICIENCY AS A PROD
TO SOCIAL ACTION

Kenneth B. Clark

Kenneth B. Clark is Professor of Psychology at The City College
of New York.

BUSINESS AND INDUSTRY must not commit themselves to social
change for sentimental reasons. Commitment must make sense in
relation to criteria and standards that are relevant to the normal
requirements of business and industry—namely, effectiveness and
efficiency.

Gunner Myrdal states in his book, *Challenge to Affluence*, that
the modern technological revolution has had one highly
significant consequence—the ideals of democracy and the practical
imperatives of survival of the technological society are now one.
They are indistinguishable. Ironically, perhaps, efficiency, ethics,
and survival are now part of the same amalgam.

Survival depends on the ability of modern man to stimulate, to
reinforce, to nurture, to create positive social change, to engage in
a social revolution that matches the technological revolution of
our times, that makes life more possible than death, that elimi-
nates hunger and disease and all exploitation of human beings by
other human beings.

I would argue that oppression and cruelty, which seem to characterize even the most allegedly civilized societies, are not merely
morally unacceptable, but practicably unacceptable. The oppressed are not merely a goad to conscience, a nagging discomfort,
an inconvenience; they are a threat to the stability, the
well-being, the growth potential of society as a whole.

Business and industry have a great deal at stake in this enterprise. In the United States the business and industrial community,
in terms of its own criteria of effectiveness and efficiency, must
now address itself to methods of remedy and change in the cyclic
system of racism and urban pathology. The requirements of indus-

Reprinted, with permission, from the *Monthly Labor Review*, August 1969.

trial business and commercial efficiency are inconsistent with urban instability.

For several years I have argued that the American business and industrial sector is the last hope for any serious, realistic, hard-nosed attempt to change the predicament of life in American ghettos. I do not come to this conclusion in the conviction that business and industrial communities are more empathic to the day-to-day problems of the ghetto, nor because I believe that they are more idealistic or morally or ethically sensitive than others.

I took this position rather because they are clear about their goals. They are not bemused with moral self-righteousness. They are usually unsentimental about their concern for profits and productivity. Even racial discrimination may fall victim to their single-minded search for efficiency and economic viability. Or so I believe may be possible.

What must one know about the style of ghetto youth, the more severe casualties of this peculiar American system of democratic racism, if one is serous about developing training programs in business and industry that are not tokens or gestures? If industry is going to have any hope in addressing itself to this problem of adapting ghetto youth to a constructive role, it must prove, by the nature of its program and by its initial formulation and presentation, that it is genuine; that the program is not a glittering word promise-tokenism program; that it is really serious in its intent, serious in its method, and if it is serious, it will demonstrate this by the structured specific planning of the program; that the nature of the training must be an integral part of the jobs which allegedly exist and will be offered. Otherwise, pre-job training is not likely to be considered serious by ghetto youth, who are suspicious and hypersensitive and who expect that promises will not be honored.

Training that is an integral part of the job, training in which the training and the job and the remuneration are all part of the same package, can be a concrete and serious demonstration that the promise and the performance are one. Also, the training must be real. Real training is not just job-skill training. These young people know better than anyone else that they are basically deficient in reading, arithmetic, and communication skills. Industry will not be taken seriously if it pretends that it is training him for a job that has mobility without simultaneously addressing itself to his fundamental deficiencies. These youngsters will exploit the alleged training program as long as it is beneficial for them—and then they will get out.

Business and industry must build into industrially structured training programs remedial compensations for the inefficiency of the public schools—reading, arithmetic, oral and written communication, the major defaults of the American public schools. Academic training, job training, and jobs must be part of the total package.

The default of the American public school system is directly related to the interests of business for several reasons: First, a substantial proportion of the tax dollar paid by industry goes to support public schools. Second, inner city public schools are producing human casualties who cannot be effectively integrated into the industrial and economic segment of society without the expenditure of additional funds by business and industry to compensate for the inefficiency of the public schools. Business and industry are, in fact, subsidizing inefficiency if they continue to permit public education to spawn hundreds of thousands of functional illiterates each year. If they comply with equal-employment demands of the Federal Government in terms other than token terms, business and industry are caught in a double taxation bind. In sheer dollars-and-cents terms, this is an area that calls for intervention from the business and industrial community.

Business and industry are being offered shoddy products and being asked to use them as if they were not. This is an unnecessary burden. If a consortium of big business and industrial firms is really serious in bringing in previously rejected minority groups as an integral part of the hierarchy of employment, it should and must address itself to this basic question of increasing the efficiency of public education.

Once industry accepts its responsibility to train and employ the educationally and economically deprived, it must exercise it in an empathic, understanding way. It cannot be done sentimentally. It cannot say, "You poor disadvantaged youth, I will accept any kind of production from you. I will accept any kind of performance." Any sentimentalism will be exploited and seriousness will be eroded and rejected. Specifically, the importance of time, production standards, structured standards of performance—standards that have been found to be important in general industrial efficiency—must be clearly understood and clearly articulated and demanded.

Industry must demonstrate its seriousness by not accepting from the Negro youngster any lower level of academic performance than is expected from white youngsters, at the same time that it takes into account the fact that the public education of Negro youngsters has made them inferior in certain academic areas, a deficit which business will now make up for by its on-the-job training. It must demonstrate its seriousness by requiring and obtaining from the Negro youngsters precisely the same standards of manner, style, dress, punctuality that it requires from others of whatever level of job. I cannot express vehemently enough my abhorrence of sentimentalistic, seemingly compassionate programs of employment of Negroes which employ them on Jim Crow double standards or special standards for the Negro which are lower than those for the whites.

This is a perpetuation of racism—it is interpreted by the Negro as condescension and it will be exploited by them. Those who have been neglected and deprived must understand that they are being taken seriously as human beings. They must not be regarded as peculiar human beings who cannot meet the demands more privileged human beings can meet. This is an important but subtle point. I suspect that the significant breakdown in the efficiency of American public education came not primarily from flagrant racial bigotry and the deliberate desire to create casualties, but from good intentions, namely, the sloppy sentimentalistic good intentions of educators to reduce standards in the education of low income and minority group youngsters, to leave them in a state of amorphousness and, thereby—on the grounds that teachers should not demand of these children what they demand of suburban children—make it possible for noneducation to be alibied.

I urgently warn business and industry not to follow this pattern of sentimentalism under the guise of doing good, under the guise of compensating for guilt and past injustices. As a psychologist, I know that this pattern will have detrimental consequences. But I do it on even more empirical grounds, that it will fail the ghetto youths' test of seriousness.

They will know that the standards for them are different. This is part, if not the whole of the problem.

They cannot and will not accept condescension although they might exploit it.

They will accept only evidence of respect for their humanity, their capacity as human beings, their ability to learn the way people learn, they ability to perform with the same standards by which other people's performances are evaluated. And in respecting these, business and industry will be giving not verbal, but genuine acceptance of them as human beings.

They must be provided also with realistic rewards and incentives for meeting single standards of performance and achievement. They cannot be rewarded, and believe that they are being taken seriously, for double standards which are inferior standards of achievement. They will accept the same gold medal for clearly inferior work, but they will know that it is a Jim Crow medal whites would not award to whites for the same level of performance. They must be provided with the opportunity to move upwards, but as far as I see and understand these youngsters beneath their words, they do not want to be relegated to another track. They do not want the continuation of Jim Crow seniority or promotion systems. Deep down, these youngsters want the opportunity and the equipment to determine the extent to which they can compete with other human beings without special gimmicks or crutches, however necessary aids may be at an interim stage.

The goals of a serious program to bring ghetto youth into business and industry cannot be attained without understanding, patience, guidance, clarity as to human requirements for genuine dignity. Whatever these are, they are not likely to be qualified by the color of skin; they are the same for all human beings. All human beings share a basic sense of their worthiness or unworthiness, a basic problem that will be settled only by constructive achievement, not by pretense.

The degree of seriousness and success of any program will be determined by how short a time is required for special programs. Once these youths are brought into business and industry and given whatever they require to function and to be judged as individuals, from that moment they must have the same degree of freedom of choice which other human beings appear to have.

The ultimate test of success will be when whites and Negroes observe the range of individual differences among Negroes with the same degree of acceptance that they grant to individual differences among whites; when we will be able to note that an individual Negro is inferior in intelligence, or has questionable character, without being required to wonder, with a sense of guilt, whether his inferiority or questionable character is the result of racial oppression or is the reflection of the "fact" that all Negroes are inferior. Whites have questionable characters, because nature was not democratic. Nature distributed abilities along normal distribution curves. We need to accept the normal distribution curve principle with the same freedom from guilt in regard to Negroes as it now appears to operate among whites.

And what is true for Negroes and whites in America is true for all human beings everywhere. The cost of oppression degrades the victim and the oppressor. When the victim is freed the oppressor is freed also. All human beings must be accepted in terms of their humanity and not rejected in terms of the irrelevancies of race or class or sex or religion or geographical accident of national boundary. What is at stake is nothing less than human survival. If the world deserves to survive it will mobilize the intellectual, the economic, the practical planning resources which will make survival possible. This will be the ultimate and practical morality.

14. PURISTS AND POLITICIANS

Don K. Price

*Don K. Price is Professor of Political Science
at Harvard University.*

SOMETIMES the tone of a headline tells you more than the news.
Last summer a New York *Times* headline read "Pure Physicists
Stay That Way: Vote to Remain Out of Politics." The story was a
straightforward account of the decision by the members of the
American Physical Society that it would adopt no resolutions on
political issues.[1] The flavor of the headline suggested a great deal
more: that the typical newspaper readers and perhaps even a
good many scientists are still inclined to think that the moral obligation of a scientists is to remain aloof from policy issues and
political controversy.

Since I applauded the tactical decision of the physicists but deplored the implications of the headline, it occurred to me that this
apparent contradiction was worth some further thought. Perhaps
it is the crux of the apparent dilemma which the entire scientific
community shares with the physicists. The dilemma is ages
old—the dilemma between truth and power, or, rather, between
starving in the pursuit of truth and compromising truth to gain
material support. But it takes its new form in the delimma posed
for the scientific community as it now comes under attack simultaneously from two sides—from a political reaction and from a
new kind of rebellion.

This attack from the two extremes makes it hard for the
scientific community to continue its traditional political strategy,
especially since—as sometimes happens in politics—the two extremes may in effect be allies, even though superficially in
conflict.

The traditional political strategy of scientists has been to keep
their sights set firmly on the advancement of basic knowledge in
the conviction that their mode of thinking is in the vaguard of
political and economic progress, and at the same time to persuade

---

Reprinted, with permission, from *Science*, January 1969; copyright 1969 by the
American Association for the Advancement of Science

[1] *New York Times* (July 14, 1968).

politicians and philanthropists to support science for its indirect payoffs in power and wealth.

This strategy was based on a belief in automatic progress that had its orgins in the same way of thinking that produced economic laissez-faire. Scientific knowledge, like economic initiative, could be relied on to produce progress if government could be persuaded not to interfere, except with the necessary subsidies.

But now, under attack on two fronts, scientists find this strategy harder to sustain.

On one side, the attack comes from a political reaction, which has three main purposes. Politicians want to cut down on the appropriations for research, to have more of the money spent on practical technology and less on academic theory, and to break down the degree of autonomy which the leaders of the scientific community gained a generation ago in the procedures by which research grants are distributed. On each of these points the reaction conforms to the best American tradition of the political pork barrel.

On the other side, the rebellion is a cosmopolitan, almost worldwide, movement. One is tempted to identify it with its violent and fantastic and adolescent fringe—flower power and student insurrections. Obviously, the young are the ones who charge the cops in Chicago and barricade the buildings at Columbia or Berkeley. They have to be: my contemporaries no longer have the muscle and the wind for such exertions. Today's youth are indeed the student activists, just as today's youth are the infantry in Vietnam. But it would be as much a mistake to give the student leaders credit for the ideology of the rebellion as to give the G.I.'s credit for the war plans of the Joint Chiefs.

The ideology of the rebellion is confused; you can find in it little clarity or consistency of purpose. Its mood and temper reflect the ideas of many middle-aged intellectuals who are anything but violent revolutionaries. From the point of view of scientists, the most important theme in the rebellion is its hatred of what it sees as an impersonal technological society that dominates the individual and reduces his sense of freedom. In this complex system, science and technology, far from being considered beneficent instruments of progress, are identified as the intellectual processes that are at the roots of the blind forces of oppression.

For example, André Malraux, denying that the problem is one of conflict between the generations, says that "the most basic problem of our civilization" is that it is "a civilization of machines," and that "we, for the first time, have a knowledge of matter and a knowledge of the universe which . . . suppresses man".[2]

Jacques Ellul, one of the heroes of alienated young Europeans, presents a more systematic indictment of scientists as "sorcerers who are totally blind to the meaning of the human adventure," whose system of thought is bringing about "a dictatorship of test tubes rather than hobnailed boots".[3]

The theme was echoed by Erich Fromm in his support of Senator McCarthy's presidential candidacy, in a public protest against the type of society in which "technical progress becomes the source of all values" and we see as a consequence "the complete alienation and dehumanization of man".[4]

Herbert Marcuse, who is of course the favorite philosopher of the rebels, reduces the issue to its fundamental point[5] : "the mathematical character of modern science determines the range and direction of its creativity, and leaves the nonquantifiable qualities of *humanitas* outside the domain of exact science . . . [which then] feels the need for redemption by coming to terms with the 'humanities.' "

In one sense, the challenge does indeed come from the humanities. The student rebels and their faculty sympathizers, at home and abroad, are found more conspicuously in the departments of humanities and in schools of theology than in the natural sciences or engineering.[6] If the danger comes from the humanities, however, it comes not because they are politically powerful but, rather, because, as Mr. Marcuse suggests, they may have convinced scientists themselves that science is an inhumane discipline. The case for laissez-faire vanished when businessmen themselves became

---

[2] *Ibid.* (Oct. 22, 1968), pp. 49 and 56.

[3] J. Ellul, *The Technological Society* (Knopf, New York, 1964), pp. 434-35.

[4] Statement in campaign advertisement, New York *Times* (May 22, 1968).

[5] H. Marcuse, "The Individual in the Great Society," in *A Great Society?*, B. M. Gross, Ed. (Basic Books, New York, 1968), p. 74.

[6] For a confirmation of this impression, see D. W. Brogan, "The Student Revolt," *Encounter,* July 1968, p. 23; and S. M. Lipset, "Students and Politics in Comparative Perspective," in *Daedalus,* Winter 1968, p. 1. A similar observation regarding the lack of participation in Germany by young scientists, technologists, and medical students may be found in M. Beloff, "Letter from Germany," *Encounter,* July 1968, p. 29. It seems likely that the difference in this respect among the disciplines is less important than that between the academic disciplines and the various types of professional training.

aware that unregulated initiative brought depressions and economic disaster. The potential effects of the power created by modern science and technology are so obviously dangerous to the modern world—whether in terms of the cataclysm of war or the slower but equally disastrous degradation of the environment—that it would not be surprising if even scientists should wonder whether we have been reduced to these dangers by the reductionism of their system of thought.

Most scientists try to avoid thinking about this basic problem very much because they are apt just now to worry more about the reaction than the rebellion. For the reaction touches sensitive budgetary nerves in anyone who is a laboratory director or a department chairman or even an aspirant to a fellowship.

I think this choice is a mistake. The reaction is a tolerable discomfort, the rebellion a fundamental challenge—and a challenge that poses problems scientists should think about critically rather than dismiss with contempt.

It is easy and misleading to blame the reaction on the Vietnam war and therefore to sympathize with the antimilitary sentiments of the rebellion. But this view overlooks the facts that two earlier wars produced more money and autonomy, not less, for science, and that the civilian agencies of government (including those with some of the most generous and humane purposes) have been more likely than the military to insist that research funds be spent on practical problems, and that they be distributed more evenly among universities and regions.

Indeed, it seems to me that the reaction mainly uses the war as an excuse, and it is hard to see how the reaction could have been so long delayed. In slowing down the rise in appropriations, congressmen were reacting naturally to the projection of curves on the budgetary graphs that lumped basic science together with engineering development. In emphasizing application, they responded to the salesmanship of scientists who told them in congressional hearings a great deal about how science would make us healthy and wealthy, and very little about how it would make us wise. And, in their avarice on behalf of their own districts and institutions, congressmen differed only in degree from scientists themselves. In these practical ways, the reaction is in the highest tradition of the English-speaking scientific world, which has always assumed that science was justified in large part by its contribution to material welfare—the tradition of Francis Bacon, who caught cold and died while trying to learn how to refrigerate poultry, and of the Royal Society, with its initial interest in "Manufactures, Mechanick practices, Engynes, and Inventions," and of Ben Franklin's American Philosophical Society, "held at Philadelphia for promoting useful knowledge."

But the rebellion is a different matter. It is the first international radical political movement for two or three centuries (I am tempted to say since Francis Bacon) that does not have material progress as its purpose. Far from proposing to use science and technology to improve the material welfare of the poor, it rejects technological progress as a political goal. Far from calling on government to distribute the fruits of technology more equitably, it denounces big organization in government and business indiscriminately. For three centuries science has worked on the comfortable assumption that it could pursue fundamental truth and at the same time contribute to human welfare and humane values. Since Bacon, revolutionary leaders have accepted this assumption and considered science to be in the vanguard of political progress. But now the rebels say that science, by its intrinsic nature, has reduced itself to an inhumane mode of thought, and our polity to an engine of oppression, and so they conclude that humane feelings demand the overthrow of the whole system, if necessary by an irrational rebellion.

Even though many of the young rebels call themselves Marxists, the guiding spirit of the rebellion is as much in conflict with Marxism-Leninism as with Western democracy—perhaps more so, because communism believes that science can provide the basis for political values, and the New Left considers the degree of scientific influence over our political system a disaster. Communism is a system of rigorous discipline and meticulous dogma; the New Left has neither. It is more like a religious heresy, renouncing a concern for power and wealth, than like a political movement, and even its emphasis on drugs and sex is reminiscent of the antinomian rebellions of the middle ages.[7]

The rebels are right when they complain of the symptoms of sickness in modern society—symptoms that afflict the Communist as well as the capitalist world. We have not learned how to make our technological skills serve the purposes of humanity, or how to free men from servitude to the purposes of technological bureau-

---

[7] On the distinction between the new rebels and Communists, see P. Goodman, "The Black Flag of Anarchism," New York *Times Magazine,* July 14, 1968; on its antinomian overtones, see D. P. Moynihan, "Nirvana," *American Scholar,* Autumn 1967. For a fuller account of the medieval rebellions, see N. Cohn, *The Pursuit of the Millennium* (Essential Books, New York 1957).

cracies. But we would do well to think twice before agreeing that these symptoms are caused by reductionism in modern science, or that they would be cured by violence in the name of brotherhood or love.

As the first step toward a diagnosis of our problem, we must admit that, as scientists, we have not been very clear in the past as to the basic relation of science to politics. When the rebels charge science with destroying freedom by subverting moral values or controlling policy decisions, we cannot dismiss the charge by repeating the old principle that political authorities determine policies on the basis of philosophical or moral values, and that scientific knowledge only tells us how best to carry out those policies—that is, tells us the best means to those ends. This reply will no longer do. In Marxist countries official dogma holds that science determines the basic values, and in America many scientists have been hypocritical on the issue; they use the old formula as a defense for public relations, even though they realize that science has, and must have, a profound influence on values, and are inclined to believe that science could provide the answers to policy questions if politicans were not so stupid.

It is high time that we become more critical—instead of hypocritical—in facing this fundamental issue. As we do so, we should remember that the relationship of science to politics has at least three aspects. They are knowledge, institutions, and policy.

Let us consider knowledge first. The way people think about politics is surely influenced by what they implicitly believe about what they know and how they know it—that is, about how they acquire knowledge, and why they believe. In traditional political systems—a few still persist in the world—issues were decided on the basis of immemorial custom, religious tradition, or the divinely sanctioned will of a ruler. Before this could change to a system in which elected assemblies could consider facts—perhaps even on the basis of scientific evidence—and then deliberately enact policies, a revolution in the nature of knowledge had to take place. That long slow revolution went along with the progress of science, and the main line of progress has of course been that of *reduction*—the change from systems of thought that were concrete but complex and disorderly, and that often confused what *is* with what ought to be, to a system of more simple and general and provable concepts.

It is clear, as Mr. Marcuse points out, that this reduction of knowledge to its abstract and quantitative bases is a calculating

approach to reality that makes no allowance for humane sentiments or moral judgments. It is also clear that serious practical
politicians who disapprove in theory of Mr. Marcuse may agree
with him in practice, and may fear that reductionism will impair
our political responsibility. For example, leading candidates for
political office have charged that the Supreme Court's weakness
for sociology and statistics is eroding the moral fiber of the nation,
and congressmen in committee hearings have expressed concern
that the new mathematical techniques of systems analysis may
dominate our strategic decisions.

But it is not at all clear to me that reductionism is a threat to
political freedom or responsibility. In their practical political behavior, scientists are not quite so consistent or doctrinaire. To say
that science feels the need for redemption seems to me (if I may
use a technical literary term in addressing a scientific audience) a
pathetic fallacy. Science feels nothing. Scientists have feelings,
and on political issues their feelings seem to me to be just as varied and moralistic as anyone else's.

On a more theoretical level, it seems to me that reductionism
has not been pushing scientists generally toward a belief that science as such can solve the issues in which the average man is
most interested, or can determine the nature of the political system. Although other branches of science admit their growing reli-
ance on mathematics and physics, they seem no more likely than
they were a century ago—perhaps less likely—to assume that they
can solve all their problems by reducing their disciplines to
atomic or subatomic bases.

The notion that scientific advance cuts down the freedom of
the human spirit, and reduces the range of choice open to mankind, is an obsolete idea; on the contrary, every new grand
simplification opens up a new range of complex questions for exploration. Man found it hard to change from the astronomical
conception of a closed world to one of an infinite universe; the
notion that scientific advance on reductionist principles will cut
down our freedom, in either intellectual or political terms, seems
to me the result of hanging onto an obsolete and narrowly me-
chanistic nineteenth-century conception of science.

Before we decide that the remedy for our present disorders is to
put moral sentiments back into science, it may help us to remember that science is not the only mode of thought which has gone
through a reductionist trend and then found that the simpler abstract concepts provided less specific guides to action than one

might hope. If reduction is the change from complex and disorderly ideas that confuse what *is* with what men would like, to more simple and general (if not always provable) beliefs, the change in theology from polytheism to monotheism was reductionist, and so was the change from the Ten Commandments and the intricacies of the Talmud to the simpler commandment to love God and your neighbor as yourself. And in theology, as in science, reductionism brought a shocking denial that natural laws were in harmony with human righteousness: "for He makes His sun rise on the evil and on the good, and sends rain on the just and on the unjust."

If science can learn any lesson from theology on this point, it is that reductionism does not cause the political problem, nor can it solve it. For the simple law of love was taken, over the centuries, as the antinomians' justification for the abandonment of all moral laws as well as for the rigorous moralism of Calvinist Geneva and the Spanish Inquisition, for the anarchy of the hermits and the Ranters as well as for the ruthless tyranny of the Byzantine emperors.

The trouble with reductionism, as far as politics is concerned, is not that it gives *all* the answers to the important issues but that it gives hardly any. I suspect that the current attacks on science come less from those who have always feared it than from those who were frustrated when they tried to put too much faith in it. To them, it was another god that failed. Science is quite impartial in debunking idols—its proudest claim is that it is always debunking itself.

If we are concerned with political freedom we cannot concern ourselves only with the theory of knowledge. Reductionism in science is not the real problem. We do harm not by reducing science to its mathematical bases but only by reducing men to a concern for nothing but science. As we ponder the political status of science it may help us to recall that freedom of religion resulted less directly from the reformation of theological thought than from the competition of dissenting churches and from changes in the political system itself. That brings us to the second aspect of the relation of science to politics—institutions. And so we must face the question whether a scientific and technological establishment, or the aggregate of scientific and technological institutions, is a threat to freedom, especially because of its intimate alliance with a bureaucracy managed on scientific principles.

At the same time that science has been reducing knowledge to fewer and simpler general concepts, society has been expanding the number and the variety of the institutions that develop and apply that knowledge. From the traditional community ruled by a priest-king, combining in one set of institutions political power and the preservation and transmission of traditional knowledge, has been evolved the complex structure of modern society. This process of *specialization* has separated from the center of political power various more or less autonomous institutions that are then permitted to operate according to their own functional requirements.

The fundamental basis for the freedom of specialized institutions is that the public recognizes that they can do their particular job better for society if they are not immediately controlled by those who hold ultimate political power. The business corporation can be more efficient, the scientific laboratory can be more innovative, if it is granted substantial autonomy. And the same principle works, within limits, within the formal structure of government itself; it is the justification not only for a nonpolitical judiciary but for a professional diplomatic or military service and for a civil service run on merit principles.

But the free institutions' role in serving society is not merely to be more efficient within their specific functions. It is also to serve as a source of independent criticism of those who hold power. It is, in short, to prevent centralization of authority. Scientific and technological competence is so necessary today for understanding the complex programs of government that scientists who are employed by institutions outside the immediate executive hierarchy have an important role to play in criticizing official policy and checking centralized power.

If they are to play that role, they must be close enough to the big issues to understand them, but they must have enough independence of action to speak without fear of damage to their status or careers. But how can they be closely enough involved without sacrificing their independence? Logically, the dilemma seems absolute. The judiciary cannot get into the fight over civil rights without being accused of usurping the power of the legislature. Churchmen cannot preach social justice without coming under political attack. And scientists cannot get involved as consultants to government, or universities accept contracts for applied research, without being accused of prostituting themselves to political power.

Obviously, an institution can be more surely free of political influence if it deals with pure science and shuns the competition for power. But absolute purity is a delusion. It is a delusion partly because every institution needs material support and cannot isolate itself from the society that supports it. Even more important, absolute purity is a delusion because it is a refusal to serve one of the essential purposes of an independent and nonpolitical institution, that of providing some independent standards of criticism of public policy.

You can resolve the dilemma in one of two ways. If your approach is doctrinaire, you can try to resolve it by forcing the competing elements together within a single institutional system. Politics and religion are obviously related, so church and state cannot be separated. Economic and political power are related, so the state must own the means of production. Political decisions must be made scientifically, so science must provide a theory of politics and a methodology for deciding public issues, and then must be controlled by the state. That way, of course, lies totalitarianism.

But if you are sensitive to the danger that any single doctrine or theory may be perverted in the interests of power, you will take a more pluralistic and more discriminating approach. You can distinguish between different types and degrees of political involvement on the part of nonpolitical institutions; even more important, you can distinguish between what it is prudent and effective for an institution to do and what that institution's members are free to do in their capacity as private citizens or as participants in other institutions. (I hope it was this line of reasoning, more than any fundamental distaste for politics, that led the American Physical Society to abstain from political resolutions.) A member of a church may also be a member of a political party, and need not expect both institutions to play the same roles. A professor in the university may also be a consultant to a research corporation or a government agency and a member of a scientific society. His freedom to play different roles in these different institutions—and to defend the autonomy of each institution against the others—is one of the most important safeguards of freedom in modern society.

Independent institutions are not, of course, the fundamental basis of freedom. Their independence comes from their roots in the way people think and what people believe. You will not want to let a university or scientific society function free from governmental direction if you think its work will immediately determine the major political decisions of the day.

We believe in free academic and scientific institutions not be-cause we consider them irrelevant to practical political concerns but because we tacitly understand that their type of knowedge does not directly and clearly provide the answer to any complex political issue. Does this contradict the power of the reductionist approach that has given science its great effectiveness in dealing with practical as well as theoretical problems? I think not. Reduc-tion in knowledge and specialization in the definition of institu-tions and their roles go hand in hand. Just as the zoologist or bo-tanist may admit the great contributions that biochemistry and biophysics have made to biology and still see that tremendous problems remain at the more complex levels of organization, to be dealt with by different modes of thought, so the politician (and his scientific adviser) may make full use of analytical science and yet be left with difficult problems of synthetic judgment in making his decision.

The type of thought that, in the style of the Marxist dialectic, rejects traditional dogma in favor of reductionist science, and then tries to make science the basis of a new dogma, is not reduction-ist, but only dogmatic. Reductionist knowledge provides no ratio-nale, and no rationalization, for centralized authority. Like the specialized institutions in which it is developed, it tends to be a check on general political power, an impediment to sovereignty rather than a tool of tyranny. Reductionism and specialization have indeed biased our political system toward some of the practi-cal abuses of power that the rebels deplore, but they have done so not by creating a centralized system. On the contrary, they have so greatly strengthened the productivity and power of specialized concentrations of economic wealth and technological competence that our general constitutional system is incapable of controlling them.

This brings me to the third aspect of the relation of science to politics—policy, or the definition of public purpose by responsible authority.

As a complex civilization has developed its system of knowledge by *reduction*, and its institutions by *specialization*, its policy has moved over the centuries toward *generalization*. The purposes of politics have broadened from the tribe to the feudal community to the nation, and are beginning dimly to be perceived in terms of world interests; they have broken down the rigid lines of caste and class, and are beginning to transcend differences of race. With almost as much difficulty, the general purposes of responsible politics must now try to control the specialized functions and institutions of government in the general interest.

This movement toward political concern for all men, and toward the sharing of power with them, was perhaps made possible by the other two aspects of politics—the reduction of knowledge to a more effective scientific basis and the transfer of specialized social functions away from the general system of sovereignty to institutions less concerned with power and more with material welfare. Without new techniques of communication to let men share ideas from place to place, and new techniques of production to give them enough material goods to share, the broadening of political concern would have been impossible.

I am also inclined to believe that this broadening of public purpose was encouraged by that earlier form of reductionism, the theological reductionism that slowly and partially converted religion from a complex of local superstitions to a broader and simpler faith. As far as the general evolution of public policy is concerned, the processes of reduction toward simpler and more fundamental ideas in science and in religion have had similar effects.

But I must qualify this assertion of faith with a cynical concession. Science has an intellectual advantage over religion: a reductionist science comes out with grand generalities in the form of mathematical equations that the layman reveres because he cannot understand them; a reductionist religion comes out with grand generalities in the form of platitudes that only embarrass the layman because he thinks he understands them all too well. For example, the tough-minded ghost writers for one of our leading politicans, I am told, were always annoyed at being required to put into each of his speeches a reference to what they call BOMFOG—their derisive acronym for the Brotherhood of Man and the Fatherhood of God.

As scientists we are apt to take pride in this distinction: even pious people, unless they are simpleminded, can laugh at BOMFOG, but nobody makes fun of $E = mc^2$. But such pride is ill-founded. If we ridicule BOMFOG, it is not because we do not believe in God or human brotherhood; indeed, the more we believe, the more we are likely to see that such belief does not solve practical political problems, and that a politican who appeals to such abstractions for self-serving purposes is absurd. It seems obvious to us that $E = mc^2$, while it may be the fundamental equation of atomic energy, does not tell us even how to make atomic bombs, much less how to get international agreement against their use; no politican would win votes by using a basic scientific formula as an incantation.

But this is a parochial idea. We may not make a political slogan out of a scientific concept, but others do. We find it hard to imagine the political quarrels that took place in Russia over the scientific philosophy of Mach or Einstein[8] , or to understand how Soviet scientists give credit for their discoveries to Marxist-Leninist doctrine, and Chinese scientists give credit to the thoughts of Mao. But, at least in Russia, the more sophisticated scientists react to the scientific dialectic the way we react to BOMFOG—with an appropriate mixture of reverence and ridicule.

If, as Americans, we have escaped the Communist habit of muddling scientific theory with political practice, we cannot claim too much credit. We had been inoculated, so to speak, by the English-speaking historical culture against the translation of the great simple truths into practical policy. We had tried that under Puritanism—under Oliver Cromwell and John Winthrop—and had had enough. So Jefferson, as clearly as Burke, was against the Worship of Reason in the French Revolution, and T. H. Huxley opposed Comte's conversion of science into a political dogma—the dogma (which Lenin later enforced) that diversity of opinion was no more to be tolerated in politics than in chemistry.

With respect to knowledge and institutions, politics becomes more civilized as it moves in the analytical direction—toward reduction and specialization. But policy is a synthetic process: generalization requires more than analytical skills. Indeed, it demands special care with respect to analysis and specialization, not to prevent but to control and use them, and not to be misled by thinking that any one type of basic knowledge or institutional skill will solve the problems of a complex political organization. Reduction is the prescription for basic knowledge, but reductionism—taken neat—can be poisonous for policy.

America is not entirely free of the idea that some scientific formula will guarantee our political salvation. The president of the AAAS gets frequent letters outlining such schemes. If I were not too honest to steal such secrets from their authors, I could tell you how to provide unlimited energy without cost, and thus eliminate poverty, and how to remove all feelings of hatred and aggression, and thus guarantee universal peace. But it is typical, I

---

[8] D. Joravsky, *Soviet Marxism and Natural Science* (Columbia University Press, New York 1961).

think, that most of those American scientists whom their colleagues consider crackpots are interested, not in basic theory or ideology, but in gadgetry—in finding gimmicks to cure the world's ills.

This taste for the so-called "practical," of course, the crackpot shares with his fellow countrymen. In America, we are not dialectical materialists, only practical materialists. We do not convert our science into political faith—only our technology into business profits. We do not make our political theory into a revolutionary crusade; we only assume that technical assistance and more calories will make peasants contented, and that B-52's are cost-effective in pacifying jungle villages, and that welfare payments will remove racial hate in our urban ghettos.

The philosophers who blame such blunders on scientific reductionism—who believe that the mathematical and fundamental approach to knowledge is the basic flaw in modern politics—are themselves reducing the problem to a more abstract level than is useful. We get into political difficulties less because our method of knowing is wrong than because we put too much confidence in specialized programs and institutions and show too little concern for the processes of government that relate those specialties to general policy. It is true, of course, that many political controversies are over meaningless issues or insoluble problems, and new "technological fixes" [as Alvin Weinberg called them[9]] are often useful ways out. But this approach will work best if it is tried by some responsible authority who is thinking about the problem as a whole, as a part of the general political system; it can be disastrous if it is peddled to politicians by a special interest in the business or bureaucratic world that is concerned only with increasing its own profits or professional influence.

To deal with any public issue of any consequence, we need to bring science and politics together in all their aspects. We need more precise knowledge. We need more effective institutions. And we need both the will and the competence required for the synthesis of general policy. Of these three, the most difficult is the policy aspect, for generalization cannot be reduced to precise techniques, or delegated to a specialized profession or institution.

But synthesis and analysis are not incompatible processes of

---

[9] A. M. Weinberg, "Social Problems and National Socio-Technical Institutes," in *Applied Science and Technological Progress* (National Academy of Sciences, Washington, D.C., 1967) (available from the Government Printing Office, Washington, D.C.).

thought, any more than facts and values are totally separated from each other. The new techniques for the analysis of complex systems developed by mathematicians, physicists, economists, and other scientists have become the most powerful tools for the critical study of the components of policy, and hence for the development of general policies.

You cannot synthesize a sensible policy unless you have first analyzed the problem. Reductionism is not the enemy of humane political thought; it is the first practical step toward it. To take both steps is hard work, and requires the scientist to share the complexities and uncertainties that harass the politician, and to join in compromises that offend the purist in either science or morals.

From these uncertainties, the human mind is tempted to seek refuge in phony reductionism—the new rebels reducing the complexities of policies to the simplicities of moral feeling, the scientists taking shelter in the purity of research. Both these paths to purity are like BOMFOG—you feel obliged to respect them, but the trouble comes in putting them into effect.

What is wrong with the purists, on both the moral and scientific sides, is not that their objectives are evil but that they tackle the problem at the wrong level of abstraction. In the United States we are in no danger of using science to deny political freedom, or of rejecting BOMFOG in favor of a theology that would support a caste system. But there is a real danger, it seems to me, that the two types of purists—the scientist and the moralist—will withdraw from public affairs and leave responsible political authority without support against the powerful combination of technological skill and special industrial and bureaucratic interests.

For example, take the Institute for Defense Analysis. IDA is a prime target for the new rebels; to them it symbolizes the corruption of the purity of scholarly institutions by military power. IDA is also not very popular among theoretical scientists; it represents the kind of applied work with government support that does little for pure science. Yet IDA was not created in the interest of irresponsible military power. On the contrary, it was a part of the effort to give responsible civilian political authority the ability to control the competing special military interests. The constitutional authority had always been there, but without the special knowledge or the special institutional controls needed to make that power real, and hence to make possible the synthesis of the independent missions of our Army, Navy, and Air Force into a general policy.

Even before 1961, IDA was one of the tools the Secretary of Defense used as an aid in the synthesis of general policy. There was no antithesis here, in either theory or practice, between, on the one hand, reductionist knowledge and specialized staff institutions and, on the other, an effort to make general policy supreme over special technological interests.

In opposition we saw officers from the most powerful and independent segment of American bureaucracy, the career military services, supported by industrial clients who disapproved on principle of any not-for-profit corporation, rise to denounce the whiz kids in the research corporations and the Office of the Secretary of Defense. The use of mathematical and scientific techniques to deal with military policies, such as strategic plans and weapons systems, was a cold and calculating and heartless approach, they said to what ought to be an affair of the heart—a vocation to be followed on moral rather than quantitative principles. Or as Admiral Rickover, put it[10], "The Greeks at Thermopylae and at Salamis would not have stood up to the Persians had they had cost effectiveness people to guide them."

I find much of Admiral Rickover's critique of our overemphasis on technology and bureaucracy refreshing—especially coming from an Admiral. What other Admiral would ask[11], "Does man exist for the economy or does the economy exist for man?" and charge that the "larger bureaucratically administered organizations" in which most Americans now work, as a result of the Industrial and Scientific revolutions, "are in every respect the obverse of a free society"?

But I doubt that this rhetoric, which ought to endear the Admiral to the new rebels, really advances our understanding of the nature of freedom in modern society. Whenever a powerful special interest begins to appeal to basic moral or philosophical principles in an effort to escape subordination to general policy, we are entitled to be skeptical if not cynical. The new purists in

---

[10] Testimony, May 11, 1966, on Department of Defense appropriations for 1967, before the House Committee on Appropriations Subcommittee on the Department of Defense, 89th Congress, 2nd Session, part 6. I do not argue here that the systems analysts have been right, only that they have been attacked for the wrong reasons.

[11] H. G. Rickover, "Technology and the Citizen," address before the Publishers' Lunch Club, New York, January 7, 1965.

morals and in science who join with rebellious segments of the
Air Force and Navy in attacks on IDA and the Office of the Secretary of Defense are in much the same position as the contemporary religious fundamentalists who become allies of reactionary
industrialists by seeing social security, the income tax, and the
regulation of business as the work of Godless communism.

In the current state of the world the question whether scientific
societies should pass political resolutions is a trivial tactical issue;
the community of science needs to look to its broader strategy.

In this strategy the idea of scientific purity—of avoiding involvement in political compromise—was once a useful notion. It
helped to free science from the teleology of the earlier philosophers, and scientific institutions from the obligation to work on
practical problems as practical men defined them.

This reductionist strategy, while protecting the freedom of
scientific institutions, did not slow down the practical application
of science in political systems that had shaken off feudal or bureaucratic constraints in an era of optimism about material progress.

But the new rebels are right in thinking that that era of
optimism—that blind faith in automatic progress—has ended.

That optimism misled Western thought in two ways for a century or two after the Enlightenment.

After the French Revolution there spread eastward through
Europe and Asia the optimistic notion, stemming from the Enlightenment, that science, by perfecting our philosophy and our
values, will teach us how to revolutionize society and eliminate
the corruptions of politics; in its Marxist form, that notion proposed to let the State itself wither away.

After the American Revolution, the pragmatic West came to a
less doctrinaire but almost euqally optimistic conclusion: that the
advancement of science would lead to the progress of technology
and industry and an increase in material property, and to a
withering away of governmental interference with private initiative.

The rebels are right in being pessimistic about such notions. I
do not think they are even pessimistic enough. To me it seems
possible that the new amount of technological power let loose in
an overcrowded world may overload any system we might devise
for its control; the possibility of a complete and apocalyptic end of
civilization cannot be dismissed as a morbid fantasy.

And the rebels are far too romantically optimistic in their remedy. Mere rebellion to destroy the existing order—mere purposeless violence to upset the establishment—assumes that those who gain power by violence will be nobler and more generous in purpose than those who now try to hold together the delicate web of civilized institutions.

If scientists wish to maintain the freedom of their science and, at the same time, play a rational and effective role in politics, they need to adopt a strategy that is more modest in its hopes for the perfectibility of mankind and more pessimistically alert to the dangers of power—not only power that is obviously political but the power that calls itself private as well. They should start by acknowledging in theory what in the United States we have always taken for granted as a practical matter: that reductionism in scientific knowledge, while it may provide the fundamental advances in scientific theory, does not alone provide the answers in the realm of policy, or the basis for a political ideology.

If this point is clear, no one will need to take seriously the charge that the scientific mode of thought is a fundamental threat to humane values. The threat comes not from the theoretical reductionism of science but from the very pragmatic reductionism which assumes that applications of advanced technology are automatically beneficial, or that we are always justified in granting special concentrations of technological and industrial power freedom from central political authority.

If everyone understands that sciense, as such, does not control policy decisions, scientists will then be free—and, in my view, will be morally obliged—to devote their synthetic as well as their analytic skills to the formulation and criticism of policies by which the nation may control technology and apply science in the public interest.

In an era which is beginning to be alert to the threats posed by modern technology to the human environment, the role of science in politics is no longer merely to destroy the irrational and superstitious beliefs which were once the foundation of oppressive authority. It is, rather, to help clarify our public values, define our policy options, and assist responsible political leaders in the guidance and control of the powerful forces which have been let loose on this troubled planet.

V

CAMPUS REVOLTS

15. A FOOLPROOF SCENARIO FOR STUDENT REVOLTS

John R. Searle

John R. Searle is Professor of Philosophy at the University of California at Berkeley and formerly administrative assistant to the Chancellor.

IN SEVERAL YEARS of fighting for, fighting against and simply observing student revolts in the United States and Europe, I have been struck by certain recurring patterns of action and internationally common styles in the rhetoric of confrontation. Leaving out student revolts in Turkey, Czechoslovakia and Spain—all of which have rather special features—and confining ourselves to the United States and the advanced industrial democracies of Western Europe, it seems to me to be possible to discern certain family resemblances in the successful campus rebellions. In general, successful student revolts in these countries tend to occur in three identifiable phases or stages.

In the beginning, the revolt always has—at least in the mythology of local administrations—the same two features: there is only "a very small minority" of troublemakers, and "they have no legitimate grievances." These conditions, I have found in visits to

Reprinted, with permission, from the *New York Times*, December 29, 1968.

campuses all over the United States and Western Europe, are, by common administrative consent, universal. They are also the reasons why "it won't happen here"; that is, they are always the reasons why "this campus won't become another Berkeley" or, lately, "another Columbia." I have discovered, incidentally, that a legitimate grievance is defined as one in which the students win. If you win, it turns out that your grievance was legitimate all along; if you lose, then alas for you, you had no legitimate grievance.

"The small minority with no legitimate grievance" starts out by selecting an issue. Curiously, almost any old issue will do. At Berkeley it concerned the campus rules on political activity; at Columbia it was the location of a gym; at Nanterre, a protest at the offices of T.W.A. and the Chase Manhattan Bank; at Essex it was a visit by a representative of the Ministry of Defense, and many places have used recruiters from the Dow Chemical Company and other variations on the theme of the war in Vietnam.

Almost any issue will do, provided it has two crucial features: (1) It must be an issue that can be somehow related to a Sacred Topic. In the United States, the Sacred Topics are the First Amendment, race and the war in Vietnam—in that order, though I believe that in the last year race has been pulling ahead of the First Amendment. (In France, *la révolution* is itself a Sacred Topic.) If the issue can be related to a Sacred Topic, then the majority of students, even though they would not do anything about it themselves, will at least be sympathetic to the demonstrators' position in the early stages. (2) The issue has to be one on which the university authorities cannot give in. The authorities must initially refuse your demands. If you win, you have lost. If the authorities give in to your demands there is nothing for it but to pick another issue and start all over.

The demand, therefore, has to be presented in the maximally confrontationalist style. This usually requires a demonstration of some sort, and sit-ins are not uncommon at this stage, though a "mass meeting" or march to present your demands will often do as well. The number of people in Stage One is usually small, but they serve to "educate" the campus, to "dramatize" the issue. It is a good idea, though not always necessary in Stage One, to violate as many campus rules or civil laws as you probably can, in as visible a manner as you possibly can, during the initial presentation of your demands. In other words, you should challenge the authorities to take disciplinary action against you, and generally they will oblige by suspending a few of your leaders.

Stage One closes when the administration rejects your demands, admonishes you to better behavior in the future and, if possible, brings some of your leaders to university discipline for rule violations in the demonstrations. Berkeley 1964 and Paris 1968 are the models of a well-managed Stage One. At Berkeley, one of the weaknesses in the issue of Eldridge Cleaver's invitation to lecture in an accredited course on racism is that university discipline has never been effectively tied to the substantive question, as it was in 1964. True, the regents, in ruling that Cleaver could give only one lecture in a course for university credit rather than the ten for which he'd been invited, did "censure" several members, but no students were involved in rule violations in Stage One, and it has subsequently proved very difficult, in spite of hard rule-violating efforts in Stage Two, to meld university discipline into the Cleaver issue.

In Stage Two the original issue is transformed so that the structure of authority in the university is itself the target. This is achieved by the following method. The fact that the university rejected the original demands and, even more, the fact that the university disciplined people for rule violations in making those demands are offered as conclusive proof that the university is the real enemy of the forces of truth and justice on the Sacred Topic. Thus, if the original demand was related to the war in Vietnam, the fact that the university disciplined a student for rule violation in making the demand is proof that the university is really working for the war and that it is out to "crush dissent." If, for example, the demonstrations were against Dow Chemical Company recruiters on campus, the fact of university discipline proves that the university is really the handmaiden (or whore) of the military-industrial complex. And the fact that the university refuses to cancel plans for the gym (Columbia) or does cancel plans for the Cleaver course (Berkeley) demonstrates that the university is really a racist institution. Why would anybody try to discipline our fellow students and refuse our just demands if they weren't racists, warmongers or dissent-crushers, as the case might be? And, indeed, can't we now see that the university is really just a part of much larger forces of oppression (imperialism, racism) in our American society? In the face of such proof, only the most callous or evil would fail to join us in our struggle to make this a livable university, a place where we can be truly free.

If this attempt to make the university the primary target is successful, the number of people involved in Stage Two will increase enormously. Large numbers of students who will not demonstrate illegally against the war in Vietnam or for free speech will demonstrate illegally if they can demonstrate against someone's being disciplined for illegally demonstrating against the war in Vietnam or for free speech. The original issue is made much more personal, local and "relevant" to their life as students by being redefined, with the university authorities as the main enemy. The war in Vietnam is a long way off, but Grayson Kirk's office is just across the campus. This redefinition of the issue so that the university authorities become the main target is crucial to the success of the entire operation and is the essential characteristic of a successful Stage Two.

Speeches, leaflets, meetings and articles in student papers all serve to create a certain rhetorical climate in which charges that would normally be thought to verge on the preposterous can gain currency and acceptability. Thus, the president of the university is a racist, the board of regents is trying to run the university for its personal profit, the university is fundamentally an agent of the Pentagon and so on. Anyone who remembers the witch hunts of the 1950s will recognize the distinctive features of this rhetorical atmosphere: the passionate conviction that our side is right and the other side not only wrong but evil, the urgency of the issue, the need for all of us to stand united against the threat (of Communism or the military-industrial complex, depending on your choice of era) and, most important, the burning sincerity of all but the most intelligent.

To accuse a professor of doing secret war research for the Defense Department nowadays has the same delicious impact that accusations of secret Communist party membership did a decade ago. And one even reads the same sort of nervous, apologetic prose on the part of the accused: " 'I was consultant [to the Institute for Defense Analysis] from 1964-67, when I went to meetings and listened and offered comments; however, you will not find my name on the reports,' he said" (The Daily Californian, Tuesday, Nov. 5, 1968, p. 1). The ultimate in such accusations—leaving out such horrendous charges as "He worked for the C.I.A."—are "He's a racist" and "He is in favor of the war." We are, incidentally, going to see a great deal more of this left-McCarthyism in the next few years on college campuses, especially in the United States.

In Stage Two certain new and crucial elements enter the fray—television and the faculty. It sounds odd to describe the jobs television does but here they are: it provides a leader and it dignifies the proceedings. The mechanisms by which television provides the movement with a leader are not generally well-understood. It looks like the movement chooses a leader and he addressed the TV cameras on its behalf. But that is rarely what happens; in fact, that almost never happens.

What happens is that among the many speakers who appear at rallies and such, some are more telegenic than others; and the TV reporters and cameramen, who can only use a small amount of footage anyway, are professional experts at picking the one who will make the most interesting news shots. The man they pick then becomes the leader or spokesman or symbol of the movement. Of course, his selection has to be approved by the movement, so any TV selection is subject to ratification by the crowd. If they don't like him, the TV people have to find somebody else, but among the many leaders who are acceptable to the demonstrators, television plays an important role in the eventual success of one or another.

Thus Mario Savio in Berkley, Daniel Cohn-Bendit in Paris and Mark Rudd at Columbia were people with relatively little leadership position prior to Stage One, but who, as a result of their own qualities and the fact that the television people chose them to present as leaders, were elevated to the status of leaders, at least symbolically. Both Savio and Rudd have complained of this television exaggeration. Actually, Cohn-Bendit is the purest case of mass publicity as a factor in selecting a leader, for Jacques Sauvageot, the leader of the student union, and Alain Geismar, the head of the teachers' union, were both authentic campus leaders and organizers well before Stage One ever got going, but neither is much good on TV, so neither ever attained Cohn-Bendit's symbolic stature. In a sense, the fact that television plays such an important role in the selection of the leader doesn't much matter because it is a feature of this type of political movement that leaders don't lead (they may manipulate, but lots of people who are not "leaders" do that as well); unfortunately it would take me another article to explain why this is so.

In a crazy kind of way, television also dignifies the proceedings. If you are at a demonstration at noon and you can go home and watch yourself on the 6 o'clock news, it suddenly means that the noon behavior is lifted out of the realm of juvenile shenanigans and becomes genuine historical stuff. If you are there on the box it must be pretty serious, an authentic revolutionary event.

This is a McLuhanite generation, raised with a feel for publicity in general and TV in particular. When I was an undergraduate, if you got kicked out of school you went somewhere else and tried to forget about it; nowadays you would immediately call a TV news conference and charge that you did not get due process. As a news medium, television requires the visually exciting, and campus demonstrations are ideal telegenic events; they are dramatic, colorful, often violent, and in slack moments the cameras can rest on the bearded, barefoot hippies or the good-looking, long-haired girls. In return for useful footage, the media men provide the dignity and self-respect that ordinary people derive from mass publicity.

It is very important in Stage Two that a few faculty members side with the demonstrators "on the issues." In general, they will not directly condone rule violations, but by supporting the issues of Stage One they add a stamp of approval to the whole enterprise and thus have the effect of indirectly excusing the rule violations: "It is unfortunate that there should be any disruption of the university, but it really is awful that the administration should kick poor Smith out just for sitting peacefully and nonviolently on the dean's desk for a few hours, especially when Smith was only trying to end racism and the war in Vietnam."

More important, the approval of faculty members provides a source of security and reinforcement of convictions. An undergraduate engaging in a disruption of university operations is not (at least, not yet) engaging in a conventional and established form of political behavior. He feels deeply insecure, and the stridency of his rhetoric should not conceal from us the depth of his insecurity. The apparent passionate convictions of most university demonstrators are in fact terribly fragile, and when away from the crowd many of them are fairly easily talked out of their wildest fantasies. A few faculty members can provide security and reinforcement, and are therefore a great aid in recruiting more student support. Old-fashioned people, Freudians and such, would say that the student needs the faculty member to play the role of an older sibling in his revolt against the administration-parent.

At the end of Stage Two, there is a large-scale demonstration against the university on the issue of Stage One as transformed by the rhetorical impact of Stage Two. In the United States it takes the form of a large sit-in, though this has recently been developing into the seizure ("liberation") of a building, complete with barricaded doors and windows. (In Paris, it was also a matter of building street barricades, but street barricades are a French tradition, not easily exportable, that somehow seems to survive; the survival is aided by the presence of small cars that can be used as building material.) When the sit-in or seizure occurs, the university authorities are strongly inclined to—and usually do—call out the police to arrest the people who are sitting in. When that happens, if all has gone according to the scenario, we enter Stage Three, and we enter it with a vengeance.

The first characteristic of Stage Three is an enormous and exhilarating feeling of revulsion against the calling of the police. The introduction of hundreds of policemen on the campus is regarded as the ultimate crime that any university administration can commit, and a properly led and well-organized student movement will therefore direct all of its efforts in Stages One and Two to creating a situation in which the authorities feel they have no choice but to call the police. Large numbers of faculty members who have so far watched nervously from the sidelines, vaguely sympathetic with the students' rhetoric but unwilling to condone the rule violations, are suddenly liberated. They are rejuvenated by being able to side with the forces of progress against the forces of authority; the anxieties of Stages One and Two are released in a wonderful surge of exhilaration: we can hate the administration for calling the cops instead of having to tut-tut at the students for their bad behavior. On the students' side, there is a similar euphoria. In Berkeley, the student health service reported in 1964 a sharp decline in the number of students seeking psychological and psychiatric help during Stage Three.

In the transition to Stage Three, the more police brutality you can elicit by baiting and taunting (or the more the police are able to provide by themselves in the absence of such incitement), the better, but, as any competent leader knows, police brutality is not, strictly speaking, necessary because any large-scale mass arrest will produce accusations of police brutality no matter what happens.

In the face of the sheer horror of the police on campus, the opposition to the movement, especially the opposition among the liberal and moderate students, becomes enfeebled and usually collapses altogether. At this point, there is a general student strike with fairly strong faculty support, and quite often the campus will be completely shut down.

Furthermore, the original demands of Stage One are now only a small part of a marvelously escalated series of demands. Sometimes, as in Paris, the Stage One demands may be pretty much forgotten. Who, for example, could remember on the barricades what Cohn-Bendit was agitating for back in Stage One? A typical list of Stage Three demands would comprise the following:

The president must be fired (he usually is, in fact).

There must be amnesty for all.

The university must be restructured so as to give the students a major share in all decision-making.

The administration has to be abolished, or at any rate confined to sweeping sidewalks and such.

The university must cease all cooperation with the Defense Department and other official agencies in the outside community.

Capitalism must end—now.

Society must be reorganized.

Meanwhile, interesting things are happening in the faculty: committees are meeting and drafting resolutions, alliances are being formed and petitions circulated. The faculty government, by tradition a sleepy and ill-attended body that gently hassles about parking and by-laws, is suddenly packed with record numbers of passionate and eloquent debaters. There are endless amendments and fights over the symbolism of a "whereas" clause. Great victories are won and symbolic defeats sustained. Also, in the general unhinging of Stage Three many faculty members discover all sorts of long-forgotten grievances they have against the administration. There is simply no end of good grievances; indeed, in our best universities I believe this could be one of the conditions of continued employment: if you can't think up half a dozen really good grievances against the place you are probably not intelligent enough for continued employment in a university of top caliber.

More important, deep and abiding hostilities and hatreds grow up among various factions in the faculty. Those who are active find that their political role is more important to their standing in the community than their scholarly achievement. No matter what the issues, more energy is expended on hostilities within the faculty than on battle with any nonfaculty foes, and the passionate feelings usually go far beyond those found in the democratic politics of the real world. Like nuns struggling for power in a convent, professors seem to lack the distance and detachment to see Stage Three university politics for the engagingly preposterous affair it usually is.

So now we have come from the halcyon days of Stage One, in which there was "only a small minority with no legitimate grievances," to the full-blown revolutionary ecstasy of Stage Three; the place is shut down, the president is looking for a new job and the *effective* authorities are a handful of fairly scruffy-looking and unplausible-sounding student leaders. How does it work? What is the fuel on which the mechanism functions?

Before I answer that, I need to make the usual academic qualifications about the model: it is intended only as an analytical framework and not a complete empirical generalization. Certainly, not all successful student revolts go through these three stages, and I can think of many counterexamples, and so on. Furthermore, I do not mean to imply that anybody on either side actually plans his behavior with these three stages in mind; I am not suggesting that student leaders sit in cellars asking themselves, "Are we in Stage Two yet?" Furthermore, I am not saying that the demonstrators are either in the right or in the wrong on the demands they make. Student demonstrators, like university administrators, are sometimes right, sometimes wrong; on some occasions, such as the Free Speech Movement in Berkeley, the demonstrators have, in my view been overwhelmingly in the right. I am just trying to describe a common pattern of events that has recurred in many places and with quite different issues, but it will be obvious from what I have said that I find it at least an *inefficient* method of resolving campus disputes.

Getting back to the question—What makes it work?—the unique feature of the present situation in universities is the pervasive dislike and distrust of authority. Far more students in the western democracies today—more than, say, ten years ago—hate their governments, police forces and university administrations (there are complex historical reasons for this, most of which have nothing to do with universities). I can, for example, remember when it was quite common for university presidents to be respected and admired, even on their own campuses. Now it is almost unheard of (except after they have been fired).

The strategy of a successful student movement is to unite this existing mistrust of authority with genuinely idealistic impulses on one of the Sacred Topics in such a way that assaults on university authority become a method of expressing that idealism.*

---

*In France, because universities are part of the Government, assaults on university authority are *eo ipso* assaults on the Government. In that sense, de Gaulle is a university administrator.

Each new exercise of authority then becomes further proof that the administration is an enemy of the idealism, and this serves to undermine authority even more. The transition from each stage to the next, remember, is produced by the exercise of authority, and eventually—with the use of masses of policemen—if all has gone according to plan, campus authority collapses altogether. The strategy, in short, is to pit "the students" (and not "the radicals" or "the small minority") against "the administration" in a fight that appears to concern a Sacred Topic, and then to undermine the administration by provoking exercises of authority that will serve to discredit it. The three stages, then, should be seen as a continuous progression, beginning with the creation of an issue (or issues) and ending with the collapse of authority.

The demonstrators are always puzzled by the hostility they arouse among the liberal intelligentsia outside the university. But what the demonstrators perceive as the highest idealism often looks from the outside like a mixture of vandalism and imbecilic dogmatism. Though they can convince *themselves* that, say, Columbia, Stanford and Berkeley are racist institutions, few on the outside ever accept this view.

When administrations are defeated, they almost invariably go down as a result of technical mistakes, failure to grasp the nature of the struggle they are engaged in and, most important, their own demoralization. A confident administration bent on defending intellectual values, and consequently determined to destroy the power of its essentially anti-intellectual adversary, can generally win. Victory for the administration requires a readiness to deal with each of the three stages on its own terms and certain overall strategies involving internal university reforms and the intelligent use of discipline (even including the police when it comes to the crunch). Curiously, many college administrations in America don't yet seem to perceive that they are all in this together. Like buffaloes being shot, they look on with interest when another of their number goes down, without seriously thinking that they may be next.

Arnold Beichman

Arnold Beichman, closely associated with the trade-union
movement as editor and research scholar, is now a member of
the Department of Political Science at the
University of Massachusetts.

*A state never is, nor, until mankind are vastly improved, can
hope to be, for any long time exempt from internal dissension;
for there neither is nor has ever been any state of society in
which collisions did not occur between the immediate interests
and passions of powerful sections of the people. What, then,
enables society to weather these storms, and pass through tur-
bulent times without any permanent weakening of the ties
which hold it together? Precisely this—that however important
the interests about which men fall out, the conflict does not
affect the fundamental principles of the system of social union
which happens to exist; nor threaten large portions of the
community with the subversion of that on which they have
built their calculations, and with which their hopes and aims
have become identified. But when the questioning of these
fundamental principles is not an occasional disease, but the
habitual condition of the body politic; and when all the violent
animosities are called forth, which spring naturally from such
a situation, the state is virtually in a position of civil war; and
can never long remain free from it in act and fact. . . .*
—John Stuart Mill, *Coleridge* (1840)

THE LEAST IMPORTANT question facing Columbia University this
spring is whether or not another shutdown will take place; certainly a student attempt will be made to prevent the University
from functioning, and thus to transform it into the "East Coast
San Francisco State." Columbia's acting president has stated that
he would not "allow" a major disruption but has declined to say
in advance what he would do to prevent it. The most important

Reprinted, with permission, from *Encounter*, May, 1969.

question (and not merely for Columbia but for most of the large prestigious American universities) is what to do about the latest fact of American politics and culture: the rise of a cohesive radical student movement, unrelated to adult and traditional politics, as a *permanent* apparatus on the American campus.

What creates this cohesion is not some highly structured political philosophy or platform. Rather the cohesion comes from a mood, the self-validating premises of youth, a battery of marching slogans, and a life-style and culture exemplified in particular kinds of clothes, hair-do's, eyeglasses, music, and vocabulary which has altered psychological distances. Above all, this cohesion is strengthened by the certainty that whenever a university is transformed into a campus jungle there will always be one group of faculty members to support the "non-negotiable" student demands and another faculty group of benevolent neutralists, who will be seeking peace and fellowship and honorable compromise.

By now it should be obvious that the day-to-day and coast-to-coast presence and activity of revolutionary-minded, activist students is no longer a temporary affair. It should be further obvious, but it is not, that the objective of the radicalized students (and some faculty) is total change, total seizure, total paralysis, total alienation, total totality. And while some people seem to have problems about defining the ultimate aims of the proposed revolution, it would appear to be simply this: to overthrow existing democratic societies in the name of more democracy. Or in the words of Robespierre, one of the founding fathers of totalist democracy, *"Le gouvernement de la Révolution est le despotisme de la liberté contre la tyranni. . . ."* These radicalized students have decided that the university must be made the permanent base and concentration center for an American revolution of "the Left."

As a result, negotiating "demands" with the Students for a Democratic Society has proved to be a pointless exercise except as it represents a struggle for the loyalties of the great middle of the seven million college and university students now enrolled in U.S. educational institutions.

How many radicalized university students are there? It is difficult to estimate. The *New York Times* (November 10, 1968) reported a survey of 860 campuses by the Educational Testing Service of Princeton, New Jersey. It showed that while the number of radical left organizations has almost doubled in the last three years, the percentage of activists among students has remained unchanged—about 2 per cent, or 134,000 of the total enrollment. An additional 8–10 per cent are described as strongly sympathetic to the "movement for social change [and] capable of temporary activation depending on the issues." Daniel Seligman in *Fortune Magazine* (January 1969) estimates campus activists as less than 2 per cent but argues that "behind this minority is a much larger, much less conspicuous group with similar dissident attitudes. . . . Something like 750,000 students now identify with the movement."

No matter how the negotiation with the representatives of these forces turns out, the end is the same—there is always another and even more unacceptable "non-negotiable" demand. If the demand for "a faculty-student tribunal" and "open hearings" in the name of "due process" is granted, the accused student and his allies at the hearing accuse the panel of prejudice and illegitimacy. Thus the student newspaper, the *Spectator,* in an editorial (Dec. 6, 1968), wrote:

> As illegitimate bodies, the disciplinary tribunals are now in a position to take but one legitimate action—the action of disbanding. . . . As illegitimate bodies, they have only the right to consider their illegitimacy and declare themselves illegitimate. They do not have the right to conduct hearings or to demand cooperation from students.

With such editorial support, the next step is inevitable—breakup of the panel hearing by disruption. I have before me the transcript of a disciplinary hearing (November 19, 1968) of a Columbia Law School student who had, with other *SDS* followers, tried to prevent registration for the Fall semester and had himself fought with a campus policeman. The transcript reads like a scene out of Bert Brecht by early Clifford Odets. Three senior Law School professors were part of the student-faculty panel. Whenever one of the professors asked the student's defence counsel a question about a point of law or fact, the *SDS* audience—I quote directly from the transcript—shouted:

> "None of this bullshit about procedure."
> "Are you cats getting off the bench or not?"
> "Murderers! Up against the wall!"
> "We want a revolution now."
> "Shit or get off the pot."

The transcript concludes: "Whereupon a man from the audience seized the gavel from the Tribunal's desk and walked along the desk kicking aside the papers thereupon. The Tribunal left their places briefly and conferred." The hearing was adjourned to December 18, 1968 when it was disrupted again, this time by Mark Rudd, leader of the campus disorders last Spring, who called the panel members "pigs." The panel decision a week later was for probation, a meaningless sanction at universities today.[1]

It was no secret that the SDS would try to break up the hearings. It was announced in leaflets and at meetings. Faculty and administration remained silent, uttered no word of warning or caution in advance of or after the event. They obviously have a healthy respect for the *apparat* of this revolutionary subculture which preaches the doctrine of permanent revolution and which in so doing has created a significant bloc of student revolutionaries comparable, say, to those who closed Tokyo University, the *Freie Universität* in Berlin, the Sorbonne, and the State College in San Francisco.

Unfortunately what seems obvious to me (for I have been a graduate student at Columbia since 1966) is not so obvious to faculty and administration, most of whom seem to believe that all the unpleasantness will blow over in time, in a year, or two. The young men and women who lead and work with SDS, and even those who have split from SDS over differences in tactics and strategy, will be enjoying their togetherness again in spring, quite unlike irreconcilable Stalinists and Trotskyites (or Khrushchevites and Maoists). These young people are a different breed of professional revolutionaries to whom the burning struggle is more important than dogma. If there is any dogma at all, it is confrontationism. By and large, they do little else day and night but plan and plot, and not very secretly, the next sortie, the next revolutionary probe, the next leaflet, the next battle. Several of them I know remind me of the old description (by Paul Axelrod) of Lenin as a man "absorbed by the Revolution twenty-four hours a day, who had no other thoughts but the thought of revolution and

---

[1] To understand the inspiration of the SDS tactic, the reader should consult the section in V. I. Lenin's *"Left-Wing" Communism: An Infantile Disorder* (1920) entitled "Should We Participate in Bourgeois Parliaments?" Khrushchev's shoe-pounding at the UN in October 1960 is an example of this tactic, which was also used at Columbia—". . . students, scattered across the auditorium, began pounding their shoes on the desks, throwing paper airplanes and yelling 'Disband!' " (*Columbia Daily Spectator*, November 20, 1968).

who even when he slept dreamt nothing but revolution. . . ."
Some of these graduate students are so immersed in revolution
that their final examinations and term papers in one course dealing with modern revolutions were replete with attacks on the
young professor who taught the course and who, of course, had to
grade this scholarly output.

Lenin, however, might have had mixed feelings about these
"infantile disorders." There is the case of one professor who opposed expulsion of one student on "dialectical" grounds. According to his theory, if Lenin hadn't been expelled from the University at Kazan, "there might not have been a Bolshevik Revolution. . . ."

These students are shrewd, very dedicated, gifted agit-prop experts. They know better than to try to seize banks or corporations,
headquarters of what they call the "military-industrial complex,"
or to occupy supermarkets, or invade police stations (all of which
are within convenient marching distances from student headquarters). They know they are fairly safe taking over colleges and
universities because they have learned well this important guide-
line for campus guerrillas. *If you can influence or, better yet, morally intimidate some part of the faculty, victory is certain.* "We live
in wondrous times," Bismarck once said, "in which the strong is
weak because of his moral scruples and the weak grows strong
because of his audacity. . . ." It is also helpful to know that if
you move against the university you will not be shot, jailed for
very long or clubbed very hard, and that if you are arrested, you
will be sprung on bail in no time at all; or if convicted, the University itself will be appealing to the district attorney or the judge
to quash the sentence. A university administration today is fairly
impotent when large sections of university faculties act as shield,
ally and buckler for any group of students which is obsessed by
utopianism, revolutionism, confrontationism, and a romantic
quasi-religious sense of a mission deriving from a credo consisting
of occult references to Che Guevara's immortality.

In addition to allies in the faculty, the radicalized students at
American universities have one other source of great support—the
vague sense of youthful solidarity among their fellow-students.[2]
The Administration is no ally, except unwittingly. The radical

---

[2] This is a potential, not often or completely realized in action. A survey at Columbia showed that while a majority of students and faculty supported the Columbia strike goals last spring, overwhelming majorities of both students and faculty
rejected the tactics. Allen H. Barton, "The Columbia Crisis: Campus, Vietnam and
the Ghetto," *Public Opinion Quarterly* (Fall 1968), pp. 333–51.

students work apart from ethnic minorities, particularly from black students who are now enforcing their own segregation, socially and politically. The revolutionaries cannot call the police or military their allies, nor the trade unions, workers, farmers, press or other media (although they are granted enormous space and visibility because they are such a dramatic story). The older intelligentsia, particularly that sector with a Stalinist/anti-Stalinist background and German émigré professors, are against "the movement," even though they do little practically to resist the disrupters. Business and industrial interests oppose them. Few religious leaders (except for a handful of swinging priests and rabbis) are on their side. Most politicians carefully avoid involving themselves in university fracas except for Governor Ronald Reagan of California and the pre-convention Richard M. Nixon.[3]

Yet despite this lack of visible means of support, these young Jacobins have cut down university administrators, forced curriculum changes, halted classes, closed campuses and sent a nationwide chill of fear through the university establishment. At Columbia they forced the resignation of President Grayson Kirk last August and, in January, that of David B. Truman (the executive vice-president who until the revolution had been understood to be Kirk's successor). Truman had no alternative but to resign after a large sector of the Columbia faculty opted for the student minority whose extra-legal excesses they could persuade themselves to forgive. Truman could not be forgiven because his very presence at Columbia rebuked faculty supineness. And, after all, he had even accepted the faculty's advice on how to handle building seizures.[4]

---

[3] Months before he obtained the GOP nomination, President Nixon called on Columbia to "rid the campus now" of student groups responsible for disruptions. He called the Columbia disorders "the first major skirmish in a revolutionary struggle to seize the universities of this country and transform them into sanctuaries for radicals and vehicles for revolutionary political and social goals." He warned that "if that student violence is either rewarded or goes unpunished, then the administration of Columbia University will have guaranteed a new crisis on its own campus and invited student coups on other campuses all over this country." Academic freedom, he said, "dictates that the rationally committed stand up and resist the dictates of [the] emotionally committed." (New York Times, May 16, 1968.

[4] Columbia Professor Arthur C. Danto has written, "The Ad Hoc Faculty Group, by opposing amnesty and bust [i.e., calling in the police], prolonged the demonstration and elevated the final violence. Had the police come that first Friday [April 26, 1968], when in deference to faculty sentiment the administration re-

Despite all that has happened and even as the *SDS* plans its *sacre du printemps,* the Columbia faculty remains split, notably that intellectual wing involved in the social sciences and humanities. It is the students in the social sciences, particularly in the graduate school, who are the most revolutionary. Surveys agree that students with "left-liberal family predispositions and backgrounds" select the social sciences. Sociology, of course, has become the war-horse of the struggle, since its subject matter covers self-involving topics—poverty, race, class, war-and-peace, anti-colonialism. Thus for student militants, the social sciences are arenas for their activism. For their teachers, many of them erstwhile "men of the Left," their chastening experiences over recent decades have made them aware of the complexities in making vast generalizations about human behavior and institutions.

"Hence, when a campus turns activist," one professor explained to me, "the tensions will be greatest within the social sciences. The faculty is likely to be divided with some adhering or returning to their old Leftism, while others adhere to the apolitical scholarly conception of the discipline. There are also likely to be severe divisions between activist students and faculty. The militant students deny the notion of a "scientific" approach to social science. Everything is "ideological" to them. The tensions which continue result in a breakdown of morale within the social sciences, and a high rate of defection by faculty from institutions where tensions run high.

"One can't have good social science in a politicized university. Social science becomes what the radical students want to make it, an arena for partisan debate and conflict. Faculty are judged by students in terms of their politics. And since social science students tend to be predominantly Left, this means that senior faculty members, particularly, feel very much under attack."

---

versed its decision to request them, the buildings might have been efficiently cleared, there being few bystanders at the time." *(New Republic,* January 25, 1969, p. 25, italics added). Danto was himself a member of the Ad Hoc Faculty Group. The administration figure who reversed the decision in deference to faculty sentiment was Truman.

One august Columbia professor I have spoken to has just begun to forgive Truman for having rejected his advice that the Columbia 1968 Commencement be cancelled. The Commencement was held indoors, not outdoors as usual, with no untoward incident. The "academic lynching" of David Truman is considered by some the most shameful aspect of the Columbia Revolution which should haunt faculty consciences for many years. An eminent political scientist and former Columbia College dean, Truman is now president of Mount Holyoke College, a Massachusetts school for women.

Columbia, like its peers, is becoming a highly politicized institution as its faculty finds it impossible to establish some kind of consensus about what should be done, say, in the event of building seizures, the breaking-up of classes, or acts of so-called "creative vandalism." As a foretaste of the future, about forty or fifty classes have already been broken up or disrupted; nothing, so far as I can judge, has been done about it. The news is even withheld from the press so as not to "aggravate" the atmosphere.

In one case, a young lecturer was subjected in advance to a taste of what he was to teach. The course was *Government 4411x,* Political Systems of Revolutionary and Post-revolutionary Societies," a brand-new entry in the Columbia catalogue, where it is described as follows:

> A comparative assessment of the effect of a revolution upon a political system, with emphasis on the French, Russian and Chinese cases. Attention is given to the foreign and domestic aims of revolutionary *élites,* the causes and consequences of widespread organized violence, and the demands upon the political system created by the rapid destruction of old values and institutions.

Within a few minutes after he had started his lecture, a minority of students began to bombard the instructor, Michael Oksenberg, with questions as well as salty comments about his teaching talent and general knowledgeability. The questions demanded his personal views on revolution, his definition of politics, and the dissolution of the lecture course (180 students) into smaller groups. Admittedly, the disruptionists were a small minority, possible no more than two dozen; needless to say, the student newspaper described the event through the eyes of one of the disrupters.

What followed this class disruption is rather indicative of the jejuneness of many of the faculty. Oksenberg was telephoned by a number of his colleagues who offered to come and "show the flag" by sitting in his lecture hall the following week. He thanked all for their offer but said he could handle it. The most conspicuous faculty failure was the absence of any public protest by the faculty, or by one single member in the student press, or elsewhere, against a "happening" that would have brought thunderous faculty outcries had the disruption been instigated by some reactionary, or Rightwing, or drop-the-bomb-now or racist group of student militants.

Last December, a month after the Oksenberg class disruption, the class of Professor James Shenton, a well-known historian of the U.S. Civil War, was interrupted by students who were not members of the class and who were unknown to Shenton. A few days later they issued a leaflet to explain why they had engaged in "classroom intervention" against a faculty member who had been "100 per cent all-out" for the student revolutionaries last Spring and who was still for them. The leaflet explained:

> We do not aim to criticize James P. Shenton as an individual; rather we aim to criticize our insane, repressive and inhumane society. Within our society, the University serves as an "Officers' Candidate School," socializing tomorrow's leaders. Shenton is one of the more appealing functionaries in this School. Like the smiling recruiting officers, he is doing his socially prescribed job in the best way he knows how. It is precisely because he is a "good teacher" and a "nice" fellow, that he is dangerous. The point is that gentle Jim Shenton is doing violence to you, and to himself, by creating a false consciousness of security within the University. . . .
> Some have called Shenton a "radical." His "radicalism" conceals the reality of his role. He accepts a position within the existing hierarchy. He lives the status of "professor" and thereby perpetuates the inferior status of the student and the custodian (who may have five kids but only one-tenth of a professor's salary). . . .

The leaflet was written in the form of a dialogue between unnamed students who presumably resented the class intervention—"You're violating the rights of the other students. . . . You're violating academic freedom. . . . We wanted to hear Shenton and you wouldn't let us. . . ." The leaflet answered:

> Of course, you have the right to do what you want, but you also have the responsibilty to ask yourself whether you *really* want what you think you want. If market research can create artificial needs (alienated desires) such as fatless fat and sugarless sugar, isn't it also likely that a similar technique has created an artificial need for a university education. . . . True, we imposed on you. Our purpose in doing so was to point out how "legitimate authority" imposes on you every day in a thousand ways, so much so that their imposi-

tions are accepted as "natural," while ours was disturbing because unusual.

Your right to do what you please is always qualified by your responsibility not to violate the same right of others (to life and sanity, for example) both in this country and abroad. Your passivity in accepting this part of the system is a political act for which you are responsible. We challenge your action. . . .

Such norms (as falling silent when the professor speaks, accepting his control of discussion, refraining from writing on the blackboard, not entering or leaving the classroom except at prescribed times, not discussing "personal" matters, etc.) serve to perpetuate the existing system and its inhumanity and injustices. . . .

You say "It's rude" to interrupt your class for ten minutes, but your probably don't bat an eye to hear that 2,000 Vietnamese have been killed and 5,000 Biafrans have starved this week. How are you protesting these "insults" to humanity? . . . It's not necessarily the responsibility of the critic to produce a solution to the problem he sees. We feel that the existing society is repressive (tolerant though this repression may seem). We seek to end this repression. This is ample work for the present. Would you ask the prisoner escaping from a concentration camp to produce a "better alternative?" (Better what? A better concentration camp?)

When I discussed this leaflet with a senior professor, he cautioned me not to blame the leaflet on the *SDS* but only on the "irresponsible Yippies." Later that day I mentioned this caveat to an *SDS* leader. He smiled as he told me that he himself had written the text, adding, "Does Professor M—— really think that the 'Yippies' are smart enough to write such a leaflet?"

This concern by a faculty member not to "blame the *SAS* unjustly" is one reason why *SDS* leaders, rightly or wrongly, have the feeling that they needn't worry about the rules of behavior for student activism as laid down by the Faculty Executive Committee. Another reason is the fact that the faculty has studiously avoided public notice of several *SDS* sorties in recent months—an unsuccessful attempt to stop registration last fall, a similarly unsuccessful attempt in January to prevent military recruiting, and the spoilage of some 30,000 registration records by activists who dumped scarlet paint over them as they were unpacked at Columbia's Teachers College. No one, however, should interpret the adjective "unsuccessful" as signifying failure. On the contrary, the morning after *SDS* failed to stop the military recruiting, an Administration official pointed glumly to a three-column photo in the *New York Times,* showing post-demonstration fisticuffs among Columbia students. The official said: "Maybe *SDS* didn't stop the recruiting but that photograph is *their* triumph, not Columbia's. . . ."[5]

After every "failure," the student insurrectionaries reform their battle-lines, find still another issue, call another mass meeting, issue yet another sheaf of leaflets and march again, two steps forward for any step backward. So an *SDS* defeat is a victory and an Administration-Faculty victory is a defeat. The *SDS* "guerrillas in the field of culture" fight an unlimited war against an institution which by its very nature can only fight—if at all—a limited campaign.[6]

It is now a year since the first Columbia takeover, the most savage attack on academic freedom at Columbia in half a century. Last year the disruptions could self-righteously be blamed on Grayson Kirk and Truman, but who will now be the scapegoat?

This year, the Faculty (or part of it) struggled for almost half a year before it was able to publish a statement of principles on how to deal with the student revolutionaries. From what I know of the preparation of this manifesto ("The University as a Sanctuary of Academic Freedom"), it was a horrendous chore for the small group of professors who felt *something* ought to be said—consensually—by the faculty on the Columbia crisis. Nights and weekends of negotiation for this word, for that phrase, for different formulations and amended punctuation—it seemed as if the statement would never emerge. When finally the statement,

---

[5] From the *New York Times,* February 5, 1969: "Applications for admission to Columbia College's freshman class next Fall have dropped 21 per cent from last year because of last spring's riots on the campus, the director of admissions said yesterday." Applications to Barnard College, Columbia's sister college, dropped 11 percent last year.

[6] From the *News-Letter* of the Graduate Student Union of Columbia University (September 25, 1968, p. 3): "The chief task, then, is to advance on the 'cultural front.' And the only current institutions capable of sustaining such an offensive seem to be the universities. Thus we must begin to create for ourselves within the universities an atmosphere where 'guerrillas in the field of culture' can flourish." (The "guerrilla" phrase is, of course, Fidel Castro's.)

signed by several hundred academicians,[7] did appear on March 10 it carefully avoided saying what ought to be done if *SDS* ignored the faculty consensus and engaged in 'revolutionary tactics similar to last year's (or worse). Despite what sounded like strong language—"the university had the right, and indeed the obligation, to defend itself"—the statement failed dismally to deal with the all-important question: *when* may a university order the use of legitimate force "to defend itself?" What is fact is that had the statement attempted to transcend its pieties and proceed towards spelling out these conditions, it would have been *impossible* to obtain any significant number of signatures. Accustomed to immunity from outside pressures, the Columbia faculty seems particularly inept at dealing with the internal pressures generated by a handful to students whose interests quite clearly are not educational reform or "curriculum building" but in avowedly revolutionary acts, *e.g.*, the abolition of Columbia's School of International Affairs, preventing the University from buying neighborhood real estate for future expansion, or abrogating the conventional Faculty right to vote on academic tenure. Were the attack on academic freedom from the John Birch Society or from followers of George Wallace or from some reactionary and philistine State Legislature, the Columbia faculty, like any faculty in America, would know exactly what to do. The response would be swift, heroic, and efficacious. Yet these same intellectuals, many of whom were able to mount a powerful propaganda assault against President Johnson and Vietnam, are still unable to contain the

---

[7] Among the singers: Jacques Barzun, Daniel Bell, Zbigniew Brzezinski, Charles Frankel, Fred Friendly, El Ginzburg, Richard Hofstadter, Donald Keen, Paul Kristeller, Paul Henry Lang, Joseph Mazzeo, Robert K. Merton, Ivan Morris, Phillip E. Mosely, Ernest Nagel, Meyer Schapiro, Fritz Stern, Lionel Trilling, Rudolf Wittkower.

---

[8] A faculty friend told me of how after supporting a resolution in his department for student participation in curriculum revision, he came to one of the first meetings only to discover that the students elected to the committee were not in attendance. They had come to the first meeting and participated in some of the discussion. The second meeting—no students. The faculty members then made the decisions on the new curriculum and adjourned. Later, when the professor dropped in at a neighboring phonograph shop, he saw one of the "no-show" student committee members listening to records. He had forgotten about the meeting. A student member of another joint committee criticized faculty members because he suspected they weren't as "frank" in the presence of student members as in their absence.

196   ARNOLD BEICHMAN

"Left" assault from within, even though the *SDS* and its allies represent little more than 5 per cent of Columbia's 17,500 students.

What has created this vacuum of leadership, this failure of nerve at Columbia and similar institutions? For one thing, few faculty members any longer expect orderly debate and intellectual discourse under recognized rules, nor does anyone expect compliance or support of such traditional liberal conventions.[9] The reason for the present collapse of compliance and lack of enforcement of normal academic discipline is that those who run the universities—and they are not the Trustees or the Administration but the faculty[10] —have quietly decided that for the foreseeable future the university is no longer a place where truth is to be pursued. What has been tacitly ratified is a decision that the American university is primarily (not secondarily) the springboard for upward social mobility as the ascriptive right for ethnic minorities.

Let me be quite clear, in these especially sensitive times, as to what I am suggesting: when universities begin to choose an increasing number of freshmen on the basis of ethnicity and a reverse *numerus clausus;* when they begin to plan curricula on the basis of student political pressure; when faculty members begin to be selected not on the basis of recognized scholarly achievement but on color and/or ideological affiliation, then the University

---

[9] The only rules which are obeyed are those which abolish rules. For example, the parietal regulations in Columbia's all-male student dormitories used to regulate visiting hours for female guests. These were amended to what is now called "24-hour parietals" which is a euphemism for no parietals at all. Female guests can come and go when they please. Some girls are living in the dormitories full-time. One official told me the university is delighted that it is no longer in "the rooming-house business." A current witticism among faculty members is to ask, "Do you believe in pre-parietal intercourse?" Evidently "sex problems" are much easier to solve than problems in politics and culture.

[10] As Professor Richard Hofstadter put it in his address at the 1968 Commencement, "Trustees, administrators and students tend to agree that in ultimate reality the members of the faculty are the university and we of the faculty have not been disposed to deny it." He went on to say:

"The technique of the forcible occupation and closure of a university's buildings with the intention of bringing its activities to a halt is . . . a thrust at the vitals of university life. It is a powerful device for control by a determined minority, and its continued use would be fatal to any university. In the next few years the universities of this country will have to find the effective strategy to cope with it, and to distinguish it sharply and permanently from the many devices of legitimate student petition, demonstration and protest."

may conceivably be performing useful, perhaps even necessary social acts, but it is no longer involved in the pursuit of truth. This is not to say that, until now, the American university has been a "parfit gentil knight." Far from it, but at least the standard was there, as an ideal goal. As Jacques Barzun points out in his recent book, *The American University,* neither scholarship nor teaching is any longer "the central concern of the university or its members." Society, he argues, has turned itself over to education and created "a mandarin system [whereby] in order to achieve any goal, however modest, one must qualify."

In this degradation of higher education, faculties participated just as lustily as did administrators and trustees, and no faculty more so than Columbia's.[11] Columbia's decline didn't begin with Grayson Kirk's tenure, although he did very little to stop the downhill slide. It began with the paralyzing interregnum following the passing of the Nicholas Murray Butler era and the appointment of General Dwight Eisenhower as University President. The faculty accepted a "public relations" appointment without a word of protest. They assuaged conscience by exercising the *ius murmurandi,* retailing among themselves Ike's gaffes, solecisms, and general philistinism.

No university is viable unless it has a sense of its own security, and only a faculty can endow the institution with this sense of security. Its own principles of solidarity are essential. When legitimized force, indispensable to the maintenance of a legitimated institution, becomes "illegitimate" at the instant of application or at the threat of application, that institution is no longer capable of ruling. This is the situation of all the large American universities today. They are subject to seizure or paralyzing sit-ins with or without notice. Courses can be cancelled by the pressure of demonstrations in a classroom.[12]

---

[11] Professor Robert Cross, an outstanding Columbia historian before he became president of Hunter College, has criticized faculty apathy (his own included) for the crisis. "The faculty simply sloughed off. It didn't bother to see where the University was moving. It's incredible that I sat there for years unconcerned. . . ." *(Columbia Daily Spectator,* November 7, 1968).

[12] "The Harvard Graduate School of Design scrapped today a course that was to have developed an action program for the effective control and eventual elimination of riots in urban areas, after more than 100 Negro students forced cancellation of the course's first semester. It substituted, under the same professor, an unstructured seminar open to all students to develop new ideas for an urban education program at Harvard." *(New York Times,* February 9, 1969). In the same edition, the *Times* reported the following incidents—a University of Chicago fac-

To make explicit what I mean by the illegitimizing of legitimacy I want to report what happened during a Columbia sit-in on February 27 when *SDS* occupied two buildings as a protest against optional military training. According to the campus newspaper report:

> Shortly after the sit-in began, Athena Constantine, director of the placement office, announced that she had been directed to tell the protesters that they were "obstructing a University office" and must leave. The students continued their discussion.
>
> Moments later, Paul Lehmann, an assistant dean of admission, told the demonstrators that if they did not leave the hall in fifteen minutes, he would ask them for their identification cards. The group voted overwhelmingly to remain past the deadline.
>
> At 1 p.m. when the time limit had elapsed, Mr. Lehmann began reciting the Interim Rules on campus protest while the crowd heckled. When he and another University official began asking the students for their ID cards, one student yielded his identification, but the rest refuses, yelling: "We're all Eldridge Cleaver!"
>
> The proctor (an Administration official) then told the crowd that if they kept cleared a path to each office, the demonstration would be declared legal. Paths were cleared, the doors unlocked, the employees entered the offices unobstructed.
>
> At 1:45 p.m., the protesters filed out of both buildings and returned to the steps of Low Library. One speaker told the crowd, "The Cordier myth has been shattered; the Cordier myth is over. We're gonna say to Andrew Cordier what we said to Kirk—up against the wall, motherfucker."

The new president of Columbia, Dr. Andrew Cordier, was arraigned last fall by *SDS* students as the man who had "mur-

---

ulty disciplinary committee chairman had been waylaid by student demonstrators who broke up the hearing; at the University of Wisconsin students disrupted classes and marched on the campus; at the University of North Carolina there was a peaceful occupation of the main administration building ground floor; Negro students at the State University, Stony Brook, N.Y., demanded Negro faculty members and Negro studies as have been demanded at other institutions with white student support.

dered" Patrice Lumumba during the time Cordier was a high UN official. Candlelight marches to "mourn" Lumumba (eight years after his assassination) and mass meetings were held on the campus to dramatize Cordier's "complicity." The only visible faculty reaction to this Goebbels-like exercise in the "Big Lie" was a letter of exculpation in the college daily by Arthur Lall, a former Indian diplomat now teaching at Columbia. When I expressed my curiosity to a senior professor at this faculty silence in the face of character assassination, he replied that "some accusations are so contemptible that we should apply the Oxford method—ignore them. . . ." Several weeks later, Cordier was confronted at a press reception on the campus by forty SDS members, one of whom presented him with a "subpoena" to stand trial for "crimes against the students and residents of Morningside Heights." When some of the guests laughed, an SDS leader faced around to them and said: "Some of you may laugh at this, but this man is a criminal." (Columbia Spectator, November 22, 1968.) Quite obviously, SDS is not to be shamed by the minatory silence of the senior professors.

What causes this paralysis of will among men of learning and decency? Is it the very idea of youth in its current romanticization as the essence of purity, freedom, virility, and the future? How is it that the teenage student seems to so many of them to hypostasize the virtues of the charismatic leader with mission announced and obedience demanded? Perhaps youth seems infallible, omniscient and incorruptible to those professors whose prestige is measured by how little time they devote to teaching and to office hours for students. I mention the case of a student in one of my seminars who had his appointment with the professor cancelled at the last minute (it had taken weeks to get it) because the distinguished man had to appear on television that night to discuss some burning issue in world affairs; another professor who, in the recent years of campus crisis, has been on yearlong leaves, and has threatened regularly to resign because of the vices of the *ancien régime*. It is not the first time in history that the guilt-ridden old seek redemption in the young, but the young also have their problematical disorders, and only a Freud of political neuroses can diagnose the point at which they both meet. Nothing from the past—neither Rousseau's youth-cult nor Bakunin's nihilism, or even Spengler's vision of a new barbarian horde of young urban vandals—satisfactorily explains the student uprisings the world over.

The university revolutionaries are unencumbered by old-style entanglements with the great ideological movements of Communism and Fascism. For them, Mao, Che, Fidel, and Ho are cultural, not political, figures. They know little of Hitler and Mussolini and care less about Nazis, Fascists, John Birchers, George Wallace-ites, racists, *et al.* Perhaps it is impossible to deal with the *SDS* because its allies and followers belong to no adult political society, no responsible subversive movement with a center or an intellectual or spiritual headquarters. The visible aim of their tactics (unlike a workers' strike where an attempt is made to improve wages and social conditions) is apocalyptic: to smash and destroy and overthrow and transcend. The evil institution must be levelled. But who is so wildly cynical as to think that their aim is to take Cordier's chair as President and to place ten *SDS*ers on the Board of Trustees?

An *SDS* member arose in the banquet room of the Conrad Hilton Hotel in Chicago where a dinner honoring the new University of Chicago president, Dr. Edward Levi, was in progress. The *SDS* youth shouted out to McGeorge Bundy on the dais: "You are responsible for the genocide in Vietnam. You're soaked in blood and your stench of death fills the room. I'm going to join my brothers in the street where the air is cleaner. . . ." (I am quoting from an *SDS* publication, *Hard Core*, December 20, 1968, p. 12.) I asked a Columbia *SDS* supporter how denouncing Bundy in this fashion would accomplish the destruction of the Ford Foundation. He answered me: "This is how we show the Establishment, and the Power Elite, how powerless they are to deal with us! . . ."

At Columbia today, as in other urban universities throughout the USA., we are witnessing the exercise of legitimated dual power, Student-Faculty as "the party of movement" and Faculty-Administration as "the party of order." But it is the student front which has learned how to convert myths into political power and how to use power to acquire more power, how to annul hierarchical structures without really trying. The student front's most important safeguard is that "military intervention" against confrontationism is no longer feasible at Columbia and at most other private universities. Thus Wayne Booth, dean of the University of Chicago undergraduate school, said: "The moment we call the police we have brought the institution downward. This would mean we are no longer able to govern ourselves. . . ." *(Newsweek,* February 17, 1969, p. 71.) The university's six-story administration building was seized on January 30 and held by students for sixteen days to protest against the dismissal of—you guessed it—a female assistant professor of sociology after the unanimous vote of the tenured social science faculty that "The intellectual quality of her work did not meet the standard required for reappointment in her deparmtent."

At Columbia, the debate as to which group—students, faculty, or administration—should run the university prevents it from being run at all. Bonapartism may work in underdeveloped countries where the military can be the party of both order and movement, but clearly it doesn't work at universities, one-time seats of high culture and academic isolationism, where the faculty resists involvement with campus and pedagogical affairs. As Professor Robert Nisbet has written, 60 per cent of all academics in American universities "have so profound a distaste for the classroom and for the pains of genuine scholarship or creative thought that they will seize upon anything . . . to exempt themselves respectively from each."

There is another reason why the radical student revolutionaries are difficult for the faculty to deal with. This is a movement, as I said earlier, which is unrelated to adult political life. It is different from the kind of extremism to which the liberal-intelligentsia has been exposed in the era of totalitarianism. The great issue of the 1940s and '50s and early '60s was Stalinism and post-Stalinism (East Germany, Poland, Hungary, Cuba). Communist totalitarianism was a cultural as well as a political entity. The liberal-intelligentsia could resist the Communist movement with political-cultural initiatives, ranging from counterdemonstrations (like New York's famous anti-Stalinist Waldorf-Astoria conference in 1949) to picketing the Soviet Embassy. (No one would suggest a demonstration or picket-line outside *SDS* headquarters because, for one thing, no one is really sure where it is!) In a real sense one always knew what the Communist Party was up to by watching the Soviet press or speeches and reacting accordingly. Everyone knew that the CP-USA was not interested in revolution but in mustering support for Soviet foreign policy. With the *SDS,* there is no *partiinost;* there is no tangible political line either to fight or to understand. Moscow means very little to them before or after Czechoslovakia. For Cohn-Bendit, Russian and French Communists are *"crapules staliniennes."* Since there is no organized focus for the international youth movement—the moment one uses the phrase one realizes there is no "international youth movement" in which a Rudi Dutschke or a Mario Savio hands down orders to his oblates—it is rather difficult to engage in political struggle and counter-struggle. So the far-sighted professor prepares for violent seizures and disruptions by removing personal files, research data, precious books and favorite pipe from his private office. After all, two professorial offices were burned during the last Columbia *putsch,* and it is little solace to be told by *SDS* partisans that the arson was committed by "police *agents-provocateurs,"* not by revolutionary students.

This political "generational gap" is exceeded by the intellectual "generational gap" which makes conversation and debate with the student revolutionaries a dialogue of the deaf. Most middle-aged faculty members of the Liberal Left have lived through or personally experienced great traumas—the disillusion after World War I, the great Depression, the disenchantment with Communism and the Moscow trials, the war in Spain, the threat of Facism, Genocide, World War II, the Joe McCarthy period with its "Age of Suspicion." It appears to be impossible for the middle-aged to communicate the feeling of being jobless, of being "betrayed" by Stalin and his epigones, the feeling of identification and choking weakness at the news of Auschwitz, the fear of ultimate weapons. The 1930–60 generations went through ordeals which simply preclude communication between those in the 40–50 age group and those in their late teens and early twenties, even with the Vietnam War. There can only be bewilderment when a greying or balding professor, who has lost faith in the miracles of government intervention and welfare statism, reads in a revolutionary student leaflet that "the politicization of the university is of prime importance for the creation of the objective and subjective conditions for building a revolutionary socialist movement in America. . . ." Short of mounting a soapbox in opposition, a professor has the options of "internal emigration" from the university, supporting such a movement, leaving university life and changing his job, or just hoping "it'll go away" as other cultural fads have done. A week before the Columbia revolt, a professor whom I respect and admire said to me as we strolled across College Walk: "You know, there's no more wonderful job in the world than being a tenure professor at a university like Columbia. You can do what you want. Nobody can tell you what to do. You can write or not, publish or not; it doesn't matter, you won't perish. . . ."

Seven months later, this same tenure professor was devoting all of his spare time to disciplinary hearings and committee meetings and assorted *ad hoc* sessions over and above his lectures and seminars. He and many of his colleagues had been forced into a new way of life by an unstructured political-cultural movement whose leaders, as Professor Stanley Hoffmann has written, "display a flamboyant ideological style devoid of ideology." Instead of reading their professional journals, or the books of their colleagues, they now read the mimeographed leaflets, the protest pamphlets, the "exposés" of the faculty in the college newspaper, and volumes like the Cox Commission's report on the Investigation into the Columbia Disorders.[13] The joys of being a tenure professor are no more. "Those were the days, my friend, we thought they'd never end. . . ."

I am writing this in February, amidst a fourteen-inch blizzard which has halted all traffic in Manhattan. One faculty member murmured, "Now is the winter of our content. . . ." But the snows will melt, the spring freshets will begin to flow. Will it all happen again? There seems to be agreement that the revolution of the millennial zealots will take place, although no one is quite certain about the role which black students will play in any *putsch*. One professor said to me, "For us the big question is what are the blacks doing and saying—no one can reach them." (One of my *SDS* friends said with a touch of malice when I asked him why Negro students were saying little—"Maybe they haven't anything to say, did you ever think of that?") *SDS*, however, will lis-

---

[13] The Cox report (named after its chairman, Professor Archibald Cox of Harvard) exemplifies something Walter Lippmann wrote in his *Drift and Mastery* more than a half a century ago: "There is in America today a distinct prejudice in favor of those who make the accusations." The Cox report seems to accept on a one-to-one basis the Columbia events—the Administration did this, the reaction was that; the Faculty did such-and-such, such-and-such followed. It is a sort of Greek tragedy written in "labor mediation" language in which everybody is right and in which everything is inevitable. The report was questioned by A. M. Rosenthal, an editor of the *New York Times*, as to its finding (p. 108) that "there was no substantial vandalism" in President Kirk's office resulting from *SDS* seizure and occupation for one week. Rosenthal queried Columbia for a bill of particulars and was told that repairs and refurbishing the President's office came to $4,572.

Vice-Provost Herbert Deane attacked Cox for having quoted from an interview in the college newspaper without checking whether the quoted material was accurate or not. Deane had protested to the college newspaper when the interview had first appeared and now was outraged that the Cox Commission hadn't taken the trouble during its hearings on the campus to verify the misquotation attributed to him. *Si non é vero, e ben trovato.* (The Cox report is titled *Crisis at Columbia*, Vintage paperback, 1968).

ten to *SAS* (Students' Afro-American Society) demands. For example, *SDS* was ready to launch an all-out attack on one
Left-Liberal professor, for much the same reason they did against
James Shenton. In fact, I heard one *SDS* speaker at a rally attack
this professor by name. A day later an *SAS* official told *SDS* to
"lay off" this professor—a white, but one who had written exten-
sively and favorably on anticolonial movements. *SDS* laid off. If
white defers to black, black no longer defers to white. Last fall,
the spokesman for *SAS* warned that Negro students at Columbia
would not become "the black tail on a white radical dog." No
melting pot for the revolutionaries! As Mark Rudd told the *New
York Times* (May 19, 1968): "I was never really attracted to civil
rights. There was too much idealization of Negroes and they
didn't seem too effective. I've always felt a tremendous barrier
between me and blacks. . . ." I have intruded this particular issue
because the *SDS-SAS* relationship may well determine the progress of the *putsch, i.e.,* whether there will be successful violent
takeovers of the Columbia buildings.[14] One of last year's *SDS*
veterans told me that the night before the 1968 disruption, Rudd
went to the *SAS* leader, told him of the *SDS putsch* programme
for the following day and said, "You're going to look awful foolish
if you guys don't come out with us tomorrow." *SAS* came out. So
far this year *SDS* has received little support on its picketlines or
during its demonstrations from *SAS* or Negro students generally.
There seems to be general agreement that the initial involvement
of Negro students in April 1968 inhibited the Administration
from an immediate call-up of the police. "The delay in calling
upon the police," Professor Truman has confessed, was "dictated
at the beginning by a desire to avoid inflaming the neighboring
black community [Harlem]. . . ." Professor Danto documents the
mythology: "Faculty believed students were really interested in a
negotiated settlement; students believed faculty were being radicalized, and hence were incipient allies; administrators believed a

---

[14] In March I was told by an academic that "it all looks good for spring—
nothing is going to happen because the blacks are talking, thank God. They're
demanding everything and that's good because it means we can negotiate."
On March 13 a meeting took place behind closed doors between the Black
Students' society and the Administration. The Negros insisted that neither side issue any press statement. They were asking for an autonomous "Black Cultural Institute," to be administered by a board of students and faculty and—I am quoting
the student newspaper—"outside experts on the black experience." Barnard College
for women has already agreed to an Afro-American study program and to segregated, separate, dormitory facilities for black students as demanded by the Barnard
Organization of Soul Sisters (BOSS).

major problem was civil strife between students; everyone believed Harlem would rise to devastate the campus. . . ."

Whether or not the black students involve themselves in the coming disruptions (the *casus belli* will probably be the Naval Training Program at Columbia and a demand for its abolition) as they did last spring, the present *SDS* leadership is committed to more than mere manifestos and verbal solutions for what they feel are the "gut issues" in American society. It is important to realize that they are thoroughly prepared to use "revolutionary violence" against the university, against dissident students and oppositional faculty. A tragedy is in the making at Columbia, and no one knows how to avert it.[15]

I asked one of the more popular graduate school professors what he would do should *SDS* (or the "Yippies") try to break up his lecture course. "I'd, frankly incite the rest of the students to beat them up," he replied. "That is, if they wanted the class to continue." His point was that since no university could be expected to police every lecture hall, it was up to the students to resist "gangsterism." The wife of one Columbia academician thought very poorly of this "solution," she said, "How would you, as a parent, like it if you heard that students were fighting in the classroom and that your son might get brained and brain somebody else?"

SDS has another asset this time. It is one they lacked last spring—a fragile relationship to an AFL-CIO trade union. I was made aware of this arrow in the *SDS* quiver during a television interview with two *SDS* leaders I conducted last fall for the Canadian Broadcasting Corporation. I asked one of them how he was reacting to newspaper reports that white workers were "flocking" to the George Wallace presidential candidacy (they never did). He answered: "That's good because it shows the workers' disaffection from the System." I suggested that the last time workers showed such disaffection from the System, it was the Weimar Republic and they bought Hitler instead. "That only means we must lead this disaffection into Left channels," he said. How? "By conducting wildcat strikes among workers and radicalizing them."

---

[15] "I reviewed the lessons to be learned from other universitity disruptions—especially Columbia. One ingredient lacking at Columbia, I thought—because of its history and organic structure—was that there was no condemnation by the faculty and the students as a unified whole of the illegal acts on that campus." Morris B. Abram, president of Brandeis University, in the *New York Times Magazine* (February 16, 1969). A Brandeis building was taken over on January 8 by Negro students and held for eleven days.

Columbia University, whose labor-management relations for decades were about as progressive as those of the early American steelmasters, now has union trouble on its hands which could lead to wildcat strikes among the cafeteria workers and library employees. Last spring when the students picketed the buildings, some students and faculty ignored the picket lines on the grounds that while they would support an economic strike they wouldn't a political strike. This spring, with *SDS* members as union organizers, there could be a strike which might be difficult to handle because of a "Student-Worker alliance," however tenuous it is. The most serious walkout could be at the Butler Library, one of the great institutions of its kind in the world. Last spring the Library was closed for a week during the disorders and there was even fear of arson.

One thing is quite clear about the young men and women who have emerged as the revolutionaries of our time. They are not concerned with reforming the university or introducing courses on revolution or receiving degrees in African history. They are profoundly unconcerned about who precisely will be the president of Columbia to replace Acting President Cordier. *Any* university president is categorically the enemy. They are concerned with the demoralization and radicalization of the American university, specifically Columbia, with the smashing of institutions that they feel oppress and frustrate and humiliate them. They are like the "possessed" ones in a Dostoevsky novel, and one is reminded of Peter Verhovensky in *The Devils:*

We don't want education. We have had enough of science. We have plenty of material without science to last us a thousand years. The thing we want is obedience. The only thing that's wanting in the world is obedience. The desire for education is an aristocratic desire. The moment a man falls in love or has a desire for a family, he gets a desire for private property. We will destroy that desire, we'll resort to drunkenness, slander, denunciations; we'll resort to unheard of depravity; we shall smother every genius in infancy. We shall reduce everything to one common denominator. Full equality.

17. "WAR OF THE FLEA" AT SAN FRANCISCO STATE

John H. Bunzel

John Bunzel, formerly Professor of Political Science and Chairman of the Department at San Francisco State College, is now President of San Jose State College.

On November 6, 1968, the leadership of the Black Students Union and the other minority groups which make up the Third World Liberation Front at San Francisco State began putting into operation their plan to immobilize the college and shut it down. Using hit-and-run tactics and terrorism, groups of black and brown students, later joined by whites, succeeded in disrupting the campus with a violence unprecedented in the history of American higher education.

It is not enough to say that the eruption which took place reflects the general crisis in higher education today. This kind of generic argument, or some variation of it, is always lying about ready to be used, attractive for its easy simplicity. In certain hands it can also become a cheap, even demagogic, appeal that attempts to diminish the accountability of participants. The fact is it has little real explanatory value (beyond the obvious) because it is too unfocused and frequently question-begging. It cannot explain, for example, why these particular leaders turned to the tactics of disruption and violent behavior. Nor can it help us understand the very different cast of mind that is shaped by the magnetic force of a powerful ideology for its perception of the world and its activist directives.

The events of a year ago cannot be separated from certain facts and some history. Consider, for example, the symbolic importance of November 6. On that very day of the previous year, at approximately 10:30 in the morning, fifteen members of the Black Students Union, silent and somber in their black leather jackets and sunglasses, had marched into the office of The Gater, the student newspaper. Stationing themselves carefully around the entry room, they asked to see the editor. A reporter glanced up

Reprinted, with permission, from the *New York Times*, November, 9. 1969.

and told them he was on the phone. Five of the group walked into the editor's office and shut the door behind them.

According to the editor, one of the intruders tore the phone from his hands and began to beat him. After a series of blows, the editor fell to the floor and was kicked repeatedly. Outside, other staff members, hearing the commotion, tired to come to his aid but found their way blocked by several of the "brothers" who had remained in the entry room. In the ensuing battle, several staffers were roughed up and an instructor in the journalism department sustained a number of bruises and a broken finger. The attackers left some five minutes later, but not before they vandalized the office.

That noon on campus a rumor circulated widely that the Black Students Union denied having any part in the beating. However, on unanticipated development turned out to be disconcerting for the intruders: Quietly but unnoticed, a staff photographer had taken pictures of the whole melee. When some of the pictures appeared in The Gater the next morning, they showed that BSU members made up the attacking force.

The college administration had learned in late summer that the black students had chosen November 6, 1968, as the day for some sort of activity to "commemorate" the beating of The Gater editors. The black students explained that "black people in this nation do not have any meaningful holiday," and they felt some should be created. The anniversary of the raid on The Gater, which coincided with the anniversary of the arrest of Huey Newton, a Black Panther hero from Oakland, would be a beginning.

On the afternoon of November 5, 1968, the Black Students Union made public their list of ten "non-negotiable" demands; two days later the Third World Liberation Front added five similar ones. Dr. Robert R. Smith, then president of the college, offered to discuss them with the black students, but they refused, insisting on a yes-or-no answer. Among the demands was one which ordered the college to establish at once a black-studies department with twenty full-time faculty members, to be completely controlled by its own faculty and staff. They also demanded that the college accept all blacks who might apply for admission in the fall of 1969 without regard to the academic qualifications of the applicants. In addition, they insisted that George Murray, 22, a graduate student and the Black Panthers' Minister of Education, be reinstated as a part-time English instructor. Murray, who had stated publicly that black students should carry guns on campus to protect themselves from "racist administrators," had been suspended with full pay on November 1 by President Smith under orders from the State College Chancellor. On November 6, the Black Students Union, their demands unmet, launched a strike against San Francisco State College.

On the eve of the strike, Stokely Carmichael, then still Prime Minister of the Black Panther party, set the ideological tone in a speech to a campus meeting of some 800 BSU and Third World students (no whites were allowed). Creating a sense of solidarity and brotherhood, he spelled out some of the components of the belief system which served to transform the strike from a dispute over specific issues into a struggle for a radical change in power relationships:

"What you have to do is work on the attitude," Carmichael said. "Not the specifics. The correct attitude. In order to do that, we must have a clear definition of what our problems are and where we're going. Now, the attitude of white America is that you must be responsible, you must love, worship, be patriotic, etc., etc. . . . The attitude of us must be that we must oppose white America on every level. On every ground. We must oppose it. . . .

"Now, the Black Students Union at San Francisco State is the *most* notorious in the country. I think that's good. I hope *you* do not think it's good because if *you* think it's good you're in trouble because you might let notoriety become your goal. If you can set the attitude at San Francisco State, it will be duplicated across the country."

And Carmichael went on: "If the Black Students Union was to say, 'We want white persons kicked out; we want them replaced with a black person'—that's not enough. It's not enough because they can replace them with any black person, and that black person will not be a black person to your liking, to your choosing, or to your same political ideology. Now, the way to insure that you get somebody who is to your liking, who is someone who will do what you want them to do, and who has the same political ideology that you have is to make sure that you can choose or you have control over that person. . . .

"There are two types of power. There is visible power, and there is real power in the sense of control. We must now go for the real control. That's got to be the word—the real control.

"When you talk about black studies you talk about methodology and ideology, not just another subject. Not the same methodology the white man uses, but a different methodology to communicate to us. Different ideology means an ideology brooding in black nationalism. Not just adding black people to white history. That's an insidious subterfuge. It is going to misdirect our struggle if we allow that to happen. A different ideology because finally we have to, and it is your job to heighten the contradictions while we prepare for the confrontation. While we heighten the contradictions, we politically awaken our people so that when that confrontation does come we become victorious. It is easy to die for one's people. It is much more difficult to live, to work, and to kill for them.

"Now, there are two things: When you fight, you depend only upon yourselves. Nobody else. That's black people, and then there's people of color outside of the circle. If you're going to start the war, then you be ready. We're not talking about a tomorrow battle. We're talking about prolonged warfare. Warfare—psychological, political, and otherwise. It means military. That's what we're talking about. And that's what you prepare yourselves for. Psychologically. . . .

"If you fall into the mistakes of other students by seizing a building for the sake of seizing a building, you have plunged your movement down one more time. Let's understand that. There've been buildings seized before. You've done it, here last year. Big deal. To come back and seize it again this year—it doesn't even excite anybody. Victory is what we want. Not notoriety. I think we get carried away with the short demonstrations and seize a building for three days and talk about it for the rest of the semester. And show absolutely nothing for it. So we must begin to understand we're talking about prolonged struggle. . . ."

Carmichael's appeal for the seizure of power in a protracted struggle against "the enemy" was echoed many times by BSU spokesmen in the months that followed. If it was perhaps too rudimentary to be termed a framework of ideology, it nonetheless seemed to provide direction and purpose for the leaders of the Black Students Union and helped to fire up those who wanted to "live the revolution."

It should be made clear, however, that the black leaders were not hostage to an explicit ideology, or even any carefully thought-out plans for the seizure of power. They were working on it, so to speak, as they went along, pretty much deciding things from one day to the next. A good deal of rationalization grew up that began to look like an ideology—but here was no Lenin.

The strike was not a strike in the trade-union sense of that term, as some among the faculty and many more in the student

body tried to convince themselves. By their own public statements, the leaders of the Black Students Union and Third World
Liberation Front made clear that their demands were not to be
discussed but implemented. "The fifteen demands are nonnegotiable," they would announce from one day to the next, "which
means we want them all . . . no piecemeal program, no
compromises—we want all of them." They purposely bypassed the
college's procedures for solving problems and reconciling legitimate grievances. In their own language, they were engaged in a
"struggle for power against the capitalist, imperialist, racist white
power structure" that was out to "exterminate" minority students
on campus. They saw themselves as directing a revolutionary
movement against the faculty, the administration and the state
college trustees—and, for some, the whole political structure of
California.

Most Americans have had little experience with the concept of
ideology. For this reason, many students and faculty who witnessed the crisis at San Francisco State had no conceptual apparatus by which the pronouncements and behavior of the Black Students Union could be understood. Lacking a basic ideational
framework, they could not see the straight line connecting the
bullhorn oratory of the black student leaders with the speeches of
Malcolm X and the writings of Frantz Fanon. For example, it
was commonplace at noontime strike rallies on campus to hear
black spokesmen invoke the model of anticolonialism to depict the
racial situation in the United States as a struggle between the
oppressed people (blacks) and their oppressors (whites), thereby
aligning the Black Students Union and the Third World Liberation Front with similar struggles of colonized people around the
world.

"We will no longer put up with this racist country living off
the poor people of the world," they would shout, depicting their
strike against San Francisco State as an extension of their opposition to American imperialism, especially in Vietnam. Many white
students, therefore, supported the blacks because they wanted to
be identified with this third-world struggle for freedom.

The anti-imperialist appeal was then given a special force: the
struggle of oppressed black people around the world against the
imperialist United States, they said, is the same struggle being
fought on campus for black studies. (Angela Davis, the black philosophy instructor at the University of California in Los Angeles
and a member of the Communist party, recently provided a varia-

tion on the same theme. "The real academic freedom," she said, "is to link up with concrete struggles, to expose imperialism.") What followed was the cry for liberation and self-determination— liberation from the oppressive rule of "that pig Smith" and his "racist administrators," and self-determination for blacks to control their own institutions.

Throughout the strike, the demand for black studies was caught up in the mythic language of black pride and identity, of "soul" needs, of black rage and violence. Anyone who expressed an interest in seeing some measure of academic substance and integrity in the black-studies program found his concern swept away in the flood of symbolic arguments seeking symbolic solutions.

I had written an article in which I was critical not of the idea of black studies, but of creating a completely autonomous Department of Black Studies in which only a totally black faculty would be hired to teach the commonly shared ideology of revolutionary black nationalism exclusively to black students who would then return to their black communities and help organize the black revolution. I did not believe that black studies should become an induction system for the revolutionary movement. But in the combustible environment of the campus, in which the mass rally replaced conversation and listening gave way to diatribe, I quickly discovered that one either supported the proposal of the Black Students Union in its entirety or was tagged an enemy. One morning, a bomb, still ticking, was found outside my office door, placed there by persons unknown. One night, after my wife and I had gone to bed, someone slashed the tires of our two cars and painted all over them: "Facist [sic] Scab."

Drawing on an ideology that has already shaped a sizable part of the world, the black militants at San Francisco State portrayed themselves as the colonized people within the mother country (the United States) fighting against the white racist establishment that would never give up its power without a struggle. Thus certain major themes repeatedly found their way into the speeches and declarations of Black Students Union leaders, ranging from the need for cultural identity and separatism to the call for armed self-defense, and (as their own battle cry for the strike): "Power to the People."

Opposed to the Sorelian emphasis on personalism and individual will that often characterizes the outlook of many white radical groups, such as the Students for a Democratic Society, the black student leadership, stressing black determination, borrowed heavily from the Marxist-Leninist-Maoist tradition, as well as from black revolutionaries like Malcolm X and Fanon, and emphasized the need for organization, discipline and unity.

Among other items in their creed was the firm commitment to take a completely uncompromising nonnegotiable position with the college administration and other authorities like the trustees, who by definition were "the enemy." At a college convocation called to discuss the issues of the strike, and with President Smith in attendance, one of the leaders of the Black Students Union spoke with unmistakable clarity:

"Until we have power, everything is ——. The dog believes we want to participate in his political games and that if we demand ten things, all the niggers really want is five. Each day the demands are delayed we will escalate our tactics. If armed struggle is what is needed for us to control our lives and our education, then that is what we will use. Peace and order are —— issues. They don't mean anything unless we have control of our lives. The pig administration has run down our attempts to win legitimate demands by peaceful means."

Stokely Carmichael had spoken about the importance of the "correct attitude" and the need for black third-world students about to go on strike to "prepare themselves" psychologically. He understood, as did the leadership of the Black Students Union, that self-discipline, self-consciousness and a passionate conviction are fundamental to success. To paraphrase Fanon, who paraphrased Marx: With a politically conscious people nothing is impossible; without a conscious people nothing of significance can be accomplished. Consciousness is the key, making it possible to pull together into the same frame white racism, capitalist injustice and imperialism, while providing the militant activists with justification not only for resisting the social system that has spawned them but for adopting the tactics of disruption and violence.

But there is something more involved here, too. There is a kind of specialized logic that is used again and again by the militants. It is a self-fulfilling prophecy which proves that once you produce a confrontation to make the college act like a fascist beast, it will respond by behaving like one.

How do they do this? By forcing the college to call the police, and by forcing the police to use violence. (Prof. Seymour Martin Lipset reports that Stokely Carmichael once said that any demonstration in which police are not involved is a failure for the demonstrators.) Most people know that a college wants to show a friendly and moderate face; it wants to have meetings and hold forums and convocations. But the radicals know that discussions are "counterrevolutionary" since they help to maintain the system.

On one of the reading lists of the Black Students Union is a book by a white journalist, Robert Ta'ber, entitled "The War of the Flea." Taber analyzes the successful liberation movements around the world and the principles by which a small, dedicated group can employ guerrilla tactics to undermine the legitimacy of the existing order and create the "climate of collapse" which leads to its final destruction. Primarily a propagandist and disseminator of the revolutionary idea, the guerrilla fighter uses the struggle itself—"the actual physical conflict"—as an instrument of agitation. While he will use whatever tactics are suitable to wear down his opponent, his primary objective is political.

"Thus we may paraphrase Clausewitz: Guerrilla war is the extension of politics by means of armed conflict," says Taber. The guerrilla fighter must "seek to aggravate social and political tensions and to raise the level of political consciousness and of revolutionary *will*." Casting himself in the role of David, the rebel "makes it his business to force the enemy into the role of Goliath in the public mind." As a revolutionist, he must "relate each incident and each phase of the conflict to a great 'cause,' so that revolutionary violence is seen as the natural and moral means to a desired end."

Taber then develops a central argument which was given its own application at San Francisco State:

"The guerrilla fights the war of the flea. The flea bites, hops, and bites again, nimbly avoiding the foot that would crush him and feed on him, to plague and bedevil him, to keep him from resting and to destroy his nerve and his morale. What starts as a local infestation must become an epidemic, as one by one the areas of resistance link up, like spreading ink spots on a blotter."

Taber's book seems to have become a kind of strike manual for the Black Students Union, whose leadership devised the strategy of the strike, made the major tactical decisions and planned the disruptive action. Immediately after Carmichael had finished his address at the college, one of its more prominent spokesmen went to the microphone to explain what would happen the next day:

"It just so happens that the members of the BSU Central Committee have been analyzing how student movements have been functioning. Take over buildings, holding it for two or three days, and then the thing is dead. Most of your leaders are ripped off and thrown in jail, or the masses are thrown in jail, and there's no one to lead them.

"From our analysis of this, we think we have developed a technique to deal with this for a prolonged struggle. We call it the war of the flea. . . . What does the flea do? He bites, sucks blood from the dog. Dog bites. What happens when there are enough fleas on a dog? What will he do? He moves. He moves away. He moves on.

"What the man has been running down on us—he's psyched us out, in terms of our manhood. He'll say, 'What you gonna do, nigger? You tryin' to be a man?' Here he is with shotguns, billy clubs, .357 magnums, and all you got is heat. Defenseless.

"That's not the way it's going to be any more. We are the people. We are the majority, and the pigs cannot be everywhere, every place, all the time. And where they are not, we are. And something happens. The philosophy of the flea. You just begin to wear them down. Something is always costin' them.

"Can you dig it? . . . Toilets are stopped up. Pipes is out. Water in the bathroom is just runnin' all over the place. Smoke is coming out of the bathroom. 'I don't know nothin' about it. I'm on my way to take an exam. Don't look at me. Did I plug up the bathroom? Not me.' And when they split, it goes on and on and on. Tomorrow we'll talk more about the flea and develop it some more. . . . We can fight the racist administration on our own ground from now on, where we can win. . . ."

The strike began the following day. While white students were holding a rally and marching to the Administration Building, an activity many believe was a deliberate device to deflect attention, roving bands of black students, in groups of ten or fewer, broke into classes in progress all over the campus, demanding to know why the teachers and students were not supporting them and insisting they be given time to explain the strike. Fist fights broke out, and some of those who refused to dismiss their classes were told that tougher teams would be along to enforce the strike. There were sporadic acts of property destruction, forcing President Smith to call in the San Francisco Police Tactical Squad and close the campus for the rest of the day. But by this time, the disrupters had long since vanished, leaving the campus in a state of turmoil and successful in their first objective: to draw attention to their demands, deny the "enemy" his objective—i.e., normal operation of the college—and force the administration into the countermeasure of calling the police.

The campus reopened the next day, with more violence and some arrests. A bomb exploded in the Education Building. On Friday, November 8, the strike leaders accelerated their guerrilla tactics. Approximately fifty small fires were discovered and extinguished. Black raiding parties, some wearing stocking masks, invaded campus offices, overturning desks and smashing equipment.

Most of the vandalism was done at noon while a strike rally was going on at the center of the campus. Offices were raided and vandalized in the anthropology, psychology and other departments. In the chemistry department, five men and two women, all masked, burst into the office, turned over a desk, wrecked a duplicating machine, overturned wastebaskets, scattered files, and broke the glass in the door. Four Negroes entered the anthropology office and ordered a secretary and two men to leave. One invader cut the wires to the telephone and the electric typewriter, the secretary reported. She said a girl threw the Ditto machine on the floor and pushed over the coffeemaker. A radio was thrown out a window.

These hit-and-run attacks made people uneasy throughout the campus. Secretaries asked to go home early and many of the students were apprehensive. One twenty-two year old biochemistry major told a reporter: "There are a lot of people in my 12:30 class, and every time we heard a noise—even the wind—we looked around, expecting a mass of them to come wheeling through the door. How can you concentrate on studying? One professor told his class: "I'll teach today, but if any one comes in and asks us to leave, we'll leave. We can't afford to take chances."

In the days that followed, the same pattern of "educating" students on the aims of the strike was continued. Teams of strikers, some all black and some all white, would rush into classrooms, announce the class's dismissal and leave—often with a warning that there might be consequences if the class continued. They moved so fast that plain-clothes police could do little to catch them.

A pattern had been set. In the weeks and months to come, the strike would be used as an instrument of agitation in the guerrilla struggle not only to mobilize the already committed, but to radicalize the rest of the student body. The strike leaders understood that before they could seize power, their stated goal, they would have to employ their "flea tactics" with such effectiveness that

the college administration would be forced into repressive coun-
teraction that would build support for the strike.

I can make no attempt here to follow the strike through its
different phases to its conclusion some four months later, when
the "nonnegotiable demands" were negotiated. But before it was
over some 250 faculty members and graduate assistants were on
strike, whole departments were badly split and a few virtually
closed, and several thousand supporters marched regularly around
the campus chanting: "On Strike—Shut It Down!"

Now, a year after the outbreak of the strike, an uneasy quiet
hangs over San Francisco State. S. I. Hayakawa, now permanent
president, has brought a measure of peace—which may turn out
to be only a truce. No one can be sure. A coalition of liberals,
moderates and conservatives has taken over the academic senate
in an attempt to chart a course of reconciliation. It may work.
Only time will tell.

Some of the radicals who were active in the student strike are
gone. George Murray, the Black Panther and BSU leader around
whom so much of the turmoil swirled, has served six months in
jail for failure to disperse, unlawful assembly, disturbing the
peace and inciting to riot. Free on bail while another six-month
sentence is appealed, he has dropped out of the college and the
revolutionary movement, pleading unsuccessfully for leniency
from the court on the ground that he has "undergone a renewal
of religious faith." Nathan Hare, originally hired to run the
black-studies program, was dismissed by President Hayakawa after
he disrupted a faculty meeting.

A student government still exists, presided over by a moderate,
but it has little money. Student-government funds, once a source
of power for campus radicals, are frozen in court pending the outcome of suits and hearings. Many of the student-run experimental
programs have ended. The student daily newspaper, once the stri-
dent voice of white radicalism on campus, is no longer so daily. In
short, a reaction has set in.   It has not been possible here to consider many other elements in the crisis at San Francisco State,
including the important roles of the State College Board of Trustees, the Chancellor and the Governor of California. My limited
purpose has been to examine the ideological backdrop against
which the leaders of the Black Students Union—in their own
idiom—laid their plans for a "prolonged struggle to seize power."
It had also been their hope, as Carmichael put it, to "set the attitude" which would be duplicated across the country, and by the

example of their success to "export" the revolution and its tactical imperatives. That they could not fully deliver on their rhetoric merely confirmed the fact that what was missing among the black leadership cadre was an operating principle of reality—a clear, realistic, political sense of what was achievable.

Some further conclusions:

(1) While the hit-and-run tactics of the "war of the flea" were effective in creating confusion and disorder, they were unsuccessful in terms of the publicly announced revolutionary goals of the strikers. In spite of the fact that there really is a "third world" in the city of San Francisco, as perhaps in few other places in the country, the leaders of the BSU and Third World Liberation Front discovered that there was no single, united off-campus community, black or otherwise, waiting to send its thousands of citizens to join the militant students in their struggle for the seizure of power. No one should have been surprised to learn that that kind of revolutionary outpouring was not forthcoming.

(2) No matter how much the mass rallies may have been enlivened by the oratorical flourishes of black student leaders, it is doubtful that the anticolonial model of native-imperialist relationships was accepted by the majority of students as appropriate to a college community. Whatever else it may be, San Francisco State is not a fascist state run by racist colonizers.

(3) Among the aims of the Black Students Union was sole control over black studies. President Smith had announced the creation of a new Department of Black Studies in the first week of the fall semester, two months before the strike began. One does not make a black-studies department like instant potatoes. But if those who were in charge of its planning had been more interested in getting down to the serious business of putting together a substantive and responsible black-studies curriculum instead of playing at revolution, they would have met with far more success and the program would be much farther along today.

Again this year, the militant leadership cadre of the BSU show signs of being concerned only with getting their own hand-picked or approved ideological compatriots onto the payroll of black studies. The thought of a broad-based, independent faculty whose individual members would have a genuine and scholarly interest in their particular subject matter is apparently not acceptable. It is not enough. The BSU leaders want it understood that they are in control.

When the strike began to lose support, conflicts among the

leaders and followers emerged. Those who are disenchanted with all the talk of revolution now feel it is time to start channeling their energies into organizing some long-term programs at the college. Thus, the Chinese- and Philippine-American students have turned their attention this year to developing area study programs which from their own point of view will meet their special needs and be academically sound and defensible.

(4) Many campus observers find (or want to find) more pragmatic and rational behavior in the militancy of black students than in the radicalism of whites. It is a debatable point and has been argued many ways. A combination of many factors contributed to the pronounced pattern of violence in the Black Students Union at San Francisco State, including the ghetto-based ritualization of violence among many blacks, frustration and resentment at the life style and standards of a college environment, and the influence of the Black Panther party in the Bay Area. In addition, the BSU leadership constantly sought to legitimate their disruptive behavior by a shrewd manipulation of ideological appeals. Prof. Martin Kilson, a black political scientist at Harvard, may be right in saying the cult of violence serves to validate black manhood. At San Francisco State, it also served the proclaimed purpose of seizing power and control.

(5) During most of the last year, San Francisco State was being torn apart from the inside by the militants of the left. But off campus, watching and waiting, were the avenging furies of the right. The student radicals, with the support of some striking teachers, kept saying that what they were doing was "saving" higher education in California. The political truth is that they helped galvanize all of the conservative and reactionary forces in the state into a kind of mass public that is now motivated to act not with interest, patience and constructive concern, but out of fear, anxiety and anger. While the student militants kept shouting: "Power to the People!" I was depressed when I thought of the people who really have the power.

18. INSIDE THE BUFFALO COMMUNE:
OR, HOW TO DESTROY A UNIVERSITY

Paul Kurtz

*Paul Kurtz is Professor of Philosophy at the State University
of New York at Buffalo, and editor of* The Humanist.

I

IT WAS only a few short years ago that the State University of
New York at Buffalo was hailed as the emerging "Berkeley of the
East."

The University of Buffalo, founded in 1846, was a second-rate
municipal school until it joined the newly-established State University of New York in 1962. This merger infused massive new
funding, as New York State began to compete with California in
building a state university. Buffalo, as the largest unit in the system, had a promising future. Plans were made for a brand new
campus in suburban Amherst; its estimated cost was upwards of
$650 million; and it was said to be the largest and most extensive
educational project ever conceived, and second only to Brasilia as
the largest architectural project in the world.

The University of Buffalo, grew at a galloping pace. It attracted
internationally-known stars: John Barth, Leslie Fiedler, Sir John
Eccles, C. H. Waddington, Lukas Foss (with the Buffalo Philhar-
monic), Timothy Costello, Robert Creeley, Ludwig von
Bertalanffy, and others. There were also brilliant appointments
among the lesser-known, younger faculty. Buffalo was on the
frontier of educational innovation in America.

In 1966 it brought in a new President, Martin Meyerson
(briefly Chancellor at Berkeley during the four-letter-word upris-
ing), Warren Bennis (an "organic populist" from M.I.T.) as Executive Vice-President, and Eric Larrabee (without academic experience, but an associate editor of *Harper's* and *American Heri-*

This paper was written in May, 1970 (before Cambodia) and especially for this
volume. Since then a new administration has come on the scene at Buffalo,
promising new policies. This article is being published as an illustration of how a
great university can enter a state of decline, unless corrective measures are taken.

220

tage) as Provost. Overnight, Meyerson proceeded to divide the University into seven Faculties and to break the multiversity, which eventually was to have forty thousand students, into some twenty smaller colleges, so as to avoid the alienation so frequent in larger institutions.

The growth rate at Buffalo was phenomenal: here was instant university on the make, and everyone in the educational world knew about it. Unlike Harvard, Yale, Columbia, Chicago, or Berkeley, which had their periods of growth earlier, the University of Buffalo (although 120 years old) acquired a new sense of mission when it became part of the state university system and embraced an open future for adventure in educational experiment.

Almost all of this now lies shattered. At the present moment, the State University of New York at Buffalo is in a shambles. What happened at Buffalo is a frightening illustration of how vulnerable a fragile educational institution is when an all-out assault upon it is conducted by revolutionaries allied with radicals. It also illustrates the manner in which the sleeping dogs of political reaction can be aroused in the community and encouraged by widespread public outrage and outcry.

Martin Meyerson felt it necessary to resign after only a few short years to assume the Presidency of the University of Pennsylvania. By then he had lost the confidence of a large section of the faculty and alienated the greater Buffalo community. Warren Bennis resigned as Executive Vice-President. Larrabee gave up the Provostship. Even Chancellor Samuel B. Gould had tendered his resignation. Although he denied that his leaving was connected with the situation at Buffalo, it is undoubtedly true that he came under heavy criticism and pressure from voters in New York State especially and from members of the Legislature because of events at the largest of the campuses under his jurisdiction.

Also symptomatic of the decline of Buffalo is the fact that the construction of the new Amherst campus has been halted for over a year because of the refusal by a minority coalition to accept Governor Rockefeller's integrated work-force plan. The faculty is bitterly divided into factions, and many resignations are in the offing. There have been almost daily demands from revolutionary militants to shut down the University, and right-wing activists in upstate New York have constantly attacked the University as the major den of "iniquity" and "subversion" on the Niagara Frontier. Upstate legislators are showing an undue interest in the internal affairs of the University which may presage intervention—something uncommon in most State Universities.

II

The events at Buffalo contain the ingredients of classical tragedy: the downfall—in this case of an important, young institution—due to a defect in moral courage.

The University's decline, in the opinion of many observers, began some three years ago. The full extent of its malady did not become apparent to those on the outside until a serious outbreak of violence and dissension on the evening of February 25, 1970, which continued unabated until the beginning of the Easter vacation on March 20. During that period, the State University at Buffalo and the surrounding community were in a state of extreme convulsion. It was a period in which over one hundred students, faculty, and policemen were injured in numerous confrontations, forty-five faculty members were arrested, and scores of students were apprehended and suspended. It was a period which saw an estimated $250,000 damage to buildings, including extensive window-breaking and firebombings, and the burning of over 2 thousand books of a rare collection. The University became the scene of sniper fire, of guerrilla bands who disrupted classes and threatened unsympathetic students and faculty members. Following hard on the heels of the violence came vigorous demands from all sectors of the Buffalo community—including working people, businessmen, housewives, and members of the Legislature—to purge the University of its revolutionaries. This response to the threats against academic freedom by extremists has posed another serious threat to academic freedom.

The initial outbreak of violence on February 25 caught everyone off guard. The issue seemed negotiable: black athletes refused to play at a basketball game and sat in at the center of the gym. As a result the game was cancelled. Their demands were simple enough: the hiring of two black coaches and the development of a different method of financing black athletes. The administration agreed to meet with representatives of the Black Students Union. On the evening of February 25, Acting-President Peter Regan and Black students were conferring in Hayes Hall, the Administration building, and they were close to agreement.

Suddenly some forty to fifty militant white students burst into Regan's office and demanded an audience. Since he was in the midst of negotiations, he explained that he could not meet with them. The militant students stormed out of the building in rage and began to hurl stones and other objects through the windows of Hayes Hall, including the President's office, as well as the surrounding classroom buildings. The campus security police—some twenty in number—were called to prevent further vandalism to the buildings. They pursued the vandals, who fled into Norton Union, the student building.

Campus security entered and attempted to arrest Terry Keegan, well-known leader of this and previous disruptions on campus. A struggle ensued as the arrest was being made, and when the campus police left, they were met with a barrage of rocks, sticks, garbage cans, and pieces of ice from a large crowd of protesting students. The campus police retreated in disarray, but not before several were injured by the student assault. Fearful of a continued attack upon personnel, campus security called the Buffalo Police Department for assistance. Meanwhile, militant students hastily barricaded themselves in Norton Union, and reports circulated that they were destroying windows and furniture.

The Buffalo Police Department came on campus, immediately broke through the doors of the barricaded Union, and charged into the building. They were met by opposition, and in the process several heads were bloodied and innocent bystanders mauled. As the police left the building, they were assaulted by over 2 hundred rock-throwing students, and they in turn attacked in an attempt to disperse the crowd. Again, both police and students suffered casualties.

The black athlete issue and the unexpected battle with police sparked a steady escalation of violent events in the following week. Some radical students and faculty charged that the administration (Regan, not Meyerson, managed the University's "strategy" all during this period) had called the Buffalo Police Department with undue haste. To many others it seemed apparent that militant revolutionaries desperately wanted a confrontation and that they used the black athletes' issue as a pretext to provoke one.

Riots had broken out at Santa Barbara and elsewhere during the week to protest the verdicts of the Chicago Conspiracy trials. The issue of the black athletes was lost sight of in the desire of revolutionaries to inflame the campus for ulterior political motives. Indeed, Jerry Rubin later claimed that it was violence in the

streets that forced the power structure to grant the Chicago defendants bail previously denied.

The next day, the campus was once more in turmoil as acts of
vandalism and protest continued. The Buffalo Police Department
was again called to the campus, but this time it was confronted by
a howling mob of 500 students and some younger faculty, enraged
at what they claimed had happened the preceding night, and
screaming, "Pigs off campus!" Several police cars were attacked
and their windows broken, and a small force of thirty police were
surrounded, verbally assaulted, and menaced. In a placatory response to the demonstrators, the administration again removed all
Buffalo police from the campus on Thursday, February 26, to restore calm and avoid further exacerbations of feelings. But the
situation by now was out of hand: a new San Francisco State was
emerging.

Student militants continued to vandalize buildings. On the
night of Friday, February 27, and the following weekend, several
buildings, including the library and the faculty club, were
firebombed with Molotov cocktails. There were widespread academic disruptions: the classes of Lionel Abel, noted critic, and Se-
lig Adler, distinguished historian, and others were disrupted. Liquid
amonia was splashed on the floor, forcing evacuation of some
classrooms. The protestors ran through corridors and laboratories
ransacking equipment and terrorizing people as they went. Numerous faculty members and students who had voiced opposition
to what was occurring on the campus received death threats during this period. I had the dubious distinction of receiving five
warnings in one weekend, including a written injunction, drawing upon Conrad's *Heart of Darkness*, in which I was admon-
ished: "Mistah Kurtz—he dead." The main target seemed to be the
liberals or ex-radicals (such as Abel, Adler, or myself), who refused to remain silent and criticized the erosion of academic freedom by the violence and threats of violence of extremist students.

There were no police on campus during this period. On Monday, March 2, a Strike Committee was formed. Whereas no issues
had been formulated before, the Administration was now confronted with a list of twelve hastily-drawn demands. Some 300
faculty members and teaching assistants out of 1400 faculty announced that they would suspend classes until the demands were
met. A Provisional Revoluntionary Government and a workers'
Liberation College were established. A group proclaiming itself

"Stalinists for the Apolcalypse" was formed. Strange faces suddenly began to appear; nonstudents, high school students, and militants from other campuses augmented the strike force, which demonstrated daily. Meanwhile, in response to continued violence, Acting President Regan obtained a court injunction prohibiting disruption of classes or the blocking of entrances. He attempted to negotiate with the Strike Committee, but it was very difficult to find individuals willing to discuss the issues.

The militants apparently thought they had a good thing going and wanted to keep the pressure on. Why negotiate when they were gaining strength? One of the demands called for the abolition of ROTC, and President Regan was willing to discuss the matter with the strikers. A public meeting was scheduled to debate the issues, but Regan was hooted from the platform by a shower of obscenities, "F--- o-- you bastard!" etc. There were other demands: that Regan resign, that the injunction be lifted, that all defense contracts be terminated (there was only one, a Themis project, which measured the effects of underwater pressure on the body), that open admissions for the Third World be adopted, that the newly-established colleges be given absolute self-determination (the radicals already controlled many of them), and that two faculty members denied tenure be granted it.

Upwards of 30 to 50 per cent of the students absented themselves from classes at the height of the strike—some out of sympathy with the strike, many out of fear, and many out of indifference. By the following Thursday, March 5, the strike began to peter out, though the violence, intimidation, and vandalism continued. At this point the militants resorted to a new tactic—the blocking of Hayes Hall, key offices of which by now had been virtually gutted.

It was clear that this flagrant violation of the injunction would bring the police back on campus. Apparently the militants wanted a bloody confrontation in order to gain further support. In a desperate effort some 100 militants blocked entrances and refused to allow people to enter. With this obvious violation of the injunction came a strong demand for its enforcement from conservative forces on campus and in the community.

That morning Regan announced the temporary suspension of some twenty key militants who were involved in constant disruptions and who had been identified by witnesses, pending a full hearing by a new Temporary Commission, under the Chairmanship of Professor R. Ketter,[1] established by the University Council (the Board of Trustees) for that purpose. The next day militants donned masks to avoid identification and formed guerrilla bands, roaming from building to building threatening staff, secretaries, students, and faculty with violence if they did not vacate offices and dismiss classes.

On the next day, Friday, March 6, the violence and vandalism reached its apogee. Water faucets in Hayes Hall were deliberately ruptured, flooding the basement and endangering the complex electrical circuits. The secretarial staff in Hayes Annex, the center of records and admissions, was physically threatened and forced to flee in anguish and fear. Later the records were fire bombed and burned. That night, a mob made the rounds of the campus, attacking Themis, and leaving the campus to destroy the windows of the Manufacturers and Traders Trust Company bank adjacent to the University. Revolutionaries shouted that their real target was the capitalists and that they would bring down the banks and corporations!

All during this period many sincere faculty deplored what was going on, yet they also were reluctant to urge that police be brought back on campus. Some thought that to violate the university as a sanctuary was a far greater crime than to tolerate student vandalism: "the breaking of a few windows," said one radical faculty member. Yet the vandalism mounted continually. As a result, a 24-hour faculty-student peace patrol was established. At one point it included several hundred dedicated people, whose task was to be present at all threatened disruptions and to cool tempers. For a time the patrol seemed effective and hopes soared that a solution to the problem of violence had been found. Unfortunately it was a will o' the wisp. The patrol was unable to prevent further vandalism and disruption, particularly by marauding bands. By the night of Friday, March 6, the leader, Professor David Hayes, now at odds with President Regan, resigned in a state of near collapse, and the patrol began to disintegrate.

By this time the situation at the State University of New York at Buffalo had become headline national news. The citizens of upstate New York was protesting en masse at what was happening. Although there were efforts by the administration to minimize the extent of damage, the daily reports in the press about

---

[1] He has since been named President of the University.

the extent of vandalism and intimidation called these efforts into question and seemed to emphasize the fact that the administration was unwilling or unable to prevent it. With Meyerson no longer functioning as President, and Regan acting in that capacity (hoping that he still might be nominated as the new President), it was apparent that the University administration had lost control of the situation because of its previous indecisions.

Regan, Rockefeller, Gould, the state legislators, the University Council, and Board of Trustees by this time were being overwhelmed by thousands of phone calls, telegrams, and letters from irate citizens demanding that the administration take some decisive action and put an end to the violence. Many faculty members, students, and 1300 out of 1700 staff members demanded protection against marauding disruptive students in a petition to the President. What was now evident was a virtual breakdown of the campus as a civilized community: chaos, fear, anarchy, and terror were masters. A small vigilante band of militants had the university at its mercy—they would not negotiate, they demanded complete capitulation to their unreasonable demands.

It was at this point that the decision was taken to bring the police back on campus—after an absence of ten days. But it was also decided to do so in a manner that would reduce the danger of a physical confrontation. Accordingly, about 300 Buffalo police were quietly introduced on the following Sunday morning. They patrolled the campus regularly in small squads, thus preventing roaming guerrilla bands from disrupting classes or vandalizing buildings. (The administration had received strong indications that the same tactics would continue on Monday.) However, the presence of a large force of police on campus alarmed many faculty members and students. Some were not fully aware of the previous disruptions and of the full extent of the damage. Others, who had called for protection only two days earlier, now rebelled at the sight of patrols. They spoke as if a police state was imminent.

On Sunday afternoon a large protest rally was held. On Monday the mood of protest was still strong and a large number of moderate faculty and students in department meetings—who had been on the sidelines until that time—intervened, petitioning against police on campus. Some even objected to the temporary suspensions. With the police on campus, however, calm had been restored, and physical disruptions had all but ceased. Yet the militants waged a campaign of continued condemnation and vilification. Jerry Rubin was brought in to address a crowd of 4,000 on Tuesday night. Because of fear that his bail would be revoked if violence occurred, efforts were made to cool it. At a special Faculty Senate meeting called on Wednesday, the faculty voted to have the police removed from campus. The motion was amended to condemn violence, harassment, and disruption, but the radical faculty and its supporters managed to delete the condemnation of disruptions.

It was now obvious—to all who would see—that the violence was *not* simply student-led, but to some extent faculty-encouraged. In any case, under this pressure, President Regan, with the support of the Executive Committee of the Senate, announced a phased withdrawal of the police and the lifting of the temporary suspension—though without Executive Committee support for the latter. At the Faculty meeting, a vote of censure against Regan was introduced and defeated. Regan by this time had lost support from the Left for being too strong, but also from the Center and Right for being too weak. Yet many faculty voted for him, for they feared that to remove the Acting President at this time would be an invitation to further chaos.

Tension on the campus reached a climax on Thursday, after the announcement of the phased withdrawal. Commissioner of Police Frank Felicetta announced that the Buffalo Police Department had final responsibility for public safety anywhere in the city and that he would not remove all the police while obvious threats to life and property still existed. That evening a mob of 800 students began to gather, and again demonstrated against Themis and ROTC. The militants were itching for a confrontation: they shouted, "Shut it down!" and attacked the police patrols, hurling rocks and other objects at them. The police, aware of possible brutality that could boomerang, showed measured restraint. While the Buffalo police are no angels, and many charges of brutality have been leveled against them by the ACLU (particularly for their busts of drug users among students and for their harshness in Buffalo's black ghetto), having been on the scene as a close observer at this time, I can attest to the attempt of the police to avoid precipitous action. It was only after continuous rock-throwing that the police finally made an effort to defend themselves. At one point, for example, six students attacked an isolated policeman who would have been seriously injured had not others came to his rescue. When the evening was over about sixty to ninety students and police had been injured; many required hospitalization.

By now the temper of the Buffalo campus and the surrounding community had reached a fever pitch. The militants began to lose some support because of their unprovoked attack on the police. People earlier opposed to relying on the police to preserve peace were now not so sure of their ground. On Sunday, March 15, a new round of escalation occurred. Forty-five faculty members peacefully sat in at the President's office in Hayes Hall to protest the continued presence of police on campus and the continuance of the injunction. They said that they would stay until the police left, and they urged others to join them. (Additional faculty were waiting in a nearby building to follow them.) The faculty members were requested to leave by the administration, since they were in violation of the injunction. They refused to move and were arrested for violating the court order forbidding disruption and taken downtown for arraignment. District Attorney Dillon, a strong Democratic vote-getter in Erie County, charged them on three counts: criminal trespass, criminal contempt, and civil contempt.

A subsequent meeting of the Faculty Senate requested that the Administration drop the charges, but by this time the matter was out of the hands of the University. The DA's office and many area legislators insisted that the law had been violated and that those who broke the law must be prosecuted. It is most regrettable that the arrests were made even though technically the law was being violated. Had the University acted sooner it would not have been faced with the desperate need to apply sanctions. Some faculty members were being criminally charged, because of the great furor, for what they thought was merely a peaceful non-violent demonstration. Not all of them were aware of the legal consequences of their action.

Additional evidence of the public's mood is the fact that during this period Leslie Fiedler and his wife were convicted on maintaining a house where marijuana was used. Their case, dating back many months, had been postponed time and again. It was based on questionable wire-tap evidence, and there were strong indications that the charges would be dropped. But after the intense feelings aroused by the outbreaks of student violence, public opinion veered strongly against the University and any dissenters connected with it. The Fiedlers were convicted as much because of the climate of public opinion as on the relevant evidence.

III

The terrible events of the four-week period were, in the view of many careful observers on the faculty and administration, entirely predictable. They were the legacy of a policy of appeasement that was bound to lead to an explosion. No doubt many other explanations can be given for the Buffalo breakdown. One explanation advanced by liberals and radicals is that the confrontation on campus occurred because the University was unresponsive to social change, because a "reactionary" faculty opposed reform. This, they insist, is the source of the University's fatal blunder in calling the police and "radicalizing" a large number of moderates.

One possible explanation for faculty indecision is the widespread idea that individual responsibility or guilt is basically a social problem. This concept of "no fault" finds many liberals and radicals believing that the proper approach to violence and lawlessness is not to condemn those responsible for them, but to explain *why* the violence and lawlessness arose in the first place. This concept of "no fault" has certain legitimate applications in insurance but applied to situations in which alternative courses of action were possible, the results are bizarre. In the Buffalo situation, we are told, if there was violence, it was the fault of the university, not the students; it is *we*, the faculty, who need to change, not they, the students; the cure for violence is to *understand* and *correct* the causes of it, not to curb violence or punish the violent. But this argument is absurd. For with respect to the outbreaks of violence on many campuses today, the *contrary* more often appears to be the case, and what happened at Buffalo confirms it. Precisely *because* of the rapid tempo of change, precisely because of the failure to affix individual responsibility for criminal actions and apply proper sanctions against those who committed violence, the disruptions reached crisis proportions. These master strategists who cry that the cure for violence is reform are like those who argue that arson can be stopped only by constructing better buildings. But even these buildings are vulnerable to arsonists at large. A policy of reasonable reform without a policy of punishment for those who commit violence or break the law is doomed to failure because the reforms will become the occasion for further disruptions if those responsible for previous disruptions are amnestied.

The ingredients for revolution on the Buffalo campus had been building up for several years. From the time Martin Meyerson became President, two forces converged on the campus to form an alliance. First, there were the revolutionary militants—a melange of Maoists, Leninists, and Stalinists dedicated to the seizure of the State University of New York at Buffalo as a base for the revolutionary transformation of society. These included students, graduate assistants, teachers, and nonstudents. For example, one fiery student leader thrown out of the University of Wisconsin for disruption was admitted to Buffalo's philosophy department two years ago and immediately moved into a key position as chief orator of the New Left. Another, a Maoist sympathizer, came from Duke University. These revolutionary militants were relatively small in number—possibly 40 to 50 hard-core students and 25 faculty—yet they were able to capture 200 to 300 students and 100 faculty on crucial issues. Their main interest was not in reforming the University, but in revolutionizing society. The University was to be only a steppingstone and base for operation. Whether they came to Buffalo by design or happenstance is hard to determine. Obviously, the word had gone out that Buffalo was a groovy place, the place where the action was. Within a two or three year period, large numbers of revolutionaries materialized on the scene. They tended to predominate in two faculties, social sciences and administration, and humanities and arts, and in a few key departments, especially philosophy, English, history, social welfare, and American studies.

It is important to record the fact that they were encouraged by key persons in the administration of the university who identified with another group made up primarily of educational radicals. These radicals were interested chiefly in (a) bringing about the educational reform of the university by altering requirements, abandoning the current curriculum and loosening old structures and forms, and in (b) encouraging the values of the emerging counter-culture. These radicals included many old-time permissive liberals or ex-radicals (such as Leslie Fiedler and Edgar Friedenberg, who calls himself a "conservative," but who is an admirer of Cleaver), very concerned with innovation and experiment in education. The radical educational reformers were especially strong in the administration, and several of the people that Meyerson and Bennis brought to the University, including radical Chairmen and Deans, fit into this category.

These radicals were naturally sensitive to criticisms of the Vietnam war, poverty, the plight of the blacks in the cities. Altogether with political liberals they felt deeply involved. But they were drawn to the revolutionaries' critique rather than to the liberal program of social reform, even though their primary interests seemed to be educational reform. They exalted rapid social change. They wanted to build something new and daring, not repeat what the Ivy League was doing. Their approach at times suggested to many on the faculty a combination of the worst aspects of Madison Avenue hucksterism and a native, pragmatic suspicion of the "academic." For them, the cardinal sins of the academy were "formalism," "credentialism," "careerism," and "professionalism." They were not loath to see the university attacked from within; they wanted to liberate the schools from the dead hand of tradition; and as proponents of a vague, latter-day version of Deweyism, however uncritical, they wanted to make the University responsive to the needs of society. Interestingly, the older admirers and followers of Dewey on the campus were repelled at the things done in the name of Dewey—especially by the wholesale abandonment of academic standards, the denigration of intelligence, and the absence of rational discipline.

The point is, there was a working alliance between the revolutionaries and the radical educationists, a new popular front, that was supposed to apply dramatic therapy to the University. Buffalo presented an unparalleled opportunity; for vast sums of money were being poured into it by the State of New York, and all of the traditional constraints could be abandoned in a rapid quest for growth. No doubt the revolutionaries and radical educators had different goals in mind—at least this seemed to be the case for some. For although the revolutionary ultimately wishes to destroy the school system, the radical educator wants to save it by radical therapy. In the ensuing struggle for power in the University, the chief "enemy" of the united front of radical educators and revolutionaries were those who defended academic freedom, tenure, and standards of excellence. All of these were indiscriminately condemned as "conservative." Often no distinctions were made between genuine "liberals" and "convervatives." Anyone who opposed the new program was said to be "against progress" and to be expressing a position of "entrenched self-interest." The "wave of the future" was supposed to be tied up with the radical-revolutionary scheme, and all who raised any objection or opposed them were cursed as fingers of "the dead hand of reaction."

There was an initial honeymoon period between the faculty and administration when Meyerson first came to power in 1966. But Meyerson's educational proposals soon invited opposition from members of the old administration, and faculty, who were not dazzled by the innovations. It should be pointed out that many of the faculty, so bitterly condemned as "reactionaries" or "dead wood" (by Bennis as quoted in a Los Angeles *Times* interview), were themselves progressives in education, innovators before, during, and after the Meyerson regime: they merely insisted upon the careful evaluation of programs. To claim that one believes in experimental education means nothing, unless one is prepared to develop parameters for testing new methods of learning. Many radicals in education talk about an "experimental" approach, but they do not understand the essential ingredients of a controlled test. They are romantic reformers and poets rather than objective scientific methodologists willing to test their educational ideas in practice by means of careful observation.

In any case, Buffalo was able to institute some important and fundamental changes during the period when it became part of the State University system. A whole new dimension in international education was established, with every effort to internationalize the curriculum, providing for study abroad and various kinds of research. There was a strong emphasis on interdisciplinary studies among departments, especially in the policy sciences and urban studies; a new black studies program was established without fanfare before a black studies program was initiated at Harvard; an EPIS program for disadvantaged youth was inaugurated which brought the Freshman class in 1969–70 to an enrollment of approximately 23 per cent blacks, many of them unqualified by traditional criteria but of high potential. The curriculum was modified so that many standard requirements were dispensed with; and the first six colleges, particularly A and F, were assigned Masters, and extremely innovative methods of education were adopted. In College A, for example, there were no traditional courses, no examinations, no requirements, no distinctions between professors and students. The students were permitted to grade themselves—with the result that 94 per cent received A grades. The Master of College A, Fred Snell, quipped that a student could take a course of study in tying shoe laces, if that was what he wanted. Many students received academic credit for studying in Europe or in the Buffalo ghetto on projects conceived by themselves.

Considerable changes in the governance of the University also occurred. The Faculty Senate, which had formerly been a body of elected representatives, was expanded, largely under the presidency of Meyerson, to a full Senate comprising virtually the entire faculty of 1400; the old Student Senate was abandoned in favor of a Polity town meeting, which any student could attend to discuss and vote on issues.

Both changes played directly into the hands of the militants, who for three years were able continually to disrupt the Faculty Senate, making it difficult or impossible for it to function; they were also able to take over the Polity, by packing its meetings with militants. Early in 1968, the faculty began to show signs of resistance against two increasingly dominant tendencies: violence and the deterioration of academic standards. Those opposed to these tendencies began to make their views known in the Faculty Senate and its Executive Committee. A broad coalition of liberals and conservatives were able to win most of the elections and to predominate at the Senate meetings. This coalition was united in its opposition to disruption and in its resolve to maintain academic standards. It was increasingly suspicious of gimmicks being palmed off as "progress" by the radicals in the administration. During this period the Faculty Senate had been continuously disrupted by militant students who were egged on by radical faculty and administrators. Its proceedings were often disrupted by the rushing and sometimes battering down of doors to gain access. Vile obscenities were hurled against various members by their extremist opponents. Under such conditions it was difficult for some members of the faculty to vote without a sense of intimidation; and many began to absent themselves rather than to suffer continuing indignities and insult. Revolutionary and radical forces gradually gained ground through the use of this strategy of psychological attack and intimidation. The strategy was encouraged by educational radicals, who thought the approach could be used to serve the purposes of educational reform. The faculty, which wished to deliberate carefully about the many demands for reform, was increasingly squeezed between militant revolutionaries among the students on the one hand and the radical educational reformers in the administration on the other. There seemed to be a concerted drive to "break the back" of the faculty. The events of February 28-March 20 and earlier increased the power and influence of the New Left in the Senate. In despair, many moderate and conservative Faculty members have subsequently boycotted Faculty Senate meetings. Other faculty members of the center, horrified at the presence of police on campus, have manifested sympathy for the radical point of view. In effect, the center has collapsed. It has been pushed either to the right—with a resulting alliance of liberals and conservatives demanding law and order—or to the left—with resulting support for the radical assault on the university. The upshot has been an extreme polarization of the faculty and a destruction of whatever liberal consensus once existed.

IV

It should now be apparent that the violent outbursts of February 25—March 20 did not occur in a vacuum. They were the climax of years of chronic disruption and violence. The full story of the extent of disruption and violence was minimized or suppressed by the Meyerson administration, which claimed that it had the "answers" to the problems that other campuses were facing. Yet under this administration Hayes Hall had been seized the year before (under pressure, Meyerson had reluctantly applied for an injunction and called in the police to enforce it), many classes had been disrupted, faculty threatened, ROTC, Dow Chemical and Themis Defense Department sites damaged, Senate and Senate Executive Committee meetings disrupted. There were confrontations in the medical school, files were stolen or removed, buildings were vandalized, and the structure containing the university advocate's office was gutted by fire.

There are many who are convinced that had Meyerson been willing to˙ apply *sanctions* to students disruptions, the February-March 1970 outbreaks in all likelihood could have been avoided. But until that time there was *not one case* of a penalty imposed on students by the lax administration. Meyerson had ignored a faculty petition of 350 (the largest signed until then) that called for clear guidelines against violence and the use of police and suspension when necessary. Meyerson's theory was typical of the liberal guilt-syndrome: if the students disrupt there must be causes, and we must be to blame. Therefore, rather than condemn or punish them, we must keep one step ahead and outfox them by reforming the university. The bitter lesson is that this strategy *did not* work at Buffalo: for significant reform and significant concessions *had* been made, but appeasement only whetted the demand for more, not less. Meyerson's strategy also included shifting the blame to the faculty ostensibly for being intransigent. At one point (in 1969) when the students made demands upon him, he in turn made demands upon the faculty. He wanted to get rid of all Defense Department research on campus. The faculty thought an issue of academic freedom was involved and voted for an open campus. Meyerson wanted 50-50 sharing of student-faculty power. The faculty was considering a new form of governance, but it was fearful that that kind of governance would not bring peace but only enhance the cause of the revolutionaries and weaken standards.

The story at Buffalo is a story of escalation of demands, of a weak university response, and in consequence still more extreme demands. Indeed, by some guilt-ridden method of response, the University never said, *"No,"* but almost always said, *"Yes,* you have a just grievance and we will try to accommodate it." But as soon as one demand was met, new ones cropped up.

There were twelve demands made during the February 25-March 20 period. Many of them are familiar on other campuses. The revolutionaries have made it patently clear to anyone who would listen that the specific demands offered were *not* crucial, that they didn't *seriously* expect that they would or could be met by the university, that the major goal of their disruption was to gain control of the university so as to prepare the way for revolution. Their announced intention was to "shut the university down."

The naïveté of faculty and students who so vehemently reacted against the bringing of police on campus is disheartening. The gnawing question that they have not been able to solve is this: how can the university protect individuals from constant harassment, violence, and vandalism? As a last resort, it is *only* the civil authorities who may be able to protect the integrity of the university. One reason why so many of the faculty recoiled in horror at Buffalo (and they did so at Harvard, Columbia, Cornell, and elsewhere) is that they were not fully apprised by the administration of the epidemic of violence and vandalism that had been occurring (there were almost 1200 cases of vandalism in 1969 on the Buffalo campus alone). Nor did they fully understand or believe the revolutionary goals of the militants. Although faculties are often high in intellectual talent, courage is a rare virtue on campuses. Dedicated teachers frequently find it difficult to use the rod of criticism on their students, particularly when so many of these teachers feel the need to be popular or well-liked. Perhaps we should not expect all members of the faculty—which includes poets, engineers, scientists, artists, and classicists—to rediscover a truth of human civilization that no community is possible without certain elementary principles of just order enforced by law.

The eagerness of the revolutionaries to use any and all means to bring the university to its knees should be apparent to those who are willing to examine the evidence. No amount of rationalization by radicals or liberals can justify this fact nor explain it away.

Given their conspiratorial goals, the militants at Buffalo gradually assumed control of the Graduate Student Association; they became extremely influential in the undergraduate Student Association; and were able to dominate the editorial policy of *The Spectrum,* the leading student newspaper. The revolutionaries were virtual masters of Norton Union, its corridors and halls, so that almost no meetings by moderates, including anyone to the right of the Left, were tolerated. The revolutionaries by skillful manipulation were able to control the many mass meetings that were constantly held on campus and that were an important vehicle for keeping the university in constant turmoil.

The revolutionaries began to undermine the undergraduate college curriculum. The teaching assistants in several radical departments offered courses in "the theory and practice of revolutionary socialism," "how to make a revolution," and even "guerrilla warfare." In particular, they were able to take control of at least two of the new Colleges, A and F. In September 1969, they introduced a course called "Social Change," under the aegis of the American Studies Department, with forty-five sections, many of which taught the tactics and strategy of revolution. These courses were designed to indoctrinate and to recruit. Many instructors did not even pretend to offer an objective or dispassionate analysis of their subject matter, but simply presented their own commitments. They made no bones about their desire to develop converts to their brand of Marxism. In many departments the revolutionaries attempted radically to revamp the undergraduate and graduate curricula. There was an effort to water down graduate requirements. Spending so much time in activism, they had little inclination or opportunity for hard study. The revolutionary students and faculty attempted to gain control of the admissions and tenure committees, in order to guarantee the admission of radical students and the appointment and promotion of "politically reliable" professors.

A hard core of well-organized and professionalized students was able to whip a mob of gullible, idealistic students into a frenzied state to do their bidding. One colleague observed that what we were faced with was a political-psychiatric problem: there was the mob of students who had abandoned all pretense of reason and was in a psychotic state, and there were those in the university community who were willing to listen to them and were themselves in a half-psychotic dream state in their manner of response because they took the militants so seriously.

The strategy of the revolutionaries was obvious: there was an all-out war on the University, and rational arguments were not important. The views of the liberal that he could reason out solutions with the revolutionaries, or isolate them, failed. For the aim of the revolutionaries was to demoralize the University by constant assault, whether by epithets or threats of force—and thus compel capitulation and a new escalation of demands.

For what ends? Apparently two: first, keeping the University in turbulence in order to show the "repressive" nature of "Amerika," as a fascist state; and second, seizing control of the University in order to make it a center for Marxist revolution that would eventually fan out and control society—using students, intellectuals, and blacks as the army rather than the proletariat. The liberal belief that it can contain the attacks by meeting the demands does not deal with the existence of a well-disciplined army, trained and supported by a cadre, hell-bent on overturning the University.

Responding to the threats by undertaking reforms has merit. Surely, changes have to be made for their own sake. Moreover, by reforming, the university may be able to neutralize and isolate the political radicals and thus prevent them from finding allies among the moderates. But how far shall we go in reform? To remake the university in the way that the revolutionaries wish, would mean an end to academic freedom, as we have known it, for the university would be given a "moral," actually a political commitment: its main goal would no longer be learning or inquiry, but action to promote the radical restructuring of society.

It should be apparent to anyone who has studied the university scene that violence and revolutionaries on campus are not simply due to the Vietnam war; France, Germany, Italy, and Japan are not involved in the Vietnam war, yet have suffered the same agonies of violence imposed by a dedicated group of revolutionaries. The Vietnam war surely gains support for the revolutionaries on American campuses because it touches on a moral issue that recruits moderates to the cause, but the hope that violence will end if or when the war ends is idle fancy.

The "strategic" use of violence on university campuses is therefore international in dimension. Militant forces are skillfully organized and coordinated in their tactics and goals. Thus we face in the universities a clear and present danger: a hard, fanatical core of students and faculty wish to destroy the system. The overriding question is: how can we contain the plans of the revolutionaries, without at the same time destroying the basic values of the university? The university cannot long survive under martial law. It must be committed to dialogue, tolerance, and respect for other points of view. It cannot repress honest dissent and criticism. The dilemma is how far shall we permit those who do not believe in the rules of the game to use them to destroy us? And the lesson should be clear that at some point we must prevent those who do not believe in democracy from destroying it.

As we have seen, the strategy of some in the administration at Buffalo was to use the assault of the revolutionaries to extract reform from a "reactionary" faculty. Their view was that only by reforming the university could the revolutionaries be outflanked and their attack diffused. This strategy, rather than minimizing the power of the revolutionaries, enhanced and expanded it. Most ominously from the standpoint of the long-range good of the university, it aroused vindictive forces in the society at large who were inflamed against the university for condoning lawlessness. As a result of permissive neglect, the relationship between the University and the citizens of upstate New York is now more strained than at any time in its history. The confidence and respect in which the university formerly was held by the average person has now been turned into disillusionment, despair, even hatred. One group, calling itself the "Committee of One Hundred Thousand and One," has obtained over eighty thousand signatures on petitions to get rid of violence in the university and weed out "subversion." The entire Western New York delegation of legislators (save one), Republicans and Democrats alike, have recommended strong measures. Vigilante groups have threatened to descend on campus to restore order. The militants scream "Power to the people!" yet the people consider their enemies to be the radicals, and their heroes the much-maligned police.

Buffalo had an unparalleled opportunity to build a great univ-

ersity that would contribute to an economic and cultural renais-
sance in the region. This is now imperiled. The radicals condemn
the people in the community as "Neanderthal." But the people
are perplexed by the inability of the intellectuals, supported by
taxes and charged with the tutelage of their children, to cope with
disorder. The ordinary man may be far more sophisticated in this
regard than the intellectual. Perhaps the greatest defect of the
intellectual is that he cannot see the world as it is. He is willing
to defend civil disobedience and dissent, resistance and violence as
methods of social change, but he fails to understand that without
the confidence of the public, social change will not come about.
And unless some measure of peace and harmony is achieved, civilized life would be all but impossible and would become, in
Hobbes' phrase, "nasty, brutish, ugly and short." The radical intellectual romantically identifies with the young; guilt-ridden, he
is torn between the rewards of the affluent society and the lure of
ideological rhetoric. "Law and order" has ambiguous connotations.
In its common-sense acceptable meaning it should not be allowed
to become a monopoly of the conservatives. It needs to be defended by all men; for without it civilized life is impossible. Many
in the community are angered by the increase in drug use on campuses, by professorial permissiveness toward a growing counter-
culture, and by the increase in pornography and obscenity.
Part of this indictment is well-founded; part of it is excessive. The
danger is that those who attack the university will not distinguish
between legitimate dissent on the one hand and revolution on the
other, or between genuine liberty and anarchy. The peril is that a
respect for liberal and humane values—values that have taken
centuries to achieve—may be overwhelmed by an over-reaction. If
that occurs the intellectual who has condoned and justified violence is chiefly culpable. Indeed it may already be too late to re-
pair the damage. Unless the liberal intellectuals are prepared to
save the university by decisive action against extremists from
within, then those from without may intervene; in the process a
wave of cultural Philistinism and know-nothingism may engulf
our free universities.

There is today the widespread view that the only way to defeat
the militants and end the alienation of the student is to drasti-
cally alter university governance and extend participation. In my
judgment, this tactic contains the seeds of disaster. First, it will
tend to lower academic standards, for the university is *not* a democracy, but an institution based upon competence: its criteria

for the admission and graduation of students, and for the appointment and promotion of faculty, are demonstrated ability and
performance. If popularity is allowed to replace competence,
then the inevitable result will be domination by mediocrity.
This is already apparent in those institutions of higher learning
where participatory democracy has been adopted as a panacea.
The point is, *some* students—probably the best—will work at a
high level of self-motivation and achievement, but *many* or *most*
students may not work as hard and their performance may be
lower. The School of Social Welfare at Buffalo allowed students
to share governance equally with the faculty: unfortunately, standards have deteriorated, militancy has become the most important
requirement for faculty advancement, and the faculty, beholden
to the young, is forced to curry favor. The result is that the apprentice dominates the master. Second, participatory democracy
will not of itself buy peace for the campus, and it will not necessarily end the disruptive violence. For if what has happened at
Buffalo, Columbia, Cornell, or the French universities is any indication, then the revolutionaries—who do not believe in participatory democracy but consider it to be a bourgeois effort at
cooptation—will themselves use it to further solidify their position.
Participatory governance is the great hope of the liberal radical for
saving the university; but it also provides an added opportunity
for the revolutionary to seize control. Unless safeguards are present to prevent this, the revolutionary may be in an even better
position to destroy the university.

If the university is allowed to be politicized, the first casualty is
bound to be academic freedom. Militants either do not genuinely
believe in academic freedom or they only believe in it for themselves. It does not apply to ROTC, to research supported by the
defense department, to Dow Chemical, or General Electric recruiters; it does not apply to liberal or conservative professors or
speakers with whom the militants disagree. Militants reject the
ideal of an open campus, a free and pluralistic market of ideas or
the interplay of opposing points of view.

Radicals and revolutionaries are the first to complain bitterly
when their academic freedom is compromised by criticism from
the "far right," yet they are indifferent to pleas for the academic
freedom of those whom they hound. What they fail to see is that
if ROTC or Themis can be banned from campus on "moral" or
political grounds, then the same argument can be used to ban the

teaching of revolutionary socialism or to remove the SDS from campus.

Radicals demand the untrammeled right to teach what they wish; but they think nothing of interrupting classes of liberal professors with whom they disagree. This attitude invites disruption of *their* classes and courses at some point in the future.

Those who believe in the integrity of the university must be prepared to defend it against enemies from without and from within. McCarthyism of the left can only be neutralized *by applying sanctions and enforcing suspension and expulsion at the first outbreak* of violence, disruption, intimidation, or harassment. If the university cannot itself protect those within it, it must be prepared to summon the civil authorities and to use the injunctive power of the courts with the police to enforce it. It must be willing to *face the consequences* of its action and not to retreat at the first sign or whimper of protest from faculty or students.

Is the option then facing the university a choice between resistance and appeasement, between Hayakawaism and Meyersonism? The answer is that wisdom lies somewhere beween: we need constant reform that is rational, but we also need to apply sanctions where necessary. Meyersonism is the theory that the best way to avoid trouble is to adapt a policy of constant reformation, to stay one step ahead of the militants by anticipating what they want, and to outmaneuver them by granting their demands before they issue them.[1] But a policy of constant reform or participatory democracy may not calm the university or pacify the militants. Recent French experience is highly instructive for those who think that it will provide adequate therapy. General De-Gaulle and Edgar Faure announced sweeping reforms of the university system after the events of May 1968. These included granting of wide powers of decision-making to both students and faculty. What has occurred in France since then is hardly cause for optimism, for the universities are still in crisis. For example, Paul Ricoeur, Dean at Nanterre, and candidate of the revolutionary socialists after '68, was forced to call police on campus in March of

---

[1] For example, if you know that the militants are going to seize a building and liberate it, you announce beforehand that the new name of the building is Liberation Hall and present it to them. If they want ROTC off campus, you announce that you are against academic credit for ROTC or research funded by the Defense Department. If they are likely to demand that 10 per cent of the freshman class be composed of blacks, you give them a quota of 20 to 25 per cent beforehand.

last year in order to protect the personal safety of professors and students. This was an historic decision, for it marked the first time that a French university needed to declare martial law. Yet Ricoeur, who has since resigned, acted after extreme provocation and the emergence of right wing neo-fascist groups in the law faculty, who battled with left-wing groups.

Although Columbia University has introduced student representation in its Senate, this did not prevent disruption of the Senate recently by 150 militants and the vandalizing of university property. Cornell, even with new governance, has not been able to control its militants. Buffalo, with all of its innovation and reform, was unable to prevent violence. In short, unless universities—and this means weak administrations and confused faculties—are prepared to defend and protect academic freedom and excellence against terror, then they must not be surprised at the demands by the people for stern measures from legislative and governmental bodies, or even at the possible emergence of vigilante mobs who may intervene to restore order—a frightening option. As I write this, the radicals have been for the moment checkmated on the Buffalo campus—not by the university, but by the intervention of outside forces who have overreacted. The forty-five professors who were arrested have since been convicted and sentenced to thirty days in jail (though this is being appealed to a higher court). Leslie Fiedler's severe punishment, altogether disproportionate to his offense, reflects the community fear and reaction. The Grand Jury of Erie County is conducting an investigation and threatening indictments for many others; and the Legislature is preparing harsh legislation that may not only quell revolutionary violence but also limit dissent. Tarring and feathering—liberal or symbolic—makes no fine distinction between genuine radicalism, which must be defended in a democracy as part of legitimate dissent, and revolutionary violence, which must be prevented.

We should protest narrowing our alternatives to a simple choice between left-wing terror and right-wing repression. If only university communities will meet forthrightly the crisis that they face, this can be avoided. To defend with dignity and intelligence law and order on campus is not a "reactionary" plot, designed to "thwart reform" or to be a mask for "repression." Rather it is an essential policy of self-defense. It is vital, then, that a broad coalition of liberals and conservatives unite and adopt radical measures to defend the university against those who would destroy it.

At this moment, the State University of New York at Buffalo stands at the crossroads, as do many other institutions of higher learning. It can either resume its development as a great center of learning, build its new campus, reconcile its polarized faculty and students, and tap new areas of creative innovation; or it can collapse under the venomous attack of the extremists of the left and the right. The only hope of the university is that a vital center will emerge to embark upon reform, but *also* with enough courage to defend just law and civilized order as the essential prerequisite of academic freedom and excellence.

VI

POLITICS

AND

EDUCATION

19. CAN AMERICAN UNIVERSITIES BE DEPOLITICIZED?

The Argument of an Address by Henry Aiken as summarized by Sidney Hook

[NOTE: On February 20, 1970, under the auspices of the Center for Philosophic Exchange, a Conference was held on "The Politicalization of the University" at Brockport College of the State University of New York. Professor Henry Aiken of Brandeis University presented a paper which was then discussed by Professor Sidney Hook of New York University, among other persons. The Proceedings of the Conference are to be published soon. Professor Howard E. Kiefer, Director of the Center, has gladly given his permission to reprint the exchange between Professors Aiken and Hook. Professor Aiken, however, has categorically refused to permit the reprinting here of his paper, "Can American Universities be Depoliticized?" The combined persuasions of friendship, money, and an offer of space in which to make a final rejoinder did not avail to obtain his permission. Although the Center for Philosophic Exchange holds the overall copyright on material presented at its Conference, we do not choose to reproduce Professor Aiken's paper without his consent. Consequently, in order to make Professor's Hook's response as intelligible as it was when delivered at the Conference, in the context of Aiken's previous words, a summary is here provided of the main points of Aiken's argument—The Editor.]

"Can American Universities be Depoliticized?" begins with a criticism of the view of Morris Abram, the former President of Brandeis University, and others who have called for a "depoliticizing" of the universities in America. Such persons are described as ignorant of the fact that the golden age of political innocence in our universities is long since over. Such innocence has not existed for generations. For example, the famous "General Education" programs at Columbia and Harvard were blatantly political—intended to glorify the existing American system and cry down all others. Similar programs at other institutions were also political, but in quiet, concealed fashion.

Anyone who opposes politically-oriented educational programs is, by that very fact, himself taking a political position. It is impossible to provide education which is not political. The attempt to do so would mean the abolition of liberal education. It would mean that the state and its works could not be studied. It would involve a taboo against all normative social and political studies. In a depoliticalized university, we could not study either psychology or ethics, nor could we permit any form of religious study. Neither Marcuse nor Hook nor Chomsky nor Schlesinger could be tolerated in a nonpolitical university. The same goes for James, Dewey, and Lord Russell. Nor could we read Plato, Rousseau, or Marx.

A depoliticized university could not tolerate the SDS or the young Republicans. To do so would be to provoke students to take the place over. But then, if the state authorities or the police were called in to prevent riots and violence, that would make the university political. To preserve its nonpolitical character, the university would of necessity have to become political.

At a depoliticized university, teachers and students couldn't even discuss the aims of higher education, since such aims have political implications. The same is true for academic freedom. Such a university would have to get support for its pure research from either private or public sources. Obtaining support from either kind of source would make it political, too.

All this proves that anybody who believes that the "proper business" of universities is not politics but scholarship of a neutral kind is either intellectually dishonest or incompetent and deserves to be dismissed from his post.

This is not an extreme judgment, because such people know that grants to universities from foundations and government agencies as a rule have political strings attached to them. Such people are hypocrites because, when other faculty members or students take strong measures to break such ties, they invoke law and order. Invoking the latter presupposes government, which presupposes politics. Such persons—McGeorge Bundy, for example—become extremely hypocritical when they claim that academic power is really vested in the faculty. They know full well that the formal power of the Board of Trustees can, in the wink of an eye, be transformed into real power.

Hypocrisy is again revealed when individuals who want the university not to be political rely on the force of the police to prevent and react to the violence of students. That kind of reply is political—all the more so because the force used by the police is much worse than the violence of the students.

Professor Aiken at this point, to avoid misunderstanding, explicitly contends that this argument does not condone violence against persons or books. In situations of ultimate difficulty, the university may occasionally reply upon court injunctions to protect its records, but such legal acts show again that it is a political institution, in a political situation. Professor Aiken admitted that he once agreed with Professor Hook that professional associations should not take political positions on matters unrelated to their professional goals. He is no longer sure that this is still a valid position. Without going into the question in detail, he argues that the university is not a group of professional associations, and that, as an educational institution, it *must* take political positions, even if professional associations do not.

Universities as corporate bodies have a right to take political positions on anything that affects their basic educational commitment, to oppose state governments on domestic policies and the federal government on all policies, domestic and foreign. This is particularly true when federal, state, or local governments adopt provisions that adversely affect liberal education or the larger aims of education.

Professor Aiken emphasized again and again that every institution is political to the extent that it attempts to defend itself against criticism or attack. The church, for one; the family, for another. That every institution has a political dimension, he argued, is a truism. And of no institution is this truer than the university. The real question is not whether the university should be political—it is, willy-nilly—but what kind of politics it should have. Its political commitment should exclude from the academic community anyone engaged in research that would enhance the capacity of the United States to engage in warfare, particularly nuclear warfare. All secret work, or any work considered dangerous to man or destructive of the resources on which he depends, would—under such a commitment—be barred.

He is in favor of permitting the freedom to hold any view, no matter how unorthodox, but "in the proper circumstance and under proper auspices." Studies do not have to be "value-free" or "neutral" to be acceptable. Conflict and controversy are not to be deplored but welcomed. To be liberal-minded is to be nonconformist. Nonconformity almost always has a political dimension.

Among the positive suggestions presented by Professor Aiken to improve the current state of university life are the exchange of roles between scholars and administrators, participation of faculty in the governance of the university, student participation in teaching and in revision of curricula. Dialogue should be encouraged between radical groups and others. Disadvantaged students should be helped by special programs. Liberal education must be reformed, its ideals and practices made more relevant to modern problems and conditions. To carry out these tasks requires recognition of the fact that we are undertaking a commitment or responsibility that is completely political.

Sidney Hook

HENRY AIKEN's gush of impassioned rhetoric has carried him from a position that he himself suspects is "platitudinous"—the word is his—to one that will strike others as positively mischievous in its absurdity. How is this remarkable feat achieved? Very simply. First he disregards the specific historical context in which certain campus groups, both students and faculty, are explicitly calling *for* the politicalization of the university, demanding that the university as a corporate entity become an agency of political, even revolutionary, political change. He then proposes an arbitrary conception of the term "political," so broad that it has no intelligible opposite in human affairs, according to which "to be is to be political"—so that by definition, the university, the church, even the family and kindergarten are political institutions. Thereupon he gradually slides or slips into a more specific, conventional conception of political behavior that in effect would make the political functions and concerns of the university almost coextensive with that of a political party. There is a complete and irresponsible disregard of the overwhelmingly likely consequences of such a program, viz., opening the floodgates to a political reaction that would destroy existing academic freedoms and the relative autonomy of the university which have been so precariously won in the last sixty-odd years against earlier conceptions and practices of politicalization.

On top of all this, he scandalously misstates the position of those whom he is ostensibly criticizing, including President Abram. He stuffs figures with straw, burns them with gusto and, sheltered by the resulting thick smoke, charges that those who oppose politicalization *of* the university therefore are, or must be, opposed even to the study of politics *by* or *in* the university, and that they cannot consistently defend the principles of academic freedom when such defence has political implications. This semantic obscurantism makes it easier to blur the distinction between the study of politics and the commitment to political action.

249

Let me illustrate Aiken's method by a reference to some epi-
sodes of American higher education of whose history, to put it
most charitably, he is egregiously innocent, for he seems to believe that there was what *he* calls a golden age of freedom in the
American college (Those whom he thinks he is criticizing believe
no such thing.) There was a time when American colleges were
completely denominational—so much so that no one who was critical of Christianity could teach in them. As Professor Gildersleeve
once put it: "The teachers were either clergymen or men who
having failed to make good in foreign missions were permitted to
try their hands on the young barbarians at home." In some colleges no one could teach unless he was a Baptist; and in others
unless he subscribed to some specific dogmas and techniques of
baptism. When the proposal was made to securlarize the colleges
everyone understood what this meant. It didn't mean that religion
wouldn't be studied but only that the college as a corporate institution would take no religious position, that instruction would not
be geared to any Christian dogma, that faculty and students
would be free to believe or not to believe, and that if they were
Baptists the college would not be concerned whether they chose
to dip or sprinkle to achieve salvation.

What would we say to some spiritual forbear of Henry Aiken
who objected to the proposal that colleges as institutions be neutral in religion, and addressed us in the following words: "It is
absurd to demand that the colleges not take a religious position.
For our real choice is between one religion and another. The very
refusal to take a religious position is itself a religious position.
After all, secularism is definitely a religious position. Even those
who urge the colleges to reorganize their curriculums to permit
students to seek the truth for themselves about religion or anything else—are they not making a religion of the truth?"

What, I ask, would we say to this kind of retort that parallels
Aiken's view that the refusal of a university to take a political
position is itself a brand of politics? I think we would say with
Charles Peirce that there is such a thing as the ethics of words in
given contexts, and that Aiken has manifestly violated it. We
would say that he has missed the whole point of the controversy
which is whether it is appropriate for the college to make a
specific religious or political commitment when its members differ
widely in their religious and political views.

The illogic of the retort obfuscates political thinking, too. For
example, I believe we should tolerate in the political marketplace

the expression of any ideas. Consequently, I must also believe that we cannot suffer those who are actively intolerant of the expression of ideas, who forcibly prevent those of whom they disapprove from speaking. Along comes someone inspired by Henry Aiken's logic who charges me with intolerance, too. "You, too, are intolerant," he says, "just as much as the intolerant Nazi stormtroopers and Red Guards who break up the classes of their professors. Everyone is intolerant—only about different things. In claiming to be tolerant *you* are guilty of bad faith! For if you were truly tolerant, you would tolerate intolerance. Since you are intolerant of intolerance—you are a hypocrite!"

What does it mean when we say that the university should be depoliticalized? Nothing so absurd as Aiken pretends to believe in most of his paper. There are perfectly clear contexts in which we understand and have used the expression without difficulty. I shall give two illustrations. One from this country. One from Germany.

As everyone knows or should know, American higher education has never been free from political controls of the most blatant kind. When I began my academic career, no one who was known as a Socialist and, in many places even as a progressive, could be hired. I could cite instances galore of a political, religious, racial, and social bias that violated the principles of academic freedom. As a Council Member of the AAUP during the thirties fighting to establish recognition of these principles, we meant by "depoliticalization of the univeristy" that the university was not to penalize faculty members or students for exercising their rights as citizens, that the universities were not to make allegiances to capitalism or to any other social or political ideology a condition for membership in the academic community. These principles of academic freedom—reversing the whole course of educational history—gradually began to win acceptance. For example in 1935, together with A. J. Muste and some left-wing labor leaders, I organized the American Workers Party with a militant socialist political program. Whereupon the Hearst Press launched a national campaign demanding my dismissal. To everyone's surprise New York University refused to yield. That was a great step towards the depoliticalization of the university in America—Roger Baldwin thought it was a turning point!—for other institutions rapidly moved in the same direction. There are, of course, still abuses. But how far acceptance of academic freedom has gone is evident in the failure to unseat Professor Eugene Genovese, a public supporter of the Viet Cong, despite a gubernatorial campaign in which his right to teach was the chief issue. Aiken claims that if the American university were depoliticalized, Marcuse couldn't teach, Chomsky couldn't teach, nor could I. On the contrary. The fact that all of us, and even individuals far more extreme politically, teach is evidence of the degree to which depoliticalization has gone. *The American university is far less politicalized today than at any time in the past.*

Here is the second illustration. In the late years of the Weimar Republic the Nazis attacked the professional integrity of the German universities because of their failure as corporate bodies to condemn the Versailles *Dictat*—the peace treaty which unfairly asserted that Germany was solely responsible for the First World War. This was denounced as a betrayal of *das deutsche Volk.* The Nazis charged, with a logic and language much like Aiken's, that the refusal to take a political position, to become politically involved, was itself a political act, hostile to the German community, to German education, and to the German youth who had been branded as the offspring of war criminals in the eyes of the world. And when Hitler came to power, his minions purged those who had urged the German universities to remain politically neutral. That action was properly called "politicalizing" the university.

Those of us who oppose politicalization contend that teachers should be free to make whatever political choices or commitments they please as citizens but that the university as a corporate body should not make partisan political commitments. What Aiken contends is that it is partisan to be nonpartisan. (The same silly logic would prove that there are only nouns in the English language because when I say, " 'And' is a conjunction" or " 'From' is a preposition," etc. these words are really *nouns* because they are subjects of the sentence.)

In short, the "depoliticalization" of the university means the growth, defence, and vitality of academic freedom. The "politicalization" of the university means threats to, and erosion of, the principles of academic freedom. By academic freedom is meant the freedom of professionally qualified persons to inquire into, to discover, to publish, and to teach the "truth" as they see it—or reach "conclusions" in such fields as the fine or practical arts where the term "truth" may be inapplicable—without interference from ecclesiastical, political, or administrative authorities. The only permissible limits on the academic freedom of any teacher would flow from evidence established by qualified bodies of his peers or profession that he was clearly incompetent or had violated the standards of professional ethics. These are the current rules of the AAUP now almost universally accepted.

Today it is a fact ignored by Professor Aiken that these principles of academic freedom are being threatened more by extremist students than by fundamentalist bishops, economic royalist tycoons, and political demagogues. For these students presume to determine who should speak on campus and who shouldn't, break up meetings of those with whom they disagree, disrupt the classrooms of teachers of whom they disapprove, demand the cessation of research *they* regard as not in the public interest, and clamor for the dismissal of teachers whose views they denounce as racist, reactionary, or imperialist. On campus after campus, as the New York *Times* editorially declared when Dr. Hayakawa's meetings were shamelessly disrupted, these students acted just like the Nazi stormtroopers whose hobnailed boots and clubs broke up the classes of the Socialist and Jewish professors.

A depoliticalized university is one in which all sorts of political positions may be studied, defended, criticized so long as the ethics of inquiry are not violated. It is one in which the university as a corporate body may take a stand on public political issues that threaten the existence and operation of the principles of academic freedom. It is or should be jealous of its relative educational autonomy of the state even when it receives the support of the state. But this does not make it a political institution any more than a church which protests a measure that would restrict its freedom of religious worship therewith becomes a political institution. As an institution the function of the university is not to exercise political power but to clarify and test ideas.

This conception of the university, as I shall try to make plain, differs from that of Aiken's not only in degree but in kind. But before developing these differences I want to say something about his descriptions of American higher education past and present. He tells us he is no formalist. I don't know what he exactly means by this but if all he means is that he is indifferent to formal logic, it is apparent enough. I am not a formalist either, but I believe that a little respect for formal logic would not be amiss. It would enable him to distinguish more clearly between a contradictory and a contrary which he obviously confuses.

If Aiken is not a formalist, is he an empiricist taking his point of departure from concrete historical facts? Unfortunately not, because on critical matters he makes up his facts as he goes along. Here are three major examples.

1. He states that the programs of General Education were introduced at Columbia and Harvard "quite simply to awaken the minds of students to the transcendental virtues of our American system and the wickedness of all systems that oppose it." This is sheer invention. I know something about the Columbia system and the men who devised and taught it. Almost to a man they were critics of contemporary society. The program grew out of John Erskine's great books course in the humanities and was broadened to include social studies which were actually basic critiques. of the students' assumptions about American society. For the first time in the history of American education, Marx and Engels' *Communist Manifesto* was required reading. Many of the teachers and students in that program became the architects of the New Deal. For many years it was a genuine liberating educational experience. It received the approval of John Dewey. The major criticism of it was not that it was political but that it wasn't specialized enough, and the criticism originated with the scientists because of the great difficulties in developing general education courses in science.

2. Or take Aiken's charge that government and foundation grants have "political strings attached" to them. Just a few years ago, when Aiken was still at Harvard, a Report of a Special Faculty Committee appointed to supervise the operation of grants declared that no political strings were attached to any grant, that no government or foundation financing had subverted research. It is interesting that some research grants to Chomsky, and other critics of American foreign policy have come from Navy and other government institutions with absolutely no political strings attached.

The subject is very complex but three things are clear. No one compels a university or a faculty member to undertake any research of which it or he disapproves. The faculty as an educational body has the right to lay down guide lines governing the use of its facilities, the time of its members, the limits of secrecy, et cetera. No accredited university I know of accepts grants to prove a point of view in advance or to inculcate opinions or conclusions specified by the donor. Subject to these conditions it is perfectly permissible for a person passionately concerned for the education of free men in a free society to accept research bearing on the defence of the free society without which academic freedom and the free university cannot survive. To leave the free *society* defenseless and vulnerable to totalitarian aggression is to imperil the survival of the free *university*, too. Defense-related research initiated by Einstein in this country and other scientists in England enabled the Western world to turn back the threat of Hitler whose victory would have meant the end of all basic freedoms—in the academy and out. Neither Aiken nor I would be talking here tonight if universities had been forbidden to engage in any research "designed to enhance the [democratic] state's military power" during the years when totalitarianism threatened to engulf the Western world.

3. Finally, take Aiken's charge that faculties have no real academic authority over curriculum or conditions of tenure, that overnight "the formal powers can always be reconverted by university presidents and governing boards into actual power." This is wrong about things that matter most. Aiken is simply ignorant of the fact that in most legal jurisdictions in the United States today the tenure rules adopted by the AAUP and the AAU have the force of law. President Abrams holds *his* post at the will of his Board but happily for us Professor Aiken cannot be deprived of his tenure either by the will of the President or the Board of Brandeis. And if he doesn't believe that this represents real progress and power for the faculty, I recommend that he read Hofstadter and Metzger's book on *The History of Academic Freedom in American Higher Education* or Upton Sinclair's *The Goose-Step.*

There are many things wrong with American colleges and universities and you will find my criticisms detailed in my *Education for Modern Man* and *Academic Freedom and Academic Anarchy.* But Aiken's picture or map of academic reality is way off base. He himself says it is overdrawn by an inch. But on some maps drawn to scale an inch represents a hundred miles or more. Actually his is the wrong map of the wrong country. It tells us more about him than about the university. It proves that he is not a formalist, not a sober empiricist but—what shall we say?—a fantasist! And although he confesses—in an attempt to disarm criticism—that he may be "a bit disingenuous" he is obviously no judge of size or distance.

Basically the great and unbridgeable difference between Aiken's position and the view he misrepresents is that whereas the latter recognizes the right and sometimes the obligation of the university as an *nonpolitical corporate body* to take a stand on issues that threaten the integrity of academic freedom, Aiken would convert the university into a political action organization taking corporate decisions on anything which affects "the conditions of liberal learning" or "the wide and deep aims of higher education." This takes in the whole range of politics from the income tax, housing programs, interstate commerce, defence, foreign policy, disarmament measures.

Listen to this: "The great and ineluctable fact is that no institution, given its ends, is more profoundly involved in problems of politics and government than the university [note: not even our Courts, Congress and Legislatures!—S.H.] . . . Ours has become for better or worse a kind of Platonic republic whose crucial institution is the academy."

This gives the whole case away! We are *not* a Platonic republic but a democratic republic whose crucial institutions in political matters is not the academy but a Congress and Executive responsible to the electorate. This is the worst form of élitism and smacks of Marcuse, not of James or Dewey. The university is funded by the democratic community not as a corporate body to engage in politics or influence legislation but to provide opportunities for the free exploration and critical study of all ideas, political and nonpolitical, in the faith that this quest will lead to clearer ideas, more reliable knowledge, and indirectly to more enlightened policy. The university should be the locus of competent and disinterested investigation of human problems, a source and resource for the entire community, dedicated not only to the teaching and testing of known truths and accepted values but to winning new truths, broaching fresh perspectives and values on the open frontiers of human experience. The community does not look to the university as a political action group or political corporate body engaged in a struggle for political power by influencing legislation or laying down Platonic mandates for the masses of ignorant citizens. It looks to it, to be sure, to *study* political ideas among others. But to study political ideas does not make the university a political institution, to study religious ideas does not make it a religious institution, any more than to study crime makes it a criminal institution.

To politicalize the university in the manner Aiken suggests is to invite educational disaster. First of all it would lead to the loss of its tax exemption. Legal actions even now are pending against some universities which officially endorsed the "Moratorium" on October 15, 1969, by dismissing classes! Secondly, it would turn fac-

ulties into warring political factions each of which would seek allies not only among students but outside political groups—at the
cost of genuine educational activity. Intellectual controversy, of
course, is to be welcomed in the universities. But the kind of political controversies generated by concern with all the political
issues that are construed by some faculty members as having a
bearing on "the wide and deep" aims of higher education is sure
to plunge institutions into educational chaos. The results of such
politicalization are evident in some South American and Asian
universities, and manifest also in some embattled campuses in this
country.

Finally, and this is the greatest danger of all, the attempt to
politicalize the university along Aiken's lines is sure to inspire a
reaction from the larger political community resentful of the political intrusion of a publicly subsidized educational institution.
Political majorities, local, state, and national, will themselves
move to politicalize the universities to prevent educational resources and opinions from being mobilized against them. There
are some evidences of this at hand already. Colleges and universities will be politicalized with a vengeance. The first casualities of
this vegeance will be the principles of academic freedom and tenure themselves, won after such bitter battles, and among the victims will be not only the Aikens—who know not what they do
when they needlessly rouse by their provocations the sleeping furies of American vigilantism—but those of us who wish to preserve the autonomy of the educational process at its highest levels.

Aiken is blind or reckless about the educational direction of his
policy of politicalization. What he proposes is to set back the clock
to the days when the cultural Babbits and the economic Bourbons
declared that scholarship and teaching must be kept in leading
strings to good citizenship—except that his conception of good citizenship differs from theirs.

The view I oppose to his is that the university does not have to
choose between one conception of good citizenship or another,
that what makes a man a good citizen is no more the affair of the
university than what makes him a good husband, that its primary
concern is whether he is a good teacher and scholar. Just as I
have no right when I take a political stand as a citizen to commit
the university, so the university as a corporate body of which I
am a member, except on matters of academic freedom, has no
right to take a political stand that in the eyes of the public commits me.

Sidney Hook

THE FOREGOING ESSAYS—and the tragic events that have occurred on both the national and international scenes since they were written—are compelling evidence that college and university life in the United States has undergone a mutation. From now on, the pattern of American higher education will resemble more closely the European pattern. Even if efforts to resist the politicalization of the university succeed formally and institutions preserve an official fig-leaf of corporate neutrality, political issues will affect university life with great frequency and intensity. It has accordingly been necessary for those who wish to preserve the university as an institution for discovery and scholarship, for teaching and learning, to devise an effective defensive strategy.

The strategy upon which in the end everything depends is to *prevent* the outbreak of violence on campuses, so far as possible, and, whenever violence occurs, to limit and contain it by methods acceptable to the overwhelming majority of the academic community. The following tactical proposals are suggested not as panaceas to be blindly followed anywhere and everywhere. They represent findings that have emerged from a union of experience and common sense, and are based on study of scores of situations during the past few years. Knowledgeable persons on the scene will discern how best to adapt the proposals to specific contexts.

(1) The first thing to do is to assemble the constituent bodies of the university community—the faculty, students, and administration, or their representatives—in order to draft the principles that are to govern the expression of dissent on matters of interest to the academy, be these matters great or small. Once the principles have been laid down, specific rules implementing them should also be drawn up, rules that spell out clearly the kinds of conduct and behavior that shall constitute *prima facie* violations of the limits of legitimate dissent. At the beginning of each academic
258

year, the principles and rules should be criticized, modified as necessary, and reaffirmed. Pains should be taken not to make this reaffirmation a mechanical ritual of academic piety. Academic due process should be linked up with the rational process and with due process generally—*mutatis mutandis.*

(2) The rules implementing the principles should make provision for the establishment of a representative faculty-student discipline committee. The procedures for conducting hearings and the rules of behavior for defendants, complainants, and witnesses should be explicitly endorsed by the academic community or its representatives. These rules of behavior should clearly set forth the sanctions to be taken against members of the academic community, students or teachers, who disrupt the judicial proceedings of the disciplinary committee.

(3) Violations of the rules should be met promptly with appropriate sanctions.

(4) In the event of forcible disruption of the academic process, the first line of defense should be faculty and student marshals, empowered by the academic community to maintain order, report participants, etc. The marshals should be equipped with cameras.

(5) When a situation acquires a gravity beyond the power of the faculty and student marshals to cope with it, the administration, after consulation with the executive or other appropriate committee of the academic community, should apply to the courts for injunctive relief.

(6) If the court injunction is disregarded, its enforcement should be left to the civil authorities.

(7) If and when matters reach an extreme pass, and hazards to life and limb—whether in the form of assault, arson, vandalism, or whatever—can only be contained by use of police power, faculty and student marshals should accompany the law enforcement officers so that their mission can be accomplished without force where resistance is *not* offered, and with minimum force where resistance *is* offered.

(8) When the scale of violence reaches a magnitude that makes the previous steps inadequate—for example through intervention by large, outside, non-student forces—the university may have to be shut down and the preservation of life and property entrusted entirely to the civil authorities. In such a case, before the campus is reopened, academic sanctions against those members of the academic community who were guilty of violence—whether students or members of the faculty—should be

strictly enforced. Amnesty for "crimes of academic genocide" can only invite their repetition.

Although the prevention and containment of violence is indispensable, violence is not the only danger. We can list here only a few signs of a threatening pattern that undoubtedly will become more pronounced in the future. This ominous pattern will require a second line of strategic defense.

(a) A drive has been started to undermine and politicalize the conditions of academic tenure. Admittedly, there are many legitimate problems connected with the question of lifelong tenure for teachers. The abuses that have arisen in connection with it should be corrected, first of all in the educational interest of our students, who have been the main sufferers from the abuses. At the same time, it needs to be made clear to all concerned that academic tenure is indispensable to the maintenance of academic freedom. Because it is indispensable, particular attention should be called to proposals recently put forward by coalitions of student and faculty extremists on several of our campuses—proposals that exploit concern with abuse of the tenure system and shape this concern into an entering wedge directed towards eventual control of both the personnel and the content of instruction. Such proposals seek to achieve by indirection, and by apparently politically disinterested educational reform, what at present cannot be accomplished within our universities by direct action and confrontation under unconcealed political banners.

We refer to demands for what is called "parity," meaning the grant of 50 per cent student voting rights on all decision-making committees, whether in the university at large, in particular colleges of the university, or in departments. "Parity" is being demanded in connection with such matters as the invitation to teach, renewal of contracts, promotion, salaries, and the granting of tenure. The coalitions asserting these demands are not content with insisting upon the right of students to be consulted, their right to evaluate their teachers' abilities to communicate helpfully and effectively, and their right to have these evaluations considered by the teachers' colleagues and peers while reaching tenure decisions. These are educationally legitimate procedures for which much can be said. But current demands go far beyond them. It is asserted that students should be empowered on an equal footing with the professor's peers and colleagues to decide whether he is to teach and on what conditions. Moreover, it is asserted that tenure, once granted, should be "reviewed" every "three"—or "five," or "seven"—years by a committee made up half of students, the desired time interval being an inverse function of the political militancy of the particular coalition making the demand.

The organizers and zealous advocates of this movement towards "parity" are persons who have stressed "relevance" as among the chief criteria of satisfactory teaching. Hence, it is easy to predict the sort of decisions that would be made by such tenure committees as they are advocating; that is, committees in which political extremists and fanatics would enjoy at least equal voting power with non-extremists. In any such committee, the presence of *one* faint hearted faculty member who feared for his own tenure, or who sought to ingratiate himself with student or faculty militants, or who agreed with their criteria of political acceptability and political "relevance," would be enough to give dominant power to an intolerant orthodoxy. In practice, the creation of such "restructured" committees would have swift and far-reaching consequences. A purge of every faculty governed by such committees would immediately begin, ostensibly for merely technical, pedagogical reasons, but actually on ideological grounds. Tenure as a safeguard of academic freedom would no longer operate.

Lest anyone suppose that such a scenario could not possibly be enacted, we must report that it is close to enactment now. How little regard our extremist political students feel towards academic freedom is continuously evidenced in their demands for the dismissal of outstanding scholars whose views they caricature and denounce as "fascist" or "racist," and whose classes they disrupt. The campus of the University of California at Berkeley and several campuses of the City University of New York have been the chief but not the only loci of such actions.

(b) In some pretigious institutions engaged in technological and scientific research, questionnaires have been circulated to members of the faculty, requesting them to indicate what controls, other than the judgments of their scientific peers, should be established to govern research projects. Here, too, there are many legitimate problems concerning which men of good will and intelligence may differ. But there also is reason to believe that, under cover of plausible criteria of selection, a program is being developed to eliminate all research on "war-related problems"—a catch-all phrase for a vast number of actual and potential projects, including many that have no bearings, or extremely peripheral bearings, on national defense.

This attack on "war-related" research is coupled with the suggestion that "the community" or "the people" be consulted about the setting up of research projects, on the grounds that "the community" and "the people" are affected by the consequences of all research. There is an obvious danger here that the loudest and perhaps the most decisive voices in determining the legitimacy of particular research projects will be, not the professionally trained and responsible scientist, in consulation with qualified colleagues, but persons whose moral and political judgments will coincide with those of a small activist élite, desirous of imposing its own political line of domestic or foreign policy upon the nation. In this way, basic decisions on research may be subjected to artfully concealed political commitment or allegiance to an overarching political bias, rather than to the advancement of scientific knowledge.

(c) There is also a grosser and more manifest threat to academic freedom, one which increases in boldness and arrogance every day. This threat expresses itself as the intolerance of the self-righteous. It is similar to, and no less dangerous than, the barbarism of the virtuous in previous ages.

As society in America shed its philistinism and outgrew its cultural vigilantism, we took it for granted as axiomatic that in centers of learning and teaching, of discovery and evaluation, reasoned discourse would be the method by which conclusions were reached and disagreements resolved. This axiom, in turn, presupposed that persons representing different points of view would be free to set forth their positions, marshal their arguments, and offer alternatives to any policies and proposals in any field. But today on many American campuses this freedom has disappeared. Extremist groups have destroyed the rights of students and faculty to hear views that challenge or even vary from their own. The rights that such extremist groups have enjoyed and exploited to the fullest possible extent—rights that were won for them, at considerable cost, by earlier academic generations—they now flagrantly deny to others. It is hardly an exaggeration to say that after the victory of the so-called Free Speech Movement at Berkeley, a movement which actually had very little to do with free speech, free speech became impossible on the Berkeley campus. It has been especially hazardous at Berkeley to speak in criticism of extremist causes or groups. No one, for instance, can present positions there that favor American policy. On the campuses of hundreds of colleges and universities in this country, revolutionary or subversive speakers are made welcome, but speakers representing other groups are not tolerated. Such speakers are harried, shouted down, sometimes assaulted. While spokesmen of movements hostile to the "Establishment" have unlimited freedom to incite to violent action in opposing prevailing policies, advocates of these policies are often barred from campuses or appear only with the help of military cordons. By and large, faculties and administrations in such institutions remain silent about these matters or issue deprecating but ineffectual news releases. Even when official guests of the university, including present or past government officials, have been insulted or scandalously mistreated, the same faculties and administrations have been fearful of initiating disciplinary action, lest their doing so exacerbate campus unrest.

(d) All of these threats to academic freedom have come to a head, as this volume goes to press, in climactic and precipitate determinations to politicalize our institutions of higher learning in the aftermath of the easily predictable events at Kent State University and Jackson State College. The movement towards politicalization might have been effectively resisted in other circumstances. As events have actually shaped themselves, a second tragedy has been piled on the first. Scholars and administrators who until very recently had regarded it as unthinkable that any university should take a stand as a corporate body in behalf of any cause, no matter how exalted, have capitulated literally in thousands to the demands of their vociferous opponents, urging that an exception be made, that support be given to the "national student strike," or that some similar action be voted, with or without debate.

It is indicative of the extent to which the feelings of concern and indignation of student bodies and faculties have been politically manipulated by various factions of the New Left that there has been no outpouring of mass protest at the murder and wounding of students at the University of Madison and elsewhere by revolutionary extremists. The relative indifference of the campus response to the outrage at Madison, the cruel comments that dismissed the holocaust as an unfortunate interruption of research or as a regretable incident in a worthy movement of resistance suggest that the mass student protests of May 1970 were not altogether spontaneous. There was very strong evidence of organized activity. Even the demands, down to the very wording, contained in resolutions of protest from New York to California, were identical. Tensions do not always erupt into riots.

But when even a handful of persons are planted ready to pull the trigger of words or action, the eruptions is certain.

Grant that there are many worthy causes in the world. Grant, since we believe in academic freedom, that all faculty members, students, and administrators are free to devote themselves to the promotion of worthy causes. Grant also that the exercise of one's rights as a citizen in a free society should not in the least jeopardize a scholar's standing in the academic community. But granting all these things does not entail in the slightest that the university is thereby politically committed, nor that it should be.

As *individuals*, faculty members and students have a perfect right to support any position with respect to American involvement in Vietnam and Southeast Asia. But when a *university*, as a corporate body, takes a stand in behalf of one political position, rather than another—save when the principles of academic freedom are directly affected—that university inescapably is being partisan, and hence unfair to those among its faculty and students who disagree with that stand, or who, whether agreeing or not, regard it as a betrayal of the function of the university to take any stand. And when our universities formally and officially shut down in protest, and on top of that declare that *university resources* are to be devoted to the speedy termination of America's involvement in Southeast Asia by bringing organized pressure to bear upon Congressmen, Senators, and the Executive Branch, then it becomes more than apparent that the universities have performed a political act.

Every such act undermines the educational capabilities of the institutions concerned. Obviously, with respect to any political issue, a university could fairly claim to be neutral only if it permitted those who held different positions on the issue to use its resources. But the variety of possible positions on most important issues makes such a course absurd. If all parties and groups used university resources for political purposes, educational life would come to an end.

As *individuals*, if they so desire, faculty members and students have every right to throw themselves into the maelstrom of political activity during electoral campaigns. But when *universities*, as corporate bodies, decide to shut down for two weeks in October and November, to permit their faculties and students to engage full time in political activities, perhaps at places remote from the campus, they are betraying their responsibility to serve as "citadels of reason, sanity and civility in a deeply troubled world." There very probably are scholars—whether teachers or students—who wish *not* to take part in campaigns, except as voters and conscientious observers of current events, or who prefer to choose *other* times than October-November, or *other* means than campaigning, to influence political decisions. No institution has a right to restrict their freedom of choice in these respects, yet precisely this restriction has in many instances been moved and approved by some faculties and administrations.

The depth of our newest tragedy may be made clearer if an example is offered using *religious* commitment, instead of political. Were any of our universities to shut down officially for two weeks so that its teachers and students could give their full time to prayer and religious worship, there would be an immediate outcry from the unbelievers among the academic community to the effect that their rights had not been respected, indeed had been trampled underfoot. We are all agreed that no university is justified in determining whether, when, or how we should worship at the alter of our faith, or of any faith. Likewise, we should recover our former conviction that no university is justified in determining how and when we should think and act in the field of politics.

It is shabby pretense to assert, as some administrators have done, that shutting the university down for a fortnight "neither commits the university to any particular political position nor interferes with its prime education responsibilities." It is no secret that the universities in May 1970 planned a pre-election shutdown to mobilize their students and teachers for the election of one set candidates over another, specifically of so-called "peace" candidates—as if all candidates were not peace candidates, differing only on how best to achieve it. And for those teachers and scholars who prefer not to engage in any political activity at this time, or in this fashion, the assertion that the closure of the university is no interruption of prime educational responsibilities is the sheerest mockery. Clearly a college or university that announced as many did in May 1970 that its corporate resources would be devoted to the promotion of a partisan political position, or that it intended to close so that its faculty and students could "march" for political purposes, or descend on Washington, has violated the plainly stated rules by which it must abide, if it is fairly to remain entitled to its educational tax exemption. Every such college and university is inviting taxpayer's suits.

The threatening pattern here described, a pattern made up in the main of attacks on the tenure system, attempts to undermine the independence of academic research, suppression of free speech, and the employment of corporate university resources and influence for partisan, political purposes, is one which challenges our teachers, even more than our administrators or our students, to devise and implement appropriate defenses. But our college and university faculties will not succeed in such efforts without the understanding and support of other persons. What really is at stake in our current crisis is both our pluralistic educational system and our political democracy. The two go together. An open society is preserved and strengthened by what Justice Oliver Wendell Holmes called the free market of ideas, which is not to be identified with the free market of commodities. To keep our institutions of higher learning open and free, to assure that our colleges and universities will be communities of independent seekers of personally discovered truths, is the task of *all* citizens, not only of professional educators.

Those whose support is needed most are the young. They do not have to be told that they will inherit the world. Whether the world they inherit will be free or given over to authoritarian dogmas and practices, and whether the universities will be free or given over to ideological indoctrination, very largely depends on them.